OXFORD STUDIES IN POSTCOLONIAL LITERATURES

The *Oxford Studies in Postcolonial Literatures* aim to offer stimulating and accessible introductions to definitive topics and key genres and regions within the rapidly diversifying field of postcolonial literary studies in English.

Under the general editorship of Professor Elleke Boehmer, the *Studies* in each case elucidate and explicate the informing contexts of postcolonial texts, and plot the historical and cultural co-ordinates of writers and of the leading movements, institutions, and cultural debates situated within those contexts. Individual volumes reflect in particular on the shaping effect both of international theory and of local politics on postcolonial traditions often viewed as uniformly cross-cultural, and also on the influence of postcolonial writing on the protocols of international theory. Throughout the focus is on how texts formally engage with the legacies of imperial and anti-imperial history.

OXFORD STUDIES IN POSTCOLONIAL LITERATURES

GENERAL EDITOR: ELLEKE BOEHMER

PACIFIC ISLANDS WRITING

The Postcolonial Literatures of Aotearoa/New Zealand and Oceania

Michelle Keown

OXFORD

UNIVERSITY PRESS

OXFORD

UNIVERSITY PRESS

Great Clarendon Street, Oxford OX2 6DP

Oxford University Press is a department of the University of Oxford.
It furthers the University's objective of excellence in research, scholarship,
and education by publishing worldwide in

Oxford New York

Auckland Cape Town Dar es Salaam Hong Kong Karachi
Kuala Lumpur Madrid Melbourne Mexico City Nairobi
New Delhi Shanghai Taipei Toronto

With offices in

Argentina Austria Brazil Chile Czech Republic France Greece
Guatemala Hungary Italy Japan Poland Portugal Singapore
South Korea Switzerland Thailand Turkey Ukraine Vietnam

Oxford is a registered trade mark of Oxford University Press
in the UK and in certain other countries

Published in the United States
by Oxford University Press Inc., New York

© Michelle Keown 2007

The moral rights of the author have been asserted
Database right Oxford University Press (maker)

First published 2007

British Library Cataloguing in Publication Data

Data available

Library of Congress Cataloging in Publication Data

Data available

Typeset by Laserwords Private Limited, Chennai, India
Printed in Great Britain
on acid-free paper by
Biddles Ltd., King's Lynn, Norfolk

ISBN 978-0-19-927645-5 (Pbk.)
ISBN 978-0-19-922913-0 (Hbk.)

1 3 5 7 9 10 8 6 4 2

This book is dedicated to my partner, Jonathan Wild

ACKNOWLEDGEMENTS

As with my previous book, *Postcolonial Pacific Writing* (2005), this text has emerged from the experience, in the late Michael King's words, of 'being Pākehā' during the Māori Renaissance of the 1970s. During my childhood, my parents were both secondary school teachers, and I was privileged to accompany them on a number of live-in marae trips during the 1970s and 1980s. My early experiences triggered a lifelong interest in, and respect for, Māori language and culture, and I was fortunate to study the Māori language throughout my schooling and my undergraduate years at Waikato University. Kia ora to Pari Kana, Kingi Turner, and Aroha Yates-Smith for their teaching and support, and to Ralph Crane for supervising my Masters thesis on Māori literature.

Heartfelt thanks to Ken Arvidson and Mark Houlahan, longstanding friends and mentors who generously read and commented on this manuscript in its entirety, and to Rod Edmond, who introduced me to a wider range of Pacific writing during my doctoral studies, and who offered expert advice on Chapter 2 of this book. I also wish to express my immense gratitude to Elleke Boehmer, who invited me to contribute to the Oxford University Press series in which this book appears, and provided invaluable advice and support throughout this project, as did Tom Perridge and Jacqueline Baker at Oxford University Press.

This book could not have been completed without the assistance of the many Indigenous Pacific writers, scholars, and film-makers who generously shared their knowledge with me along the way. Particular thanks go to Barry Barclay and Vilsoni Hereniko, who sent me copies of their films and offered advice on sections of the manuscript; to Epeli Hauʻofa, for his generous advice and hospitality; and to Dan Taulapapa McMullin, who sent me a whole range of his creative and critical work. I also wish to thank many other friends, writers, and scholars who offered advice on this project: these include Julie Barbour, Joe Bray, Ian Conrich, Jan Cronin, Terry Crowley, Stu Dawrs, Steven Fischer, Nicholas Goetzfridt, Richard Hamasaki, Witi Ihimaera, Don Long, Paul Lyons, Kirstine Moffat, Sudesh Mishra, Rodney Morales, Satendra Nandan, Steph Newell, Robert Nicole, David O'Donnell, Antoinette Padgett, Som Prakash, James Procter, Adam Reed, Paul Sharrad, Catherine Silverstone, Angela Smith, Regis Stella, Konai Helu Thaman, Larry Thomas, Bronwyn Tweddle, Bob and Nancy Weber, Janet Wilson, and Steven Winduo. Kia ora koutou katoa.

I am also sincerely grateful to the Arts and Humanities Research Council, the British Academy, and the Carnegie Foundation of Scotland for their generous financial support, which allowed me to undertake vital research trips to the Pacific during this project. Many thanks to the staff of the USP library (Fiji), the Hamilton library (University of Hawai'i), the Alexander Turnbull library (Wellington), and the University of Waikato library for their assistance with research. I am also grateful to the staff of the English department at the University of Waikato, who provided me with an office and access to resources during my research trip to New Zealand, and of course to students and colleagues at the Universities of Stirling and Edinburgh, with whom I was able to discuss and refine my ideas.

Many thanks to Fatu Feu'u, who granted permission for me to include an image of his painting, 'Tautai Matagofie' (1990), and to Kate Button at Te Papa Picture Library (Wellington) for supplying the photographic reproduction. I am grateful to cartographer Max Oulton for supplying his map of the Pacific Islands upon which Map 1.1 is based. Thanks also to Auckland University Press for permission to reproduce the line drawing of the whare whakairo (carved meeting house) discussed in Chapter 6. The drawing is reproduced from Hirini Melbourne's essay 'Whare Whakairo: Maori "Literary" Traditions' (1991), and originally appeared in *Tānenuiarangi Booklet* (1988), by Paki Harrison.

Finally, thanks most of all to my partner Jonathan Wild, and to my parents (Paul and Robin Keown) and siblings (Dallas, Hayley, Natasha) for their unstinting love and support over the years, and for their help with the preparation and proofreading of this manuscript.

CONTENTS

LIST OF MAPS AND FIGURES

PACIFIC ISLANDS TIMELINE[1]

Year (BC/AD)[2]	Literatures[2]	History, politics, and culture
c. 48,000 BC:		The ancestors of today's Melanesian peoples arrive in (Papua) New Guinea from south-east Asia.
c. 1,500–2,000 BC:		The ancestors of today's Polynesian and Micronesian peoples arrive in (Papua) New Guinea and the Mariana Islands from south-east Asia.
c. 500– 1200 BC:		The ancestors of today's Polynesians settle in Fiji, Tonga, Samoa, and some neighbouring islands.
c. 1–5 AD:		Polynesian migrations eastwards to the Cook, Society, and Marquesas Islands. Later migrations to Easter Island, Hawai'i, and Aotearoa/New Zealand, where landfall was made between 800 and 1300 AD.
1521:		Spaniard Ferdinand Magellan leads the first European expedition through the Pacific.
1565:		Spain annexes Guam and the Northern Mariana Islands. Spanish attempts to settle the Solomon Islands (in 1595) and Vanuatu (in 1606) are abandoned.
1642:		Dutch explorer Abel Tasman 'discovers' New Zealand.
1754:	Jean-Jacques Rousseau, A Discourse on Inequality.	
1767:		English explorer Samuel Wallis reaches Tahiti; French navigator Louis-Antoine de Bougainville follows suit nine months later.

1769–79:		Captain James Cook's Pacific voyages take place. Cook is killed on 14 February 1779 after a skirmish on the Big Island of Hawai'i.
1788:		British annexation of Australia begins. Norfolk Island (previously uninhabited) becomes a British colony and is populated by naval, convict, and free settlers.
1797:		The London Missionary Society (LMS) establishes its first Pacific mission in Tahiti.
1814:		The Church Missionary Society (CMS) arrives in Aotearoa/New Zealand.
1828:		The Netherlands claims West New Guinea (later renamed Irian Jaya, then West Papua).
1829:	William Ellis, *Polynesian Researches*.	
1832:		French explorer Jules-Sébastien-César Dumont d'Urville systematizes the geocultural categories of Polynesia, Micronesia, and Melanesia.
1835:		CMS missionary William Colenso sets up a printing press in Aotearoa/New Zealand and begins circulating copies of the Bible translated into Māori.
1837:	John Williams, *Missionary Enterprises*.	
1838:		Pitcairn Island (settled by the English *Bounty* mutineers and their Tahitian wives) becomes a British colony.
1840:		The Treaty of Waitangi secures British annexation of Aotearoa/New Zealand.

(Contd.)

PACIFIC ISLANDS TIMELINE (*Contd.*)

Year (AD)	Literatures	History, politics, and culture
1842–1901:		France takes possession of the various island territories (including the Marquesas, Tahiti, and the Society, Austral, Tuamotu, and Gambier Islands) which eventually become known as 'French Polynesia' in 1957.
1846:	Herman Melville, *Typee*.	
1848–50:		The Māhele division of Hawai'ian land takes place, eradicating the system of communal land tenure and expediting land sales to Euro-American investors.
1853:		France annexes New Caledonia.
1856:		The US begins taking possession of various Pacific Islands in Micronesia for guano phosphate mining and the establishment of naval bases.
1857:		Waikato chief Te Wherowhero elected as first Māori King under the name Potatau.
1858:	R. M. Ballantyne, *The Coral Island*.	European settlers in Aotearoa/New Zealand now outnumber Indigenous Māori.
1860–72:		A series of 'land wars' rage between Māori and the colonial government in Aotearoa/New Zealand.
1863:	Frederick Maning, *Old New Zealand*.	
1864:	John Gorst, *The Maori King*.	

1867:		Māori male suffrage introduced; four Māori seats are established within the New Zealand parliament.
1874:		British annexation of Fiji.
1875:		Japan annexes Ogasawara (Bonin Islands).
1879–1916:		Over 60,000 Indian indentured labourers arrive in Fiji to work on colonial plantations.
1880:	Pierre Loti, *Le Mariage de Loti*.	
1884:		British annexation of Papua (Southeast New Guinea). Germany establishes a protectorate over Northeast New Guinea and the Marshall Islands.
1887–8:		France establishes protectorates over the Wallis and Futuna island groups (which eventually become a (unified) French overseas territory in 1961).
1888:		British annexation of the Cook Islands and Niue. France and Britain declare a joint naval commission for the New Hebrides (now Vanuatu). Germany establishes a protectorate over Nauru. Chile annexes Easter Island (Rapa Nui).
1889:		Britain declares a protectorate over Tokelau (incorporated into the Gilbert and Ellice Islands colony in 1916).
1890:	R. L. Stevenson, *Ballads*. Paul Gauguin begins writing *Noa Noa*.	
1892:	R. L. Stevenson, *A Footnote to History*.	British annexation of the Gilbert and Ellice Islands (now Kiribati and Tuvalu).

(*Contd.*)

PACIFIC ISLANDS TIMELINE (*Contd.*)

Year (AD)	Literatures	History, politics, and culture
1893:	R. L. Stevenson, *Island Nights' Entertainments.*	Britain establishes a protectorate over the southern Solomon Islands (gaining control of the entire island group by 1900). Female suffrage introduced in Aotearoa/New Zealand. Hawai'ian monarchy overthrown in a US businessmen's coup backed by the US Navy.
1897:		Britain places Norfolk Island under the authority of the Australian government (as a dependency of New South Wales).
1898:		The US takes Guam from Spain and formalises its annexation of Hawai'i. Germany purchases Spain's remaining Micronesian territories.
1899:		Following a bilateral treaty, Germany takes possession of Western Samoa and the US takes Eastern Samoa (renamed American Samoa).
1900:	R. L. Stevenson, *In the South Seas.*	
1901:		Britain negotiates treaty with Tonga making Britain the channel for foreign affairs. Britain transfers the Cook Islands and Niue to New Zealand administration.
1906:		France and Britain establish a condominium (joint) government over the New Hebrides (now Vanuatu). Britain transfers control of Papua to Australia.
1907:		Aotearoa/New Zealand gains Dominion status.

Year	Literature	Historical events
1911:	Jack London, *The Cruise of the Snark; South Seas Tales.*	
1912:	Jack London, *The House of Pride and Other Tales of Hawaii.*	
1914:	William Satchell, *The Greenstone Door.*	Australian forces take Nauru and German New Guinea from Germany following the outbreak of the First World War. Japan seizes Germany's Micronesian territories. New Zealand takes Western Samoa from Germany.
1918:	Jack London, *The Red One and Other Stories.*	
1920:	Katherine Mansfield, *Bliss and Other Stories.* Jane Mander, *The Story of a New Zealand River.*	
1921:	Somerset Maugham, *The Trembling of a Leaf.*	League of Nations mandates granted to Australia (over Nauru and former German New Guinea), New Zealand (over Western Samoa), and Japan (over its Micronesian territories).
1922:	Katherine Mansfield, *The Garden Party and Other Stories.*	
1925:		Britain transfers Tokelau to New Zealand administration.
1928:	Margaret Mead, *Coming of Age in Samoa.*	
1938:	Robin Hyde, *The Godwits Fly.*	
1939:	John Mulgan, *Man Alone.*	
1941:		Japanese attack on Pearl Harbour triggers war in the Pacific.

(Contd.)

PACIFIC ISLANDS TIMELINE (*Contd.*)

Year (AD)	Literatures	History, politics, and culture
1945:	Allen Curnow (ed.), *A Book of New Zealand Verse 1923–45*.	
1946:	James Michener, *Tales of the South Pacific*.	
1946–58;		The US conducts atmospheric tests of atomic (and later hydrogen) bombs in Bikini and Enewetak (in the Marshall Islands), Johnston Atoll, and Christmas Island.
1962:		
1947:		The South Pacific Commission (the first Pacific intergovernmental regional organization) is established.
1951:		The ANZUS pact is signed between Australia, New Zealand, and the US in the interests of maintaining security in the Pacific.
1952–63:		Britain conducts atmospheric nuclear tests at Christmas and Malden Islands and in 'remote' parts of Australia.
1957:	Janet Frame, *Owls Do Cry*.	
1959:		Hawai'i becomes the fiftieth US State.
1960:	Bernard Smith, *European Vision and the South Pacific*. Tom and Lydia Davis, *Makutu*.	
1962:		Western Samoa becomes the first independent Pacific Island nation.

1963:	Indonesia takes possession of previously Dutch West New Guinea, renaming it Irian Jaya (now known as West Papua). France begins building nuclear testing facilities on Fangataufa and Moruroa (in the Tuamotu Island group).
1964:	John Dominis Holt, 'On Being Hawaiian'. Hone Tuwhare, *No Ordinary Sun*.
1965:	The Cook Islands become self-governing in free association with New Zealand.
1966:	Founding of the University of Papua New Guinea (UPNG).
1966–96:	France conducts atmospheric nuclear tests in Moruroa and Fangataufa until 1975, then runs tests underground until 1996.
1968:	Nauru becomes independent. The University of the South Pacific (USP) is established in Fiji.
1970:	Vincent Eri, *The Crocodile*. Fiji becomes independent. Tonga resumes full self-government.
1971:	John Kasaipwalova, 'Reluctant Flame'. The South Pacific Forum established. (Renamed the Pacific Islands Forum in 2000.) Members include New Zealand, Australia, and various newly independent Pacific Island nations.
1972:	South Pacific Creative Arts Society (SPCAS) established by staff and students at USP. Witi Ihimaera, *Pounamu, Pounamu*.

(Contd.)

PACIFIC ISLANDS TIMELINE (*Contd.*)

Year (AD)	Literatures	History, politics, and culture
1973:	Pacific literary magazine *Mana* inaugurated by staff and students at USP. Witi Ihimaera, *Tangi*. Albert Wendt, *Sons for the Return Home.*	
1974:	Harry Dansey, *Te Raukura* (first performed 1972). Konai Helu Thaman, *You, the Choice of My Parents.*	Niue becomes self-governing in free association with New Zealand.
1975:	Patricia Grace, *Waiariki and Other Stories.*	Papua New Guinea becomes fully independent.
1976:	Jo Nacola, *I Native No More.* John Dominis Holt, *Waimea Summer.* Russell Soaba, *Wanpis.*	
1977:		
1978:		The Solomon Islands and Tuvalu become independent.
1979:	Albert Wendt, *Leaves of the Banyan Tree.*	Kiribati (formerly the Gilbert Islands) becomes independent.
1980:	Albert Wendt (ed.), *Lali* (the first anthology of Indigenous Pacific literature).	Vanuatu (formerly the New Hebrides) becomes independent.
1983:	Derek Freeman, *Margaret Mead and Samoa: The Making and Unmaking of an Anthropological Myth.* Epeli Hauʻofa, *Tales of the Tikongs.* Keri Hulme, *The Bone People.* Grace Mera Molisa, *Black Stone.*	
1984:	Donna Awatere, *Maori Sovereignty.*	

1985:	Satendra Nandan, *Voices in the River*.	Greenpeace flagship *Rainbow Warrior* is bombed and sunk by French saboteurs. The South Pacific Forum drafts the South Pacific Nuclear Free Zone Treaty, which is signed by Forum countries in 1986 but is not recognized by the US.
1986:	Witi Ihimaera, *The Matriarch*. Patricia Grace, *Potiki*.	The Marshall Islands and the Federated States of Micronesia gain their independence from the US. The Northern Mariana Islands become a Commonwealth of the US.
1987:	Epeli Hau'ofa, *Kisses in the Nederends*. Witi Ihimaera, *The Whale Rider*.	Fijian nationalists stage two military coups, overthrowing the Fijian Government. New Zealand bans nuclear powered/armed ships from visiting New Zealand ports.
1988:	Subramani, *The Fantasy Eaters*.	
1989:	Publication of Janet Frame's *The Complete Autobiography*. Vilsoni Hereniko, *The Monster and Other Plays*. Ngahuia Te Awekotuku, *Tahuri*. Larry Thomas, *Just Another Day*.	
1990:	Alan Duff, *Once Were Warriors*. Arlene Griffen (ed.), *With Heart and Nerve and Sinew: Post-coup Writing from Fiji*.	Sesquicentenary of the Treaty of Waitangi.
1991:	Satendra Nandan, *The Wounded Sea*. Chantal Spitz, *L'île des Rêves Écrasés*.	
1992:	John Pule, *The Shark That Ate the Sun*. Paul Theroux, *The Happy Isles of Oceania*.	

(Contd.)

PACIFIC ISLANDS TIMELINE (*Contd.*)

Year (AD)	Literatures	History, politics, and culture
1993:	Vilsoni Hereniko and Teresia Teaiwa, *Last Virgin in Paradise*. Lois-Ann Yamanaka, *Saturday Night at the Pahala Theatre*. Release of Jane Campion's film *The Piano*.	
1994:	Hone Kouka, *Ngā Tāngata Toa*. Release of Lee Tamahori's film *Once Were Warriors*.	Palau becomes independent from the US, having been administered as a US Trust Territory since 1947.
1995:	Albert Wendt (ed.), *Nuanua* (the second anthology of Indigenous Pacific creative writing).	
1996:	Sia Figiel, *Where We Once Belonged*; *The Girl in the Moon Circle*. Nora Vagi Brash, *Which Way, Big Man? and Five Other Plays*.	
1997:	John Kneubuhl, *Think of a Garden and Other Plays*. Hone Kouka, *Waiora*. Witi Ihimaera, *The Dream Swimmer*.	
1999:	Robert Sullivan, *Star Waka*. Haunani-Kay Trask, *Light in the Crevice Never Seen; From a Native Daughter* (rev. edn.).	
2000:		A military coup led by Fijian nationalist George Speight removes Mahendra Chaudry (Fiji's first Indo-Fijian Prime Minister) from power.

2001:	Caroline Sinavaiana-Gabbard, *Alchemies of Distance*. Subramani, *Dauka Puraan*.	Democratic elections take place in Fiji after the suspended Constitution is reinstated.
2002:	Imaikalani Kalahele, *Kalahele*. Victoria Nalani Kneubuhl, *Hawai'i Nei: Island Plays*. Sudesh Mishra, *Diaspora and the Difficult Art of Dying*.	
2003:	Albert Wendt, *The Mango's Kiss*. Albert Wendt et al. (eds.), *Whetu Moana: An Anthology of Polynesian Poetry*.	
2004:	Dianna Fuemana, *Mapaki*. Déwé Gorodé, *Sharing as Custom Provides* and *The Kanak Apple Season*. Dan Taulapapa McMullin, *A Drag Queen Named Pipi*. Makerita Urale, *Frangipani Perfume*.	
2005:	Oscar Kightley and Simon Small, *Fresh off the Boat*.	

[1] This timeline references key publications and events discussed in the book and is not intended to be comprehensive. Every effort has been made to ensure the accuracy of this chronology, but inevitably some of the dates listed here are contested by certain historians and cultural commentators. I have relied upon the following sources in particular: R. Crocombe, *The South Pacific* (2001); D. Denoon et al. (eds), *The Cambridge History of the Pacific Islanders* (1997); M. King, *The Penguin History of New Zealand* (2003).

[2] The 'literatures' column of this timeline is biased towards printed texts by European and Indigenous writers and does not therefore reflect the vicissitudes of the many oral literatures of the Pacific (some of which are discussed in Chapter 5). Further, the list of literary/critical texts provided here is selective, focusing on first and/or significant publications by particular authors discussed in the book.

1

Introduction:
Voyaging Through the Pacific

An identity that is grounded in something as vast as the sea should exercise our minds and rekindle in us the spirit that sent our ancestors to explore the oceanic unknown and make it their home, our home.

(Epeli Hauʻofa, 'The Ocean in Us')

> *when the soul has been wounded and the sun is keen*
> *to surface in the dark there is one place I go to*
> *that place that fills the earth's land with moisture and*
> *water, that changes the coast in a dream, that place*
> *the ancients call mother of mothers, the ocean*

(John Pule, 'Ocean Song to Myself')

1.1 'Mapping' Pacific literatures

This book takes the reader on a discursive journey through the post-colonial literatures and cultures of the Pacific. Given that the Pacific Ocean spreads across one third of the globe, and contains one of the most heterogeneous groups of cultures and languages in the world, this journey can only be a partial and selective one, taking the form of a series of oceanic trajectories which touch upon some of the major literary and socio-political trends and inter-relationships within the region, dating from the late eighteenth century to the present day. The book is, both in a geographical and conceptual sense, a regional study of a literary context that has received relatively little attention in international postcolonial studies. While the book retraces, in part, scholarly routes previously mapped out by established Pacific literary critics such as Subramani and Sina Vaʻai (who live and work within the region), it also touches upon literary and cultural

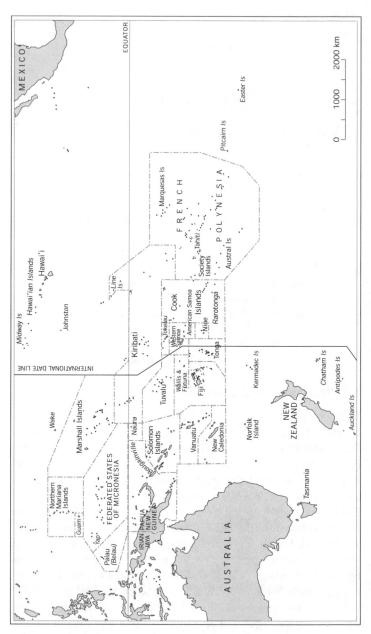

Map 1.1 The Pacific Islands (based on a map by Max Oulton)

contexts that have themselves been relatively marginal even within the Pacific itself. Most existing critical studies of Pacific literature, for example, have followed the anglophone bias that has dominated postcolonial literary criticism from its inception, and while this book focuses primarily upon literature in English—the language used by the majority of Pacific writers—it also investigates the growing corpus of non-anglophone literatures, particularly those of the francophone and hispanophone Pacific. In this sense, the book is concerned not only with the process of *cultural* translation that characterizes much comparative anglophone postcolonial scholarship; it also considers the implications of navigating through the various *linguistic* traditions of the region (see Chapter 5). Such an approach is perhaps timely, given that an increasing body of non-anglophone Pacific writing is now available in English translation (see Chapters 4, 5, and 6). Indeed, the term 'translation'—which derives from the Latin verb *transferre*, meaning 'to carry across'—seems particularly relevant to the Pacific region, a network of islands and archipelagos interconnected by criss-crossing patterns of migration and cultural exchange. The name 'Oceania', one of the established conceptual labels for the region, draws attention to the centrality of the sea for Pacific Islanders, many of whom still depend on the ocean for their livelihoods, and who possessed sophisticated maritime technologies that allowed them to navigate established trade routes throughout the Pacific long before Europeans arrived in the region. As testament to this heritage, metaphors of oceanic voyaging are central not only to Indigenous Pacific oral and written literary traditions (see Chapter 6), but also to many European narratives of exploration and settlement in the region (see Chapter 2). However, European and Indigenous understandings of the relationship between the Pacific Islands and the sea that surrounds them have frequently diverged. As Tongan[1] scholar Epeli Hau'ofa has pointed out, since the early days of European incursion into the Pacific, Westerners have commonly conceptualized the Pacific as a constellation of tiny 'islands in a far sea', remote from European colonial centres of power and dependent on 'First World' nations for their socio-economic survival. While acknowledging that many Pacific Islands are geographically 'small' and often reliant upon overseas aid to bolster their fragile economies, Hau'ofa nevertheless asserts that Indigenous Pacific oral traditions and cosmologies figure Oceania not as an assemblage of tiny, far-flung islands, but rather as part of a universe comprising not just land surfaces, but also 'the surrounding ocean as far as they could traverse and exploit it, the underworld with its fire-controlling and earth-shaking denizens, and the heavens above with their hierarchies of powerful gods and named stars... that people could count on to guide their ways across the seas'. In seeking to recuperate Indigenous ways of understanding the Pacific, Hau'ofa therefore advocates considering the Pacific Islands not as 'islands in a far sea' but rather as a 'sea of islands' seen 'in the totality of their relationships' (1993: 7). Notably, Hau'ofa's definition draws attention to the interconnectedness of land and sea as revealed in the etymology of the word 'island' which, as Gillian Beer points out, is a 'kind of pun':

'Isle' in its earliest forms derived from a word for water and meant, 'watery' or 'watered'. In Old English 'land' was added to it to make a compound: 'is-land': water surrounded land. The idea of water is thus intrinsic to the word, as essential as that of earth. The two elements, earth and water, are set in play.

(Beer 1990: 271; see also Edmond and Smith 2003: 9)

In elaborating on the interconnectedness of islands and oceans, Hau'ofa has proposed the development of a regional 'Oceanic' politico-ideological identity which will not only help to unite and protect Pacific Islanders against the vicissitudes of global capitalism and climate change, but will also serve as a source of inspiration to contemporary Pacific artists and creative writers. Hau'ofa's 'Oceanic' theories have been enormously influential throughout the Indigenous Pacific, debated by writers, artists, and theorists of many Pacific nations (see Waddell *et al.* (eds.) 1993; Subramani 2003), and in 1997, Hau'ofa himself put his ideas into practice by establishing the Oceania Centre for Arts and Culture at the University of the South Pacific (USP) in Fiji. The Centre brings together, and fosters links between, creative artists from throughout the Pacific, and appropriately, it is now affiliated to the USP Faculty of Oceans and Islands, a unique academic collective that acknowledges the importance of the sea to the island-based region of Oceania.

While Hau'ofa's theories have demonstrably inspired many contemporary Pacific Island writers and artists to explore oceanic metaphors in their work, it is also important to acknowledge that imagery of the sea has characterized Indigenous Pacific anglophone literature from its inception in the late 1960s, bearing witness to the centrality of the marine world to Indigenous Pacific oral and artistic traditions. For example, *Lali* (1980)—the first of three anthologies of Indigenous Pacific creative writing edited by Samoan author Albert Wendt—includes a variety of poems replete with sea-imagery: Wendt's 'Inside Us the Dead' and Epeli Hau'ofa's 'Our Fathers Bent the Winds' commemorate Polynesian ancestors who sought and settled 'these islands by prophetic stars' (Wendt (ed.) 1980: 284), while poems by Francis Tekonnang (of Kiribati) and Sano Malifa (of Samoa) target the movements of waves and tides as metaphors for the vicissitudes of human life (108, 276), thus indexing the anthropomorphization of the natural world in many Indigenous Pacific mythopoeic traditions. In his editorial introduction to *Lali*, Wendt describes Pacific writers as nourished by the 'warmth and love of our mother, the Pacific', and he conceptualizes the creative works of individual Pacific writers as bubbling springs of water making their contributions to the vast plentitude of the literary 'ocean' (Wendt (ed.) 1980: xix). Oceanic imagery also features in Wendt's groundbreaking essay 'Towards a New Oceania' (1976*a*), one of the earliest critical maps of Indigenous Pacific literature, as well as in various essays produced by Cook Islander Marjorie Tuainekore Crocombe, inaugural editor of *Mana* (the first regional journal of Indigenous Pacific writing, founded in 1972). Crocombe envisaged *Mana* as a newly-launched canoe richly stocked with literary cargo flowing in from 'every part of the Pacific', thus metaphorizing the patterns of travel and exchange that have linked Pacific peoples since ancient times (Crocombe 1974: 1). The title of the journal was selected because the word 'mana'—a multivalent term which carries connotations of power, psychic force, and socio-political influence—exists in almost all Polynesian and many Melanesian languages, and therefore encapsulates the journal's function as a forum for bringing together writers from throughout the region (Va'ai 1999: 27–8).

The notion of an interlinked community of Oceanic writers is central to the way in which this book is structured. Chapters are arranged chronologically or thematically, examining regional and inter-pelagic literary trajectories rather than focusing primarily upon particular 'national' traditions (see section 1.5). Such an approach seems particularly appropriate given that a large proportion of Indigenous Pacific writers and critics have, at some point in their careers, worked within the University of the South Pacific (USP), a *regional* university (established in 1968) which has brought together Indigenous peoples from eleven former British colonies in the South Pacific. (These include the Cook Islands; Fiji; Kiribati; Nauru; Niue; the Solomon Islands; Tokelau; Tonga; Tuvalu; Western Samoa; and Vanuatu.) The journal *Mana* was itself established by academics and students who formed the South Pacific Creative Arts Society at USP in 1972, and many of the contributors to *Mana*, and to Wendt's first two anthologies of Indigenous Pacific writing (*Lali* (1980) and *Nuanua* (1995)), were students on Wendt's creative writing courses at USP in the early 1970s. While relatively affluent metropolitan centres elsewhere in the Pacific (such as Aotearoa/New Zealand and Hawai'i) have spawned a rich diversity of writers from various ethnic and socio-economic backgrounds, the countries served by USP generally possess more fragile economies with far fewer resources for writing and publishing, and USP has therefore served as an important locus of creativity for writers from these nations, fostering many key authors, publications, and writers' collectives over the decades. In Papua New Guinea, where literacy rates are relatively low compared to many other parts of the Pacific, the University of Papua New Guinea (UPNG) has served a similar function for local writers (see Chapter 4).

Further, during and beyond the decolonization period following the Second World War, many writers from the less affluent island nations of the Pacific have left their countries of origin to take up secondary and tertiary education scholarships in metropolitan centres such as Aotearoa/New Zealand, Australia, Hawai'i, and the 'mainland' US, and this has contributed to the strongly 'diasporic' focus of much Pacific writing (see Chapter 6), and to the perpetually amorphous nature of literary networks within the watery domain of Oceania. This book aims to acknowledge the fluidity of Indigenous Pacific literary traditions, but also (and particularly in Chapter 4) to identify particular 'centres' of Indigenous literary activity, based on institutional, (former) colonial, or linguistic inter-relationships within the Pacific. These 'centres' include Papua New Guinea; Fiji and the USP nations; Hawai'i and the 'American' Pacific (including American Samoa and Micronesia); the 'Francophone' Pacific (including French Polynesia, New Caledonia, and Wallis and Futuna); the Hispanophone Pacific (Rapa Nui/Easter Island); and Aotearoa/New Zealand.

The focus of this book broadens even further to encompass not only the Indigenous literatures of the Pacific, but also the European settler literatures of Aotearoa/New Zealand, as well as various European discursive representations of Pacific Islanders from the late eighteenth century to the present day (see Chapter 2). This is in order to acknowledge the unique intertextual networks linking European and Indigenous writing of the Pacific, given that many contemporary Indigenous Pacific writers have engaged directly (and often critically) with European representations of the Pacific in their creative work. This is not, of course, to suggest that Indigenous writing of the Pacific is merely a form of reactionary 'writing back' to the imperial 'centre'—as we will see, many Pacific writers draw extensively upon their own precolonial oral, mythopoeic, and artistic traditions—but it is nevertheless the case that much contemporary Pacific writing is still engaged with colonialism and its legacies.

These legacies are explored in some detail in Chapter 2, which focuses not only upon *fictional* European representations of Pacific Islanders, but also upon other discourses including explorers' and missionaries' journals; the memoirs of traveller-writers; and anthropological treatises. This is in order to demonstrate the ways in which an 'Orientalist' collection of racial and cultural stereotypes about Pacific Islanders developed and has been perpetuated in various European 'texts' focused upon the region. As Palestinian intellectual Edward Said demonstrated in his path-breaking study, *Orientalism* (1978), the *material* process of Western colonization of the non-West has commonly been accompanied, justified, and reinforced by various *textual* representations which have positioned colonized peoples as politically and culturally 'inferior' or 'other' to the West. Focusing specifically upon British and French representations of India, North Africa, and the Middle East (the 'Orient' referenced in the book's title), Said discusses the ways in which various forms and genres of colonial discourse generated a collection of racial stereotypes or binary oppositions between 'East' and 'West', many of which have developed new manifestations and incarnations in modern times. As we will see, the Pacific has its own established array of 'Orientalist' stereotypes, many of which construct Pacific Islanders—and particular Polynesians—as Europe's heterosexual other(s) (see section 1.4 below). While Said's theories can usefully be brought to bear upon Pacific colonial discourse, it is worth noting that some eighteen years before the publication of *Orientalism*, Australian art historian Bernard Smith anticipated many of Said's arguments in his influential study *European Vision and the South Pacific* (1960). Smith's text analyses the ways in which late eighteenth- and early nineteenth-century European artistic representations of Pacific Islanders were inflected by Romantic and scientific theories about 'primitive' peoples, and his analysis of the *interconnectedness* of various European discourses about the Pacific provides an important point of departure for the arguments presented in this book. As we will see, nineteenth-century travel and boys' adventure writing drew extensively upon late eighteenth- and early nineteenth-century explorer and missionary accounts of Pacific Islanders, and the cultural stereotypes circulated in these writings then resurfaced in the work of twentieth-century writers, film-makers, and so on. Notably, the works of late nineteenth- and early twentieth-century traveller-writers such as R. L. Stevenson and Jack London display what Ali Behdad has termed a 'belated' orientalist sensibility (1996): these authors came to the Pacific partly in search of an 'authentic' encounter with the 'exotic', but were also acutely aware that the effects of more than a century of colonial activity in the region had (in many cases) irrevocably altered the social structures of many of the Indigenous cultures of the region. Influenced by the discourse of social Darwinism, Stevenson and London believed Pacific peoples to be declining towards extinction following contact with Europeans, and in their writings they are both critical of the colonial enterprise, but also complicit with it in their desire to memorialize aspects of the Pacific not previously documented by their predecessors. As we will see, a similar ambivalence is evident in the work of social anthropologists who undertook fieldwork in the Pacific in the early twentieth century. The Pacific was one of the last of the world's frontiers to be 'opened up' to European exploration and settlement, and in the early twentieth century the Pacific (and particularly Melanesia) became the cradle of modern social anthropology, as scholars sought new, 'pristine' cultural realms in which to test their theories.

Behdad's model of belatedness can also usefully be adapted to a consideration of Pacific literatures alongside postcolonial literatures elsewhere in the world. Indigenous Pacific literatures in English, which gathered momentum in the late 1960s and early 1970s, emerged in the wake of anti- or post-colonial literatures in many other parts of the world such as Africa, India, and the Caribbean. Although the early decades of the twentieth century witnessed the emergence (and consolidation) of robust anticolonial and self-determination movements in countries such as Samoa and Aotearoa (see Chapter 3), there were no Pacific equivalents of early twentieth-century nationalist novels such as Mulk Raj Anand's *Untouchable* (1935) or Raja Rao's *Kanthapura* (1938). When 'commonwealth' literature (as it was then called) was first taught at USP in the early 1970s, the course lists were dominated by African and Indian writers (such as Chinua Achebe, Wole Soyinka, Amos Tutuola, Raja Rao, and R. K. Narayan), and it was not until 1973 that Pacific writers began to appear on the syllabus. As we will see in Chapter 4, many Indigenous Papua New Guinean writers of the late 1960s and early 1970s drew their inspiration from African literature, while Albert Wendt has cited, *inter alia*, a range of African, African-American, Indian, and Caribbean writers as important 'influences' on himself and other Pacific writers (1995*a*: 4).

In view of these connections, this book is attentive to the inter-relationships between Pacific and other 'postcolonial' literatures, drawing upon 'international' as well as Pacific-based critical and theoretical models in its analysis of particular texts and authors. It also, however, traces trans-Pacific literary genealogies, given (for example) that the Papua New Guinean literary movement, which gathered momentum in the late 1960s, served as a source of inspiration for the USP students and academics who formed the South Pacific Creative Arts society in 1972 (Crocombe 1977: 6), while the native Hawai'ian literary renaissance of the late 1970s was energized by the Māori literary renaissance of the early 1970s, and so on. In diasporic locations such as Aotearoa/New Zealand, there are strong filial connections between Indigenous Pacific peoples from various ethnic backgrounds, and many of the 'second generation' Pacific writers who have emerged since the 1990s have drawn inspiration from—and in some cases reacted against[2]—the work of first-generation writers such as Witi Ihimaera, Albert Wendt, Konai Helu Thaman, Epeli Hau'ofa, and others. Wendt's third anthology of Indigenous Pacific literature—entitled *Whetu Moana: Contemporary Polynesian Poems in English* (2003)—features many of these new writers alongside more established figures, offering a useful index of the changing preoccupations of Pacific writers into the new millennium.

The sheer diversity of Pacific writing, and of the cultures from which this writing has emerged, makes it difficult to generalize about particular trends and developments in Pacific literature over the last few decades, particularly given the widely differing forms that colonialism—and the process of decolonization—has taken across the Pacific region. (Western Samoa, for example, was the first Pacific nation to gain its independence in 1962, but parts of Micronesia did not attain political self-determination until the 1990s.) It is, however, possible to identify—at a very basic level—some features and trajectories common to a variety of Pacific literatures produced since the late 1960s. These trends, which are elaborated in Chapters 4 and 6 in particular, can be divided into three major categories: the anticolonial and polemical 'first-generation' literatures of the 1960s and early 1970s; the post-independence shift to internal cultural politics (such as the emergence of new Indigenous 'élites'); and the 'new wave' of Indigenous Pacific creativity—featuring increased numbers of diasporic and women writers; experimentation with postmodernist aesthetics; and new initiatives in drama and film—from the 1990s and into the new millennium. Of course, it is important to recognize that not all literatures of the Pacific fit neatly into these categories, and the book does not suggest that there is any straightforward linear 'progression' between them: Albert Wendt's early writing, for example, shows ample evidence of experimentation with 'postmodernist' literary techniques, while many writers of the new millennium are still engaged with anticolonial issues. This book therefore aims to strike a balance between a genealogical or chronological overview of Pacific writing, and one which is attentive to the discontinuities, specificities, and uniqueness of individual writers, works, and cultural contexts.

In order to point readers towards these specificities, this book observes the shift towards *contextualized* (rather than purely *theory*-based) studies of postcolonial literatures as evident in the work of contemporary postcolonial scholars such as Elleke Boehmer (2005) and Paul Sharrad (2003). In particular, the book investigates various important historical events and developments, from the late eighteenth century to the present day, that have inflected the postcolonial literatures of the Pacific in various ways. This is not to suggest that Pacific literatures are merely mimetic *reflections* of socio-political developments: indeed, much of the discussion which follows investigates how imaginative literature of the Pacific transforms and contests existing narratives of history and culture, particularly those produced by the West. Nevertheless, as an (admittedly partial and subjective) introduction to the literatures of the Pacific, this book offers various contextual details about Pacific histories, cultures, and languages that are considered relevant to an 'informed' interpretation of Pacific writing.

Having mapped out some of the main contours of Pacific literature which will be further elaborated in later chapters of this book, the remaining sections of this chapter offer a series of definitions and contextual material designed to help readers navigate the geographical as well as conceptual parameters of the Pacific. Section 1.2 presents a genealogy of European and Indigenous labels for the Pacific; section 1.3 defines the three main geocultural areas of the Pacific: Polynesia, Melanesia, and Micronesia; and section 1.4 outlines some key postcolonial theoretical concepts and explores their relevance to the Pacific context. The concluding section of the chapter (1.5) offers a brief sequential summary of the remaining chapters in this book.

1.2 Defining Oceania: from 'South Seas' to 'South Pacific'

The Indigenous peoples of the Pacific possess their own labels for this vast sea of islands—in Māori it is 'Te Moana Nui ā Kiwa' (the great ocean of Kiwa, the legendary Polynesian explorer and guardian of the sea)—but Oceania has also been subject to various European forms of geographical and conceptual mapping during its post-contact history. Among the earliest European labels applied to the Pacific region were the 'South Seas' or the 'South Sea Islands': these terms, coined by late eighteenth-century European explorers, became synonymous with Romantic conceptions of the Pacific as a utopian paradise (Hau'ofa 1998: 395). After the Second World War, the 'South Seas' label was replaced by the term 'South Pacific', which was first used by the Western Alliance military forces during the war in the Pacific, and was then popularized through the wide circulation of ex-US serviceman James Michener's *Tales of the South Pacific* (1946). Richard Rodgers and Oscar Hammerstein adapted sections of Michener's text into a hugely successful stage musical (entitled *South Pacific*) that opened in 1949 and was subsequently released as a film in 1958, reaching a wide international audience and further popularizing the 'South Pacific' as a geocultural category. As Epeli Hau'ofa notes, however, the term 'South Pacific' is in fact misleading, as it incorporates 'not just those islands that lie south of the equator; it covers the whole region, from the Marianas, deep in the North Pacific, to New Zealand in the south' (1998: 396) (see Map 1.1). While the 'South Pacific' label is still widely used, since the post-war era of decolonization in the Pacific, another phrase, 'Pacific Islands Region', has also come into common use, and serves to differentiate the smaller islands of the Pacific from their larger neighbours, Aotearoa/New Zealand and Australia. This opposition can be viewed in positive terms, as a sign of the increasing socio-political independence of these smaller islands, but as Hau'ofa notes, it has also served to underscore the 'declining importance' of these islands to the West since the end of the Cold War, during which the Pacific was viewed as a key strategic site protecting the US, New Zealand, and Australia from communist military incursion (1998: 396). Hau'ofa notes that in the global political arena, the Pacific Islands are now commonly subsumed within larger geo-political entities such as the 'Asia-Pacific Region', a label widely used by international agencies (such as the United Nations) and multinational business corporations. Within this paradigm, the smaller islands of the Pacific tend to be overlooked in favour of the larger, more economically powerful south-east Asian nations. This trend is also evident in the establishment of the 'Asia Pacific Economic Cooperation' or 'APEC' (formed in 1989), which 'covers the entire Pacific rim, but excludes the whole of the Pacific Islands region' (Hau'ofa 1998: 397). As Hau'ofa argues, within such formulations the Pacific Islands region becomes an empty space, the 'hole in the doughnut' (1998: 397). Such trends have had serious implications for the people living within the region: one of the most disturbing consequences has been the use of the Pacific Ocean and various Pacific Islands as testing grounds for nuclear weapons developed by Western nations such as Britain, France, and the US. These tests have had a devastating impact upon both the natural environment and the people living in or near the test sites, and as we will see in Chapter 3, these events have given rise to a considerable corpus of anti-nuclear protest literature produced by Pacific creative writers. Many of these writers are—or have been—members of Indigenous activist groups seeking to reclaim Pacific spaces—both physically and ideologically—from these latter-day (neo)colonial intrusions.

While many of the European labels discussed above have been ascribed to the Pacific region as a whole, the Indigenous Pacific has also been divided into three geocultural subcategories known as Polynesia, Melanesia, and Micronesia. These labels, which were coined in the nineteenth century to impose imperialist geographical and racial frameworks upon the various peoples of the Pacific, are still maintained in many contemporary conceptualizations of the Pacific, and are outlined in detail below.

1.3 Polynesia, Melanesia, and Micronesia: the 'culture areas' of the Pacific

The division of the Indigenous peoples of the Pacific into racial types was systematized in 1832 by the French explorer Jules-Sébastien-César Dumont d'Urville, who identified two distinct 'races' in the Pacific. The first was the 'copper-coloured race', which he categorized into 'two very pronounced divisions' inhabiting the regions that he named Polynesia and Micronesia. The second group Dumont d'Urville identified was the 'black' race occupying the area which he called Melanesia (Dumont d'Urville 1832; B. Douglas 1999: 65). Map 1.2 depicts the three main geocultural regions of the Pacific, which are closely based on Dumont d'Urville's original categories.

Most of the islands grouped within the category of Polynesia (which translates as 'many islands') fall within a triangular geographical zone stretching from Hawai'i in the far north, to Easter Island in the east, and Aotearoa/New Zealand in the southwest. Micronesia (which translates as 'small islands') is located in the northwest Pacific and includes the Federated States of Micronesia, Palau/Belau, Guam, Kiribati (formerly the Gilbert Islands), Nauru, the Marshall Islands, and the Northern Mariana Islands. Melanesia (which translates as 'the black islands') is located in the southwest Pacific and includes Papua New Guinea, the Solomon Islands, Vanuatu, New Caledonia/Kanaky, and Fiji.

Of these three 'culture areas' in the Pacific, Polynesia is the most clearly defined and coherent, with established ethno-linguistic affiliations between its various peoples, although there are distinct variations between Western and Eastern Polynesia due to different phases of settlement. In precolonial times, most Polynesian societies were headed by chiefs ruling over communities whose members traced descent from a common ancestor. These communities lived within relatively

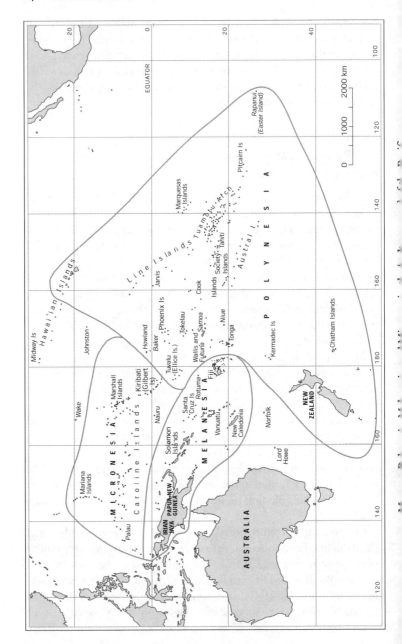

stable territories, and social rank and status depended primarily upon inheritance. Eastern Polynesians had a pantheon of 'departmental' gods with influence over human affairs and nature, while Western Polynesia had fewer gods and more spirits (many unnamed), who were attached to persons or families rather than particular roles (Campbell 1989: 15–17).

In contrast to Polynesia, the categories of Melanesia and Micronesia are less cohesive. Melanesia, for example, first settled around 50,000 years ago, is remarkably culturally diverse: its peoples range in stature from tall to diminutive, in skin colour from light brown to deep black, and there are considerable linguistic and social variations between different villages and regions. This is largely because unlike most Polynesians, few Melanesians travelled more than a few miles by land and sea in pre-European times, and there was little interaction between different village communities (Campbell 1989: 18–20). Kinship links held these communities together, but social status was earned rather than inherited: instead of being ruled by chiefs, many communities were dominated by rich and powerful self-made men (dubbed 'big men' by Western anthropologists) who maintained their status by securing the support of fellow villagers through public feasting and shrewd use of patronage (Campbell 1989: 21). Melanesian religion centred upon an assemblage of powerful and often malevolent spirits who required propitiation through ceremonies and rituals, and unwelcome events were often attributed to members of the community suspected of clandestine sorcery (Campbell 1989: 22–3).

Broadly speaking, Micronesia—first settled between 3,400 and 4,000 years ago—has more in common with Polynesia than Melanesia. Western Micronesians generally resemble East Asians physically, becoming 'progressively darker and stockier to the east' (Campbell 1989: 23). Polynesia and Micronesia show some striking similarities in material culture (witnessed in shell adzes and fishing tackle, for example), but Micronesia was also influenced by Asian material culture (such as pottery styles and looms for weaving). Micronesian religious beliefs appear to have had most in common with Western Polynesia (with a collection of spirits and ghosts, some of whom were patrons of various crafts and activities), but social organization seems to have been much more diverse than is the case in Polynesia. Like Polynesia, however, Micronesia is a region of seafarers, and Micronesian seagoing vessels (which developed into large, dual-hulled, plank-built canoes) were among the most advanced in all Oceania (Campbell 1989: 23–4).

Many historians and anthropologists view the categories of 'Polynesia', 'Micronesia', and 'Melanesia' as accounting 'neatly' for the ethno-linguistic divisions within the Pacific, but not all academics are in agreement about their efficacy. There are various theories on the exact order and direction of the various migrations within the Pacific, and the boundaries dividing the three regions are open to dispute (King 2003: 32–7; Krupa 1982: 2).[3] In spite of their limitations, the terms 'Polynesia', 'Melanesia', and 'Micronesia' are retained in this book as labels denoting the three putative geocultural regions of the Pacific, while both 'Pacific Islands' and 'Oceania' are used as general labels for the region.

A few final words need to be said about the semantic properties of the labels 'Pacific Islands' and 'Oceania', particularly as they feature prominently in the title of this book. Although the term 'Pacific Islands' is often used to differentiate smaller Pacific nations from larger neighbouring western settler nations (such as New Zealand, Australia, and the United States), in this book New Zealand is included as a 'Pacific Island' nation. This is largely because Aotearoa/New Zealand was first settled by Polynesians who have close racial, mythological, and linguistic affiliations to the peoples of other Polynesian nations such as Samoa, Tonga, and the Cook Islands. Samoan writer Albert Wendt discusses Aotearoa/New Zealand in these terms, pointing out that 'when I talk about the Pacific, the Pacific Islands, I include Aotearoa. Aotearoa is a group of islands in the South Pacific; its oldest cultural maps and fictions are Polynesian and at least 1000 years old' (1995b: 16). Aotearoa is the Māori name for New Zealand, and is most commonly translated as 'land of the long white cloud', as according to legend, Māori explorer Kupe and his wife Hine-te-Aparangi discovered the country after catching sight of a long plume of cloud hanging over the land. In this book, 'Aotearoa' is used alongside 'New Zealand' in accordance with contemporary common usage.

The label 'Oceania'—which derives from 'Océanie', a label adopted by French explorers in the Pacific—is commonly used by anthropologists, geographers, cultural theorists, and international organizations to refer to Melanesia, Micronesia, and Polynesia (including Aotearoa/New Zealand), but in some cases, the term encompasses Australia as well (Hauʻofa 1998; Crocombe 2001). This book, however, does not investigate Australian culture(s) or literature(s) in detail, partly because the racial and linguistic origins of Australian aborigines are not closely connected with those of the Indigenous peoples of Melanesia, Micronesia, and Polynesia (who arrived in the Pacific many centuries after the Koori peoples), and also because Australian literature is discussed in detail in another book in this series (by Graham Huggan). Since the arrival of its European settler population, however, Australia (like New Zealand, Spain, France, Germany, the Netherlands, and the United States) has itself operated as a colonialist force within the Pacific, and these connections are touched upon at various points in this book, particularly with reference to Papua New Guinea, over which Australia exercised colonial jurisdiction until 1975.

1.4 **Key concepts and theoretical frameworks**

This penultimate section of the chapter identifies key postcolonial concepts and theories which are relevant to the literary and cultural contexts explored here and in later chapters of the book. In each case, concepts and models drawn from 'international' postcolonial theory are situated alongside those that have been produced within the Pacific itself, in order to investigate the intersection between the 'global' and the 'local' in postcolonial Pacific literature and theory. In particular, the discussion below focuses on three key areas and sets of terms: race and forms of representation in colonial and postcolonial writing; imperialism and colonialism; and postcolonialism and its relevance to the Pacific. Later chapters of the book engage with a range of other theories and concepts not discussed in detail here: Chapter 5, for example, investigates theoretical frameworks relevant to the analysis of language strategies in postcolonial writing, while Chapter 6 engages with gender theory, diaspora theory, and transculturalism in contemporary Pacific writing.

1.4.1 *Race and representation*

The first theoretical category to be discussed here, and one which is central to much of the material discussed in later chapters of this book, is the concept of race—and the racially-inflected representation of Indigenous peoples—in colonial and anticolonial discourse. As revealed in the discussion of Said's *Orientalism* earlier in this chapter, one of the main fields of inquiry within postcolonial studies is colonial discourse theory, which examines the way in which '*representations* and *modes of perception* are used as fundamental weapons of colonial power to keep colonised peoples subservient to colonial rule' (McLeod 2000: 17, *sic*). From the late eighteenth century in particular, representations of non-Western peoples in European colonial discourse have centred on the issue of race, which has been represented as a scientific method by which to distinguish between different peoples. As John McLeod reminds us, however, the category of race is based upon 'human invention and not biological fact': there are no objective criteria by which human beings can be classified into separate 'races'. The category of race is therefore essentially a 'political construction' which serves the interests of particular groups of people (2000: 110).

Within the Pacific context, as outlined above, the division of Indigenous Pacific peoples into various racial categories—Polynesian, Melanesian, and Micronesian—formed the basis of an assemblage of racial stereotypes about Pacific Islanders that began to accumulate in European discourse from the 1830s. As a general rule, the lighter-skinned Polynesians and Micronesians were commonly considered 'racially, morally and politically superior' to the darker-skinned Melanesians as well as the Australian Aborigines (B. Douglas 1999: 65). In late nineteenth- and early twentieth-century Western literatures, Polynesian cultures (and peoples) were persistently stereotyped as 'paradisiacal', 'gorgeous', 'fertile', and 'idyllic', while Melanesian islands were represented as 'fetid', 'decaying', and 'hellish', and their peoples viewed as hostile and culturally 'backward' (Kjellgren 1993: 99; see also Hau'ofa 1975: 286). But even before Dumont d'Urville developed his tripartite racial model of the Pacific, the peoples of the region had been subject to various racial and cultural stereotypes in European discourse.

Many of those stereotypes became focused upon peoples living within the region which Dumont d'Urville called Polynesia. Since the late 1760s, when increasing numbers of European travellers visited the Pacific, Polynesia (above other regions within the Pacific) proved to be of particular fascination to European travellers and writers (B. Smith 1985: 1; Edmond 1997: 16). The perceived physical beauty of

Polynesians—and in particular Tahitians—led eighteenth-century explorers such as Louis-Antoine de Bougainville (a French captain) and Joseph Banks (the naturalist who accompanied Captain James Cook on his first Pacific voyage) to draw parallels between Tahitian culture and classical Greek culture. The region was frequently represented, in Romantic terms, as a South Seas Eden inhabited by 'noble savages' untouched by the corruptions of the 'civilized' European world (B. Smith 1985: 42; Keown 2005: 1–2). The concept of the 'noble savage' was in wide circulation at the end of the eighteenth century, popularized by the theories of the French Romantic philosopher Jean-Jacques Rousseau, who argued in his *Discours sur l'inégalité* [*A Discourse on the Origin of Inequality*] (1754) that 'natural man'—a term which came to be associated with 'primitive' or non-Western peoples—was in a pure 'state of nature' or ideal condition of humanity from which Europeans had been distanced due to the corrupting effects of 'civilization' and modernity. In late-eighteenth-century European discourse focused on the Pacific, the 'noble (Polynesian) savage' was frequently represented as the inhabitant of a tropical paradise abundantly stocked with food and all things necessary for a pleasurable, languid existence. Tahiti, described by Bougainville as 'la Nouvelle Cythère' (the new Cythera, based on the legendary home of Venus)[4] was also accorded a reputation as a sexual paradise, and as Bernard Smith points out, the island 'became notorious throughout Europe in the popular mind as a land of free-love' (1985: 47). Such stereotypes have fired the imaginations of generations of European artists, writers, and film-makers (see Chapter 2), and these idealized constructions have persisted into the contemporary era, fuelled by media and tourist-industry representations of the Pacific as a timeless paradise within which Western desires and fantasies may be played out (Wilson 1999a: 10; Keown 2005: 2). In a memorable passage from 'Towards a New Oceania', Albert Wendt discusses some of the common colonial stereotypes of Pacific Islanders which 'linger on' to this day in literature, popular culture, and tourist advertising:

There was no Fall, no sun-tanned Noble Savages existing in South Seas paradises, no Golden Age, except in Hollywood films, in the insanely romantic literature and art by outsiders about the Pacific, in the breathless sermons of our elite vampires... Our islands were and still are a goldmine for romantic novelists and film-makers, bar-room journalists and semi-literate tourists. ... Much of this literature ranges from the hilariously romantic through the pseudo-scholarly to the infuriatingly racist; from the *noble savage* literary school through Margaret Mead and all her comings of age, Somerset Maugham's puritan missionaries/drunks/and saintly whores and James Michener's rascals and golden people, to the stereotyped childlike pagan who needs to be steered to the Light.

(Wendt 1976a: 52–3; 58)

Here, Wendt specifically identifies the role that Euro-American anthropologists (such as Margaret Mead) and fiction writers (such as W. Somerset Maugham and James Michener) have played in the perpetuation of cultural stereotypes about Pacific Islanders, and these issues are taken up in more detail in Chapter 2.

While the 'noble savage in paradise' stereotype that Wendt satirizes here has proved to be one of the most pervasive images of the Pacific in European discourse, it has also been accompanied, since its inception, by a contrasting stereotype of the 'ignoble savage' which has similarly endured into modern times. In the late eighteenth and early nineteenth centuries, for example, damning accounts of the 'primitive' social practices of Pacific peoples began to filter back to the European metropolitan centres through the writings of European explorers and missionaries. The missionaries, who came to the Pacific in increasing numbers following the establishment of the London Missionary Society in Tahiti in 1797, frequently represented Indigenous Pacific Islanders as ignoble, savage heathens—who indulged in '[a]bhorrent social practices such as cannibalism, infanticide and tattooing'—in order to justify native conversion to Christianity (Edmond 1997: 9; Pearson 1984: 27). As we will see in Chapter 2, various skirmishes between European explorers and Pacific Islanders gave rise to the stereotype of the warlike, hostile Pacific Islander, a trope which persists in modern popular culture, evident (for example) in the reputation of Polynesian rugby players as fearsome sporting 'warriors', or in the international success of Lee Tamahori's 1994 film *Once Were Warriors* (discussed in Chapter 3).

Unsurprisingly, a considerable proportion of Indigenous Pacific literature takes a counter-discursive (oppositional) approach to these various racial stereotypes imposed by Europeans. Given, however, that 'Orientalist' discourse in the Pacific has targeted certain aspects of Oceanian life as *positive* alternatives to the limitations of Western cultures, it is not surprising that Pacific Islanders have at times endorsed colonial stereotypes for strategic purposes. The myth of the easy-going, sensual 'noble savage' in paradise, for example, is often invoked in order to bolster the tourist industry upon which many Pacific Islanders depend for their livelihoods. This strategy, by which aspects of Pacific cultures are valorized against perceived limitations in 'Western' cultures, bears some resemblance to the 'négritude' ideology expounded by black intellectuals such as Aimé Césaire and Léopold Senghor during the 1930s and 1940s. In order to counter negative Western stereotypes of black peoples, proponents of 'négritude' celebrated 'blackness' as an essential racial category and emphasized the putative sensuality, intuition, and innate sense of rhythm among black peoples in Africa, America, and the Caribbean. Similar stereotypes have been adopted not only within the Pacific tourist industry, but also, at times, by Indigenous Pacific writers such as Alan Duff (Keown 2005: 179–80).

Further, it is important to acknowledge that while many Indigenous peoples of the Pacific have celebrated their affiliations with other peoples of the region—particularly as a form of resistance against European attempts to 'compartmentalize' Pacific cultures—others have drawn strategically upon concepts of racial and ethnic 'difference' in order to assert their 'First Peoples' status against the claims of later immigrants to the Pacific. One of the most notable manifestations of inter-racial conflict has taken place in Fiji, where the perceived threat posed by the descendants of Indian indentured labourers to the territorial and political 'rights' of Indigenous Fijians erupted into military conflict in the 1980s and 1990s (see Chapter 4). With this in view, it is unsurprising that Pacific academics such as Indo-Fijian scholar Subramani have advocated terms like 'culture' and 'multiculturalism' as alternatives to the ideologically charged categories of 'race' and 'multiracialism' (1995: 250). Notably, however, the transcultural and transnational affiliations that have developed between Pacific creative writers have often served to bridge the cultural schisms opened up by events such as the Fiji coups: as we will see in Chapter 4, for example, creative links between Indigenous Fijian, Indo-Fijian, and other Pacific writers based at the University of the South Pacific have endured throughout and beyond the political crises of the 1980s and 1990s, and a number of new multi-ethnic publications and writers' collectives have emerged as testament to this continuing process of cultural and literary exchange.

1.4.2 Imperialism and colonialism

In making a distinction between the related terms 'imperialism' and 'colonialism', it is useful to think of imperialism, in Edward Said's terms, as 'the practice, the theory, and the attitudes of a dominating metropolitan centre ruling over' another territory (Said 1995: 8). As Elleke Boehmer observes, imperialism is 'the authority assumed by a state over another territory—authority expressed in pageantry and symbolism, as well as in military and economic power', and it is a term 'associated in particular with the expansion of the European nation-state in the nineteenth century'. Colonialism, on the other hand, is a *material* process involving the 'settlement of territory, the exploitation or development of resources, and the attempt to govern the Indigenous inhabitants of occupied lands' (Boehmer 2005: 2). In this book, 'imperialism' is therefore used mainly to refer to the *ideologies* (or systems of belief) which underpin (and are used to justify) the *material* process of colonial settlement, domination, and exploitation. When applied to literature, the adjectives 'colonialist' and 'imperialist' refer to those texts which support, advocate, or are implicitly informed by colonial and/or imperial objectives and attitudes.

As John McLeod points out, colonialism has often been intimately connected with the rise of capitalism in European nations: one of the primary reasons behind the 'seizing of "foreign" lands for government and settlement' was the 'desire to create and control markets abroad for Western goods, as well as securing the natural resources and labour-power of different lands and peoples at the lowest possible cost' (McLeod 2000: 7). In the Pacific, this is true of many colonies which were established by European nations—climatic conditions within various Pacific Islands made them ideal locations for establishing coconut and sugar plantations, for example—but is not applicable in *every* case. The settler colonies of Australia and New Zealand, for example, were established partly in order to solve the problem of overpopulation in Britain's urban centres, while many US territories in the Pacific were acquired primarily for military reasons (in order to protect the West Coast of the United States from potential foreign attack), although in many cases these territories subsequently became markets for American products and services. Further, as Rod Edmond notes, for much of the nineteenth century in Britain there was 'considerable resistance . . . to the acquisition of colonies' in the Pacific, and countries such as Aotearoa/New Zealand were annexed only after considerable pressure was exerted by missionaries and settler groups (Edmond 1997: 12). It was not until the late nineteenth century, when Germany and the US established a firmer colonial presence in the Pacific, that Britain began to pursue a more active programme of annexation in the region (see Chapter 3).

1.4.3 'Postcolonialism' and the Pacific

The label 'postcolonial' and its various derivatives (such as 'postcolonialism' and 'postcoloniality') has, throughout its history, been a problematic and contested one. The term was originally used by historians after the Second World War (in phrases such as 'the post-colonial state'), to describe former colonial territories which had gained their independence. In this context the label had a clear chronological specificity, referring to the era of widespread decolonization that followed the Second World War. From the late 1970s, however, the term 'postcolonial' has been taken up by literary critics and theorists in order to discuss the various *cultural effects* of colonization. In this context, the term 'postcolonial' has a less historically or chronologically specific meaning, referring instead to 'the political, linguistic and cultural experience of societies that were former European colonies' (Ashcroft *et al*. 1998: 186).

Another key area of debate within postcolonial studies is whether the term should be spelled with a hyphen (as in 'post-colonial') or without (as in 'postcolonial'). Some commentators have argued that the hyphenated spelling misleadingly implies that colonialism has come to an end, when in fact it is clear that colonialism and imperialism still exist in various shapes and forms. Other critics have suggested that the two variant spellings are useful as a means of distinguishing between different types of postcolonial studies. The hyphenated term 'post-colonial' has in some cases been considered more appropriate for discussions of colonialism and independence as historical events (in other words, in keeping with the historically specific context in which post-war historians first used the term). The non-hyphenated form, in contrast, has become more widely applicable to the cultural effects of colonialism as explored and mediated through literature and other forms of representation (Ashcroft *et al*. 1998: 187; McLeod 2000: 5).

When discussing the continuing economic, political, and cultural domination of once-colonized nations by Western nations, many critics use the term 'neocolonialism' (drawn from economic theory) as a way of circumventing the problems of definition associated with the label 'postcolonialism' (Boehmer 2005: 9). Western consumer capitalism, for example, which has spread to many nations across the world through global economic and media networks, can be said to operate as a 'neocolonialist' force when it persuades people to pursue Western products and lifestyles to the detriment of their own local economies, even if these countries are no longer (or perhaps have never been) colonized by Western nations.

These debates raise interesting questions when considered in relation to the Pacific. While some nations of the Pacific (such as Samoa and Papua New Guinea) are 'post-colonial' in the strictly historical sense, others (such as Tahiti and Guam) remain European or US colonies;[5] some (such as Aotearoa/New Zealand and New Caledonia) are settler colonies with Indigenous populations; and some (such as the Cook Islands) have chosen self-government in continued political association with a former colonial power. Settler colonies such as New Zealand and Australia have been described as simultaneously colonial *and* postcolonial (or neocolonial), in that their settler populations have achieved political autonomy from Britain,[6] while continuing to exercise political and cultural hegemony over the Indigenous aboriginal and Māori populations.

In view of these complexities, the term 'postcolonial' is used in this book mainly as a conceptual (rather than strictly historical) category, and is used without a hyphen except in cases where a specific post-independence context is discussed. This more flexible use of the term 'postcolonial' acknowledges that in spite of the varying political conditions within the contemporary cultures of the Pacific, the history of colonialism in the region has nevertheless, as Robert Young puts it, helped to '[determine] the configurations and power structures' of these various cultures as they exist today (Young 2001: 4). Albert Wendt offers a similarly flexible definition of 'the postcolonial' within a Pacific context, arguing that '[f]or me the *post* in post-colonial does not just mean *after*; it also means *around, through, out of, alongside*, and *against*' (Wendt (ed.) 1995a: 3; *sic*). Notably, the final part of Wendt's definition draws attention to the way in which postcolonial Pacific texts, like those elsewhere in the 'postcolonial' world, are often polemical works, positioned in opposition to imperialist and (neo)colonialist ideologies and agendas. Elleke Boehmer has described postcolonial literature as 'that which critically or subversively scrutinizes the colonial relationship' and often 'sets out ... to resist colonialist perspectives' (2005: 3). This is a useful definition to keep in mind when reading the postcolonial literatures of the Pacific, not only because many of the texts discussed in this book engage directly with political movements designed to resist (neo)colonialism in the Pacific, but also because it allows for texts written by European New Zealanders (technically members of a 'colonizing' culture) to be categorized as 'postcolonial' when they engage critically with (neo)colonialism. However, for ease of reference, in many cases the adjectives 'Indigenous' and 'European/Western' (or 'settler') are used in this book to distinguish between the various ethnic groups and literatures in the Pacific.

1.5 Chapter overview

The multiple objectives underpinning the structure of this book have been touched upon at various points in this chapter, but for ease of reference, this concluding section offers a brief sequential summary of the content of the remaining chapters in the book. As explained above, the chapters are arranged in broadly chronological order, running from the late eighteenth century until the present day, thereby allowing readers to trace particular issues or historical trajectories running through the book as a whole.

Chapter 2, for example, investigates European representations of Pacific Islanders from the 1760s to the late nineteenth century, focusing on various fiction and non-fiction texts produced during this period of exploration, colonization, and settlement in the Pacific. The chapter also analyses the settler literatures of Aotearoa/New Zealand during the nineteenth and early twentieth centuries, investigating the ways in which an emergent sense of national identity was developed, asserted, and (at times) contested in texts by New Zealand authors. New Zealand, like Australia, can be considered both 'colonial' and 'postcolonial': its achievement of Dominion status in 1907 marked its growing separation from the British imperial 'mother country', and yet New Zealand has itself operated as a colonialist force in the

Pacific, seizing Western Samoa from Germany in 1914, acquiring the Cook Islands, Niue, and Tokelau from Britain in the early decades of the twentieth century, and continuing to exercise hegemony over the Indigenous Māori of Aotearoa. The implications of New Zealand's role as a colonizing force in the Pacific are explored not only in Chapter 2, but also in later chapters of the book.

Chapter 3 focuses more specifically upon Indigenous forms of resistance to colonialism during the twentieth century, investigating how nationalist and millennialist movements in countries such as Western Samoa and Papua New Guinea have been explored imaginatively in creative works by Pacific writers. The chapter also discusses the ways in which traditional methods of warfare, and the involvement of Pacific Islanders in various twentieth-century wars (including the First, Second, and Vietnam wars), have been explored and allegorized in contemporary Pacific writing, where warriorhood is often used as a symbol of Indigenous resilience and self-assertion.

Taking up where Chapter 3's historical trajectory ends, Chapter 4 investigates the emergence of Indigenous Pacific literatures from the 1970s, acknowledging the existence of recognizably 'national' traditions in countries such as Papua New Guinea and Aotearoa/New Zealand, but also emphasizing the regional nature of many Pacific literary networks, and exploring particular 'centres' of activity within the various linguistic communities of the region: anglophone, francophone, hispanophone. This sets the scene for Chapter 5, a more 'thematic' chapter which explores the centrality of Pacific languages, oral traditions, and myths to much contemporary Pacific writing, also undertaking stylistic analyses of selected Indigenous literary texts. The concluding chapter of the book resumes the chronological focus of earlier chapters, exploring some of the most recent developments and cross-currents in Pacific literature from the 1990s and into the new millennium, and investigating the relationship between Pacific writing and other forms of representation such as drama and film.

With the contours of our literary map established, and various relevant terminologies and contextual details on board, we are now ready to begin our journey through the postcolonial Pacific. Indexing the importance of oceanic voyaging to the peoples of the Pacific, there is an ancient Māori pēpeha (proverb) that runs as follows: 'He waka kōtuia kāhore e tukutukua ngā mimira' ('A canoe that is interlaced will not become separated at the bow'). In precolonial times, this pēpeha was often used to emphasize the importance of social cohesion—if iwi (tribes) became fragmented, they were more vulnerable to attack from outsiders—but it can also serve as a metaphor for the structure of this book. While the individual chapters of this text have their own internal structure and function, they are also lashed together in order to give readers some sense of the intricate linkages between the manifold literatures and cultures within this vast sea of islands: Oceania.

2

Europeans in the Pacific

Awfully nice man here to-night . . . Telling us all about the South Sea Islands till I was sick with desire to go there; beautiful places, green for ever; perfect climate; perfect shapes of men and women, with red flowers in their hair; and nothing to do but to study oratory and etiquette, sit in the sun, and pick up the fruits as they fall.

(Robert Louis Stevenson, letter of spring 1875)

East of Fiji, life is one long lotus-eating dream, stirred only by occasional parties of pleasure, feasting, love-making, dancing, and a very little cultivating work . . . Westward of the Fijis lie the dark, wicked cannibal groups of the Solomons, Banks, and New Hebrides, where life is more like a nightmare than a dream, murder stalks openly in broad daylight, [and] the people are nearer to monkeys than to human beings.

(Beatrice Grimshaw, *From Fiji to the Cannibal Islands*)

'Simply by sailing in a new direction / You could enlarge the world'. So wrote New Zealand poet Allen Curnow in 'Landfall in Unknown Seas', a poetic meditation on the 1642 'discovery' of New Zealand by Dutch explorer Abel Tasman (Bornholdt *et al.* (eds.) 1997: 401). Tasman's abortive voyage (see section 2.3 below) was made at a time when relatively little was known about the Pacific region: the Spanish, who led the first European expedition to Oceania in 1521, had annexed Guam and the Northern Mariana Islands, but abandoned plans to expand further into the Pacific. Tasman's endeavours added little to European knowledge of the region, and it was not until the late eighteenth century that the geographical contours of the Pacific were decisively established (by British explorer James Cook). With this in mind, and taking the 1760s as our point of departure, this chapter explores some of the major material and discursive incursions into the Pacific made by Europeans in the late eighteenth and nineteenth centuries. The opening section (2.1) investigates the way in which Enlightenment, Romantic, and missionary representations of Pacific Islanders inflected later European literature about the Pacific (including the writings of Herman Melville, Pierre Loti, Paul Gauguin, and R. M. Ballantyne). The second section of the chapter (2.2) focuses upon European literature about the Pacific in the late nineteenth and early twentieth centuries, investigating the ways in which writers and anthropologists of this period drew upon contemporary racial theories (such as social Darwinism) in their representation of Pacific peoples. The final section of the chapter (2.3) is focused specifically on the exploration, settlement, and colonization of Aotearoa/New Zealand, not only investigating literary representations of cross-cultural contact between Māori and Pākehā (European) New Zealanders, but also exploring the emerging discourse of nationalism in Pākehā settler-colonial writing of the nineteenth and early twentieth centuries. The chapter ends with a brief overview of Pākehā women's writing, touching upon late twentieth-century changes in Aotearoa/New Zealand's literary landscape which are analysed further in later chapters of this book.

2.1 European representations of the Pacific in the late eighteenth and nineteenth centuries

2.1.1 Eighteenth-century explorers and philosophers: science and the 'noble savage'

The late eighteenth century is commonly taken as a starting point in analyses of European representations of the Pacific, largely due to the fact that an important new phase of exploration began in the region during this period. Improvements in the design of ships, rigging, and navigational instruments made travel to the Pacific from Europe less hazardous and arduous than it had been before, and during the 1760s several important voyages were made to the Pacific in search of 'Terra Australis Incognita', the great 'unknown Southern Land' that was believed to exist in the southern hemisphere as a balance to the large land masses in the north. On their search for the undiscovered continent, British captain Samuel Wallis and his crew (on HMS *Dolphin*) were the first Europeans recorded to have made contact with Polynesians, reaching Tahiti in 1767. Nine months later, the French explorer Louis-Antoine de Bougainville also arrived in Tahiti, and his description of Tahiti as 'La Nouvelle Cythère' (the New Cythera) was to form a mainstay of Enlightenment and Romantic conceptions of the Pacific as a sexual and environmental paradise. It was Wallis's compatriot James Cook, however, who was to make the most extensive contribution to European knowledge about the Pacific. During his three voyages to the Pacific (between 1769 and 1779), Cook, an expert cartographer, established the extent and boundaries of the Pacific ocean, proved that the great southern continent did not exist, charted most of the major island groups in the Pacific, and provided Europe with an extensive collection of material objects as well as scientific and ethnographic data (Campbell 1989: 55).

Cook's own records were supplemented by the work of a variety of scientists, artists, and other supernumeraries who travelled with him to the Pacific. On board the *Endeavour* was the renowned English naturalist Joseph Banks, who brought with him other naturalists (including Daniel Carl Solander, a pupil of the famous Swedish naturalist Carl Linnaeus) and several artists (including Sydney Parkinson) who provided graphic records of the expedition's findings. As Bernard Smith points out, Banks 'set the organizational pattern' for subsequent exploratory work in the Pacific by England, France, Russia, and America, combining research in the biological and physical sciences, and systematically collating verbal and visual observations (Smith 1985: 7). The foundations of Pacific ethnography (the scientific description of different 'races' of people) were also laid during this period: the German-born scientist Johann Reinhold Forster and his son George, who were on Cook's second voyage, produced some of the earliest comparative studies of Indigenous Pacific Islanders. It was J. R. Forster, for example, who identified the physiognomic contrasts between eastern and western Pacific Islanders which were to form the basis of Dumont d'Urville's geocultural categories of Polynesia and Melanesia (see Chapter 1) (B. Douglas 1999: 65; Edmond 1997: 8). Similarly, Wallis's, Bougainville's, and Banks's early descriptions of Tahitians, which compared their physical attributes and social practices to those of the ancient Greeks, laid the foundations for a comparative paradigm in which the lighter-skinned Polynesians were viewed as inherently 'noble' and more 'civilized' than the darker skinned Melanesians to the west (Smith 1985: 41–2).

These scientific theories about Pacific Islanders developed alongside philosophical theories on 'natural man'. As discussed in Chapter 1, the Romantic theory of the 'noble savage' was in wide circulation at the end of the eighteenth century, popularized by the writings of the French philosopher Jean-Jacques Rousseau. Descriptions of Tahiti which reached Europe in the wake of voyages by Wallis, Bougainville, and others seemed to suggest that the Pacific, one of the last remaining regions believed to be untainted by European 'civilization', presented the ideal location in which these theories on 'natural man' might be tested. In this context, the idealized vision of the Polynesian 'noble savage' did not merely emerge *from* early contact between Europeans and Tahitians, but was also imposed *upon* the Pacific on the basis of existing philosophical theories, and as a result of earlier contact with other 'primitive' peoples in Africa and the Americas. In terms redolent of Edward Said's *Orientalism*, theorist David Spurr observes that Rousseau's 'natural man' was less a real and living presence than an abstract ideal against which to measure contemporary theories on the rights of man (1993: 126). In other words, the 'noble savage', like 'the Oriental', became Europe's binary opposite, an ideological construct against which Europe could define and assert itself.

In accounts of Tahiti produced by many of the early British and French explorers, the opposition between Polynesians and Europeans was specifically gendered and sexualized, representing the Pacific as an erotic paradise in which Pacific women freely offered sexual favours to European male visitors. The journals of Wallis, Bougainville, Cook, Banks, and others all contained observations on the willingness of Tahitian women to engage in sexual relations with European visitors during trade negotiations, and Bougainville's description of Tahiti as the 'New Cythera' alluded directly to the legendary island home of Venus/Aphrodite, goddess of love. As David Spurr observes, this 'eroticized idea of Tahiti' was appropriated in various ways by European writers and philosophers during and beyond the eighteenth century (Spurr 1993: 174; see also Smith 1985: 47). These early observations thus established the dominant vision of the Pacific as a heterosexual paradise, even though, as Rod Edmond points out, observations by the *Bounty* mutineer James Morrison on the behaviour of Tahitian transvestites known as māhu inaugurated 'a largely suppressed or covert discourse on Tahitian homosexuality that was to shadow Western writing well into the twentieth century' (Edmond 2002: 146).

2.1.2 Exoticism and eroticism: the Pacific narratives of Herman Melville, Paul Gauguin, and Pierre Loti

These interwoven discourses on Polynesian sexuality have clearly inflected the Pacific writings of American author Herman Melville and French writer and painter Paul Gauguin, both of whom visited what was later to become French Polynesia. Melville, crew member on a whaling ship that called at Nukuhiva in the Marquesas in 1842, jumped ship with a fellow sailor and spent several weeks in the Typee valley, leaving the Marquesas on another vessel a month after his desertion. His novel *Typee* (1846) was represented as an autobiographical account of his adventures in the Marquesas, and Melville's fellow deserter Richard Tobias Greene—from whom he became separated after coming ashore—later attested to its authenticity. However, there are many inconsistencies in Melville's narrative: though he stayed among the Typee for less than a month, it is claimed in the novel that Tommo (the narrator, Melville's fictionalized counterpart) stayed for four months, and his ethnography of the Typee is heavily reliant on accounts by earlier visitors to the region that Melville read only after he returned from his Pacific travels. As Rod Edmond notes, the novel falls within 'that Enlightenment and Romantic tradition which imaginatively appropriated the South Pacific in order to construct its case against the ignobility of civilization' (1997: 84). The Typee are represented, in Romantic terms, as a society living in a condition of utopian 'ease' and abundance, enjoying a free and 'natural' sexuality, and observing a marriage system based on female desire (Melville 2001: 149). Tommo's paramour Fayaway is the focus for the colonial appropriation of the heterosexual other: he offers rapturous descriptions of her 'free pliant figure' and sensuous full lips, and while he asserts that Marquesans are the most physically attractive of Polynesians (rivalled perhaps only by the Tahitians), his emphasis on Fayaway's olive skin and blue eyes locates her more specifically within the classical paradigms invoked by eighteenth-century explorers such as Bougainville (Melville 2001: 85–7; Wilson 1999*b*: 366).

Tommo's celebration of the sexual allure of Fayaway and her fellow Typee also intersects with European 'fatal impact' rhetoric (see section 2.2), representing the Typee as an enervated civilization approaching extinction. Drawing upon the work of Mary Louise Pratt, Rod Edmond argues that the text incorporates this rhetoric within the paradigm of the cross-cultural romance, in which 'a feminine Polynesian culture gives itself voluntarily to a masculine, European, colonizing one which will later abandon it on the beach, leaving it to wilt and die' (Edmond 1997: 174–5; Pratt 1992: 92–7). Such a model is implicit in the relationship between Tommo and Fayaway in *Typee*, and is incorporated more explicitly into later European representations of French Polynesia such as the French writer Pierre Loti's *Le Mariage de Loti*, a novel which first appeared in serial form in 1880. In this text, the French narrator—whose experiences are based partly on Loti's own 73-day visit to Tahiti, and partly on his brother Gustave's stay on the island in 1859—loves and eventually leaves his fourteen-year-old Tahitian lover Rarahu, who subsequently dies of tuberculosis. Loti's text prompted Paul Gauguin to visit Tahiti, and there are echoes of Loti's text in Gauguin's own book *Noa Noa* (written in the 1890s and published in several different versions), in which Gauguin describes his sexual relationship with a thirteen-year-old Tahitian girl, Tehamana. Melville's, Loti's, and Gauguin's heterosexual romance narratives have formed a satirical target in the work of a number of Indigenous Pacific writers, particularly the Samoan writer Sia Figiel. In Figiel's novel *Where We Once Belonged* (1996*a*), for example, Gauguin and Tommo are represented as voyeurs, while in her autobiographical fragment 'A Writer's Story', Melville's Fayaway is described as a literary 'figment' who has helped to fire the imaginations of countless modern-day tourists in search of 'Polynesian babes' (Figiel 1996*a*: 187 and 1998: 100–1; Keown 2005: 43).

While Melville's, Loti's, and Gauguin's narratives undeniably establish a dominant model of cross-cultural romance, Gauguin's and Melville's works in particular are not straightforward heterosexual fantasies. *Noa Noa*, for example, contains a vivid homoerotic scene in which Gauguin is aroused by the sight of a half-naked young male woodcutter. Gauguin's desire emerges partly as a result of the young man's androgynous appearance—Gauguin describes him as 'sexless'—but when the woodcutter turns around to look at him, the 'hermaphrodite' vanishes and becomes a young man once more, and Gauguin's desire abates (Gauguin 1985: 25, 28). Gauguin himself had been dubbed 'ta'ata vahine' (man-woman) by Tahitians due to his shoulder-length hair, and a preoccupation with androgyny is also evident in many of his Tahitian and Marquesan paintings, where Polynesian women often appear solid-limbed and muscular (Edmond 1997: 251–2).

Melville's *Typee* similarly engages with homoerotic desire in the figure of Marnoo, an androgynous young man whose 'rich curling brown' hair and cheeks of a 'feminine softness' elicit Tommo's admiration. When Marnoo ignores Tommo on their first meeting, the rejection is compared to the public slighting of a society 'belle', as though Tommo imagines himself as Marnoo's heterosexual other (Melville 2001: 135–6). Like Gauguin, Tommo therefore finds himself attracted to both male and female Polynesians, and it is significant that his approving description of Marnoo follows directly after a rapturous account of Fayaway's feminine charms.

In addition to complicating the myth of the heterosexual cross-cultural romance, Melville's text also contains other intriguing contradictions, most clearly embodied in the two (often conflicting) narrative voices in the novel. The voice of Tommo, for example, offers an empirical account of Polynesian cultural practices that can be contrasted with another, philosophical narrative voice that attempts to impose conventional Enlightenment and Romantic accounts of 'primitive' peoples upon the Typee. The Romantic model of the 'noble savage' is regularly called into question as Tommo discovers that the Typee also engage in 'ignoble' cultural practices such as cannibalism and tattooing. In Chapters 17 and 24, Tommo criticizes those who impose European philosophical paradigms on Polynesians (125, 170), and at one point, he also admits his inability to produce an authoritative ethnography of the Typee, revealing that 'I saw everything, but could comprehend nothing' (177). As David Spurr notes, one of the major tropes of imperialist authority in colonial discourse is the panoptic, controlling, and classifying gaze of the colonizer, who looks upon the colonized but denies the colonized the privilege of 'looking back' (1993: 13). In this context, it is significant that Tommo not only denies his own specular authority, but is also deeply unsettled by the return of the native gaze in a scene where a Typee chief regards him 'with a rigidity of aspect under which I absolutely quailed'. Tommo reflects that '[n]ever before had I been subjected to so strange and steady a glance; it revealed nothing of the mind of the savage, but it appeared to be reading my own' (Melville 2001: 71; see also Sharrad 1990: 602 and Edmond 1997: 86).

There are also intriguing contradictions in attitudes towards religion expressed in Melville's text. Chapter 24, for example, ends with a parodic denunciation of the Typee as a 'back-slidden generation . . . sunk in religious sloth' (179), while later in the novel, Tommo questions the value of Christian missions in the Pacific and suggests that 'pathetic accounts of missionary hardships, and glowing descriptions of conversions, and baptisms taking place beneath palm-trees' in missionary discourse are misleading, masking the fact that in reality, many of the missionaries themselves are in 'want of vital piety' (198). These examples reveal a playful aspect to Melville's interrogation of the dominant tropes of colonial discourse, and his satirical attacks upon missionaries prefigure those of later European traveller-writers in the Pacific such as Robert Louis Stevenson and W. Somerset Maugham. Stevenson's short story 'The Isle of Voices' (1893), for example, features a double-dealing and avaricious European missionary, while Somerset Maugham's 'Rain' (1921) traces the downfall of a censorious and tyrannical evangelist who ends up breaking his own strict moral code.

2.1.3 Missionary discourse and boys' adventure stories: Ellis, Williams, and Ballantyne

Throughout the nineteenth century, British Protestant and French Catholic missionary groups were often in fierce competition in their efforts to establish theocratic dominance in the Pacific. Tonga, Tahiti, and Hawai'i became the main centres from which Christianity spread to other island groups, and in many cases, Indigenous converts themselves became missionaries: one of the most renowned of these was the Cook Islander Ta'unga, who produced some of the earliest written accounts of New Caledonians in Melanesia.[1]

Many European missionaries also kept careful records of their experiences in the Pacific, and the published accounts of LMS missionaries William Ellis and John Williams had a particularly significant impact on later literary representations of the Pacific. William Ellis's *Polynesian Researches* (1829), which included substantial ethnographic descriptions based on his experiences in Tahiti, was a source of inspiration for nineteenth-century writers such as Herman Melville and Wilkie Collins, and scientist Charles Darwin also acknowledged that Ellis's text was one of his main sources of information on Polynesian cultures (see Edmond 1997: 105). Although Ellis's text was not aimed primarily at a mission-supporting readership, the text nevertheless establishes a paternalistic colonial paradigm which was to become a familiar tenet of much subsequent European discourse on the Pacific. Ellis offers implicit justification for his mission by condemning Polynesians as 'indolent', 'peculiarly addicted to pleasure', and prone to 'barbarous' and 'cruel' social practices such as infanticide, while also identifying their 'childlike' curiosity and aptitude for learning as guarantors of the success of Christian missions in the region (Ellis 1969: xx, 92, 193, 247–8). However, as Rod Edmond observes, the ethnographic and missionizing registers in Ellis's text sit uneasily alongside one another: Ellis's painstaking descriptions of various Tahitian cultural practices (such as tattooing) are frequently followed by vehement denunciations of the 'immorality' of these practices, and yet the ethnographic sections of the text suggest 'that far from needing to be rescued by civilization, the Tahitians already have one' (Edmond 1997: 119). The text thus betrays an 'ambivalence' which theorists such as David Spurr and Homi Bhabha have identified as a central feature of colonial discourse (Spurr 1993: 7; Bhabha 1994: 85–92).

John Williams's *Missionary Enterprises* (1837), an account of his own missionary work in the Cook Islands and Samoa, also became an important source for later European narratives focused upon the Pacific. Williams's text is less rhetorically contradictory than Ellis's, emerging as a more straightforward 'conquest narrative' in which Williams celebrates his success in converting his 'childlike' Polynesian charges to Christianity. His description of the converted Rarotongan village of Arorangi, whose 'neat white cottages', 'spacious chapel' and schoolhouse, and 'tastefully laid out' gardens are contrasted with the lack of 'uniformity' in unconverted native settlements, offers a persuasive model of the domesticated 'savage' which was emulated in a number of nineteenth-century adventure novels set in the Pacific (J. Williams 1998: 92–4). R. M. Ballantyne's boys' adventure story *The Coral Island* (1858), for example, includes an almost verbatim reproduction of Williams's Polynesian domestic idyll, and the young British heroes in the narrative manage to 'pacify' various fierce 'natives' in a manner reminiscent of their ecclesiastical predecessors (Ballantyne 1995: 326–7). Near the end of the novel, after speaking to a 'native' missionary who has followed the lead of his European mentors by burning a collection of 'pagan' wooden idols, Ralph (the narrator) silently exhorts God 'to prosper those missionary societies that send such inestimable blessings to these islands of dark and bloody idolatry' [*sic*] (336). As Rod Edmond observes, in Ballantyne's novel, and in the work of other nineteenth-century adventure novelists such as W. H. G. Kingston, the Pacific became 'the prime fictional testing site and proving ground for the reconstructed manly boy of the public school-imperial axis', linking missionary and colonial 'civilizing missions' and prefiguring the consolidation of British colonial interests in the Pacific in the latter part of the nineteenth century (Edmond 1997: 145).

Given these associations between missionary enterprise and colonialism in the Pacific, it is unsurprising that a wide range of Indigenous Pacific literature produced since the 1970s has been highly critical about the Christianization of Pacific peoples. In his essay 'Towards a New Oceania', for example, Albert Wendt cites ni-Vanuatu writer Albert Leomala's lyric poem 'Kros'—in which he accuses Christian missionaries of 'killing' Pacific Islanders and their traditions—as one of the most vehement early denunciations of Christianity as the evangelizing arm of colonialism in the Pacific (Wendt 1976*a*; Leomala in Wendt (ed.) 1980: 121). Western-educated characters in the work of Samoan writer Sia Figiel trace contemporary constraints upon Samoan female sexuality back to the teachings of LMS missionaries, while Wendt himself has denounced missionary attempts to eradicate Pacific religions and cultural practices such as tattooing and carving (Figiel 1996*b*: 10–11; Wendt 1976*a*, 1996). Yet Wendt does not go so far as to suggest that Christianity has simply eradicated and supplanted Indigenous Pacific religions: instead, his fiction points towards the ways in which Pacific peoples have *indigenized* Christianity, adapting it to existing structures of belief and social exchange. The degree to which Indigenous Pacific Islanders have successfully adopted Christianity on their own terms can arguably be measured in the fact that today, Pacific Islanders (of various Christian denominations) are among the most committed church-goers in the world (Crocombe 2001: 209–10). It is also worth noting that for over a century, Christian missionaries provided almost all formal education and most medical and welfare services in the Pacific Islands, and missionaries were responsible for developing the first orthographies and grammars for Pacific languages (see Chapter 5). Although missionaries undeniably sought to (and often did) eradicate Indigenous religious and other cultural practices, they also attempted to protect Pacific Islanders from those who wished to exploit the Pacific for personal gain, counterbalancing some of the damage caused by whalers, traders, publicans, and colonists. They could not, however, prevent the accelerating forces of colonial annexation, exploitation, and settlement that took hold in the Pacific during the nineteenth century.

2.1.4 *High/forward imperialism in the late nineteenth century: the context*

At the beginning of the nineteenth century, the Pacific largely remained the realm of solitary traders, shipmasters, beachcombers, and missionaries, but as trade activity expanded, increasing numbers of foreign settlers and traders arrived, followed by larger commercial organizations seeking to exploit Pacific commodities. In the first half of the nineteenth century, these commodities included whale-oil, sandalwood, tortoiseshell, and beche-de-mer (a type of edible sea-slug), while trade in coconut oil and copra (dried coconut meat), cotton, and sugar cane flourished during the closing decades of the nineteenth century. Throughout most of the nineteenth century, major European colonial powers such as France and Britain showed little interest in the Pacific due to its remoteness (from Europe) and its perceived lack of exploitable resources compared to other parts of the 'New World'. However, when Germany initiated an active programme of Pacific colonization from the 1870s, Britain and France, and then Spain, Chile, and the United States, began to compete for Pacific territories. By the end of the century, most Pacific Islands were under the protection or colonial jurisdiction of individual Western nations, but many of these territories, once acquired, were left, as Steven Fischer puts it, to 'languish in an economic backwater' (Fischer 2005a: 123). While Melanesia, for example, was much richer in certain resources (such as land, agricultural products, timber, and minerals) than Polynesia and Micronesia, colonization was much slower and more haphazard in the region, partly because of the absence of political centralization and attendant suspicion of 'outsiders' in the region, and also due to the presence of malaria and other ailments to which Europeans had no immunity (Crocombe 2001: 414–15). Countries such as Aotearoa/New Zealand and Hawai'i, on the other hand, where Europeans and Americans settled in their thousands throughout the nineteenth century, were subject to a more direct form of colonial rule.

Whatever form it took, imperialist expansion into the Pacific had a radical impact upon the lives of Pacific Islanders. During the whaling era (1820s–1850s), large numbers of Islanders were lured from villages to thriving port settlements in Honolulu (Hawai'i), Pape'ete (Tahiti), Levuka (Fiji), Kororareka (Aotearoa/New Zealand), and Apia (Samoa). Islander men were in demand as local labourers and sailors, while some Islander women entered into domestic service and prostitution. Islanders became increasingly reliant upon European trade items (such as cloth, alcohol, gunpowder, and muskets), and many Polynesian chiefs abandoned their traditional religious and economic systems and became capitalists, though this often resulted in heavy foreign debt and increased vulnerability to annexation by Europeans. Kinship structures were altered with the increasing numbers of mixed-race children, many of whom married Europeans and Americans, and in the closing decades of the century, populations were radically depleted as thousands of Polynesians and Melanesians were 'recruited' (and often kidnapped) to work on plantations within and beyond the Pacific (Fischer 2005a: 115, 122). However, throughout the Pacific, one of the most devastating consequences of contact with Europeans was the spread of new diseases, which decimated Island populations and, as we will see below, inspired a range of imaginative literature focused upon the putative 'fatal impact' of Europeans in the Pacific.

2.2 Disease and degeneration: the impact of social Darwinism on *fin-de-siècle* Pacific writing

Throughout the Pacific, one of the most devastating consequences of contact with Europeans was the spread of new diseases among Indigenous populations. Due to their geographical isolation, Pacific Islanders had no immunity to the barrage of Western ailments (such as measles, chickenpox, influenza, and venereal disease) brought to the Pacific by successive waves of Europeans, and the populations of many Pacific Islands were decimated after contact took place. In Hawai'i, for example, a native population of around 142,000 in 1823 was reduced to 39,000 by 1896; Tahitians were reduced from around 35,000 at the time of Cook's first voyage to around 7–8,000 by the end of the nineteenth century; and it is estimated that many Western Melanesian cultures lost around ninety per cent of their populations to disease, although mortality figures were often exaggerated (Fischer 2005a: 117–18; Campbell 1989: 154; Edmond 1997: 10). A belief that Pacific cultures were dying out as a result of contact with Europeans gained widespread currency in the latter part of the nineteenth century, reinforced by the application of Darwin's theory of natural selection to Indigenous societies that were ostensibly being overcome by stronger, putatively 'superior' European cultures. The 'fatal impact' theory (which held that Pacific populations would decline to eventual extinction) held currency well into the twentieth century, and was used to justify increasing European settler and commercial expansion into the Pacific (Fischer 2005a: 119; Keown 2005: 131).

2.2.1 'Fatal impact': the Pacific writings of Robert Louis Stevenson and Jack London

The extent to which 'fatal impact' rhetoric had inflected European discourse on the Pacific in the late nineteenth century (and into the twentieth) is clearly evident in the Pacific writings of Robert Louis Stevenson and Jack London. London, for example, read the work of Herbert Spencer, the English philosopher credited as the 'father' of social Darwinism, and in *The Cruise of the Snark* (1911), a narrative which records London's travels through the Pacific between 1906 and 1908, he makes a direct reference to Darwin during a discussion of depopulation in the Marquesas. London observes that in the half-century that has passed since Melville's visit to the Taipi Valley, the native population has been drastically reduced by various introduced European diseases, particularly respiratory afflictions such as tuberculosis and asthma (2003: 109). He attributes this in part to the warm climate, where airborne diseases 'flourish as luxuriantly as the vegetation', but identifies '[n]atural selection' as the primary explanation for the relative constitutional 'weakness' of Marquesans. 'We of the white race', he argues, 'are the survivors and the descendants of the thousands of generations of survivors in the war with the microorganisms . . . We who are alive are the immune, the fit . . . The poor Marquesans had undergone no such selection' (113).

The influence of social Darwinism is also palpable in London's Pacific fiction. A range of his short stories feature what he called 'the inevitable white man', an embodiment of the putative biological and social 'superiority' of white races, and his visit to the Hawai'ian leper colony Moloka'i (see Map 2.1) in 1906 inspired a range of stories in which leprosy functions as a metaphor for the depredations of colonialism. His short story 'Koolau the Leper' (1912), for example, draws upon the popular theory that leprosy was brought to Hawai'i by Chinese indentured labourers, but the blame is laid explicitly at the feet of the American sugar planters who enlisted the labourers to work on their Hawai'ian plantations (69). The story—which describes the resistance of a group of Hawai'ian lepers against deportation to Moloka'i—contrasts the failing health of the Hawai'ian lepers with the strength and resolve of the colonizing Americans. Koolau, the dying protagonist, concludes that the biological and mental resilience of the Americans, attributes which 'his own kind lack[s]', renders them invincible in their conquest of the Hawai'ian people (102–3). London's story is based on an actual occurrence, an account of which was published in Hawai'ian by John Sheldon (Kahikina Kelekona), who heard the story from Koolau's wife Pi'ilani in 1906. Koolau was diagnosed with leprosy in 1893—the year in which the Hawai'ian monarchy was overthrown—and it is significant that where London's narrative uses Koolau's experience to underscore the 'inevitability' of the American conquest of Hawai'i, Pi'ilani's account is defiant rather than defeatist, offering vehement denunciations of the actions of the Provisional Government and other 'plundering, burning thieving' haole [white men] who 'came to fatten on our land' (Pi'ilani 2001: 25). Further, where Pi'ilani's account is understated in its discussion of the physical symptoms of leprosy, focusing instead upon Koolau's mental resilience, London's fictional narrative offers lurid and lingering descriptions of the ravaged bodies of the lepers. One woman '[weeps] scalding tears from twin pits of horror, where her eyes had once been', while one of her companions, in a travesty of 'Polynesian' sensuality, takes up a 'gorgeous flower of orange and scarlet' to place behind a 'bloated ear

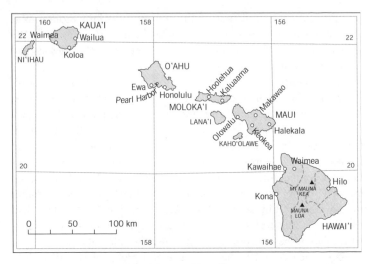

Map 2.1 Hawai'i

lobe' that '[flaps] like a fan upon his shoulder'. Significantly, London's neo-Darwinist rhetoric constructs the lepers as dehumanized and degenerate 'monsters' resembling 'huge apes marred in the making' (1912: 65), drawing heavily upon contemporary Euro-American debates about 'the apparent decline towards extinction of Polynesian cultures' (Edmond 1997: 206).

In his Pacific writings, Robert Louis Stevenson also engaged with Western theories about depopulation in Oceania. Stevenson spent his final years in the Pacific region in an attempt to improve his own failing health, and after visiting various Pacific Islands in 1888 and 1889, he finally settled at Vailima in Samoa, where he died of a brain haemorrhage in 1894. He kept a journal during his travels, using his entries as the basis for his travel book *In the South Seas* (1900), which—like London's travel narrative—includes a detailed discussion of depopulation in the Pacific. In attempting to account for the fact that Marquesans, Hawai'ians, and other eastern Polynesians are 'perishing like flies' while Samoans (for example) remain in good health, Stevenson explores and rejects various theories about the reasons for depopulation (including familiar arguments about the putative lack of hygiene and chastity among Pacific Islanders).

He eventually concludes that the degree of depopulation is dependent upon the extent of social changes introduced through European contact. 'Where there have been fewest changes,' he argues, 'there the race survives. Where there have been most [changes], important or unimportant, salutary or hurtful, there it perishes' (1987: 51–2).

While this argument reproduces familiar Romantic and social Darwinist 'fatal impact' theories, Stevenson's engagement with the adverse impact of colonialism upon Pacific cultures moved beyond mere rhetoric when he became directly involved in anticolonial politics within his adopted country of Samoa. Stevenson's 1892 publication *A Footnote to History: Eight Years of Trouble in Samoa* contained direct criticisms of the wrangling for power among British, German, and US colonial forces in Samoa. His 'outspoken' views prompted the British High Commissioner for the Western Pacific to issue *A Regulation for the Maintenance of Peace and Good Order in Samoa*, which was clearly designed to curtail Stevenson's involvement in Samoan politics (Jolly 1996: xliii).

As Rod Edmond observes, *A Footnote to History* is not a 'root-and-branch' attack upon colonialism in Samoa, but in his foreword to a 2003 edition of Stevenson's writings edited by Roger Robinson, Samoan writer Albert Wendt argues that the work demonstrates Stevenson's 'astute and perceptive and enthusiastic support for our struggle against the foreign powers and colonialism' (Edmond 1997: 169; Wendt 2003b: 10). Wendt reveals that Stevenson has entered into 'legend' in Samoa, and he draws attention to Stevenson's iconic status in his 1979 novel *Leaves of the Banyan Tree*, where a tubercular young Samoan writes an autobiographical narrative in the hope of becoming an Indigenous version of Stevenson (1979: 158).[2] Such an aspiration is particularly significant given that Stevenson himself experimented with writing narratives for Polynesian readers: his stories 'The Bottle Imp' (1891) and 'The Isle of Voices' (1893) feature Polynesian central characters and oral storytelling conventions, and copies of *Ballads* (1890), his volume of Polynesian and Highland poems and legends, were given to members of the Hawai'ian and Tahitian royal families. 'The Bottle Imp' was also translated into Samoan and circulated widely among Indigenous readers, who affectionately dubbed Stevenson 'Tusitala' (meaning 'writer of tales') (Edmond 1997: 186–8).

2.2.2 *Social Darwinism in reverse: narratives of European disease and degeneration*

While London's and Stevenson's Pacific writings clearly index contemporary theories about the 'fatal impact' of Europeans on Pacific Islanders, their work also explores another strand of contemporary social Darwinism: the perceived threat of European degeneration. Where the theory of natural selection outlined in Darwin's *Origin of Species* (1859) was used to advance arguments for the 'inferiority' of non-Western cultures in relation to more 'advanced' Western cultures, Darwin's two-volume tract *The Descent of Man, and Selection in Relation to Sex* (1871) also raised the possibility that evolution could work in reverse: in other words, that humans could *de*volve towards more 'primitive' states of being. As confidence in the British empire began to decline in the late nineteenth century, with British failures during the South African War as a particular crisis point, anxieties about European 'degeneration' became focused upon the putative risks posed by exposure to 'tropical' climates and 'savage' native customs (Spurr 1993: 162).

These anxieties are referenced in a number of Jack London's Pacific adventure stories, particularly those set in Melanesia. As outlined in Chapter 1, European racial typologies targeted Melanesians—whose darker skins and kinky hair invited comparisons with African peoples—as racially inferior to Polynesians, whose lighter complexions and dynastic social systems were compared to those of European peoples. In late nineteenth-century writing about the Pacific, anxieties about European degeneration became focused upon Melanesia, which was posited, in social Darwinist terms, as an environment within which Europeans were at great risk of physical and moral degeneration. These representations were partly motivated by the relative failures of European imperialist ventures in Melanesia during the first half of the nineteenth century. Missionary and commercial endeavours had been repeatedly frustrated by apparently hostile, 'headhunting' natives, and the Melanesian climate harboured a range of tropical diseases (such as malaria) to which Europeans lacked immunity. It was only in the 1860s, with the expansion of plantation economies and the resultant demand for 'native' labour, that recruitment agents began to call more regularly at Melanesian coastal settlements. Over the next few decades, some

100,000 Melanesians were transported to plantations in Queensland, Fiji, New Caledonia, Samoa, and New Guinea, some as indentured labourers, but many as hapless victims of the notorious European 'blackbirders', labour agents who kidnapped Islanders and sold them on to plantation owners elsewhere in the Pacific (Campbell 1989: 115).

These material details, combined with racial theories of the period, furnished Jack London with a rich source of inspiration for a range of toe-curling Melanesian adventure narratives published in his short-story collections *South Seas Tales* (1911) and *The Red One* (1918). Stories such as 'The Terrible Solomons' and 'The Whale Tooth' (from *South Sea Tales*) dwell on the putative cannibalistic 'savagery' of Melanesians, but other narratives feature a range of depraved, violent Europeans, many of whom are ruthless blackbirders who kidnap, torture, and kill Melanesian labourers. Perhaps the most memorable of London's 'degenerate' white men is Bunster, a physically powerful, sadistic German trader (in London's 1911 story 'Mauki') whose violence and volatility has led his company to post him on an 'out-of-the-way' island north of the Solomons (1939: 104). Mauki, a Solomon Islander who, after being sold to blackbirders, repeatedly absconds from various labouring posts, is (as a last resort) sent to work for Bunster 'for eight long years and a half' in punishment for his desertions (106). Bunster, described as 'a thrice-bigger savage than any savage' on the island, routinely beats Mauki and his other servants, and also takes pleasure in removing layers of skin from their bodies with an abrasive mitten made of ray-fish skin (104–5). Mauki bides his time, and when Bunster eventually falls prey to a fever, he gets his revenge, flaying Bunster with his own mitten, cutting off his head, and escaping back to Malaita (his home island) in Bunster's boat. Although the narrator describes Mauki's home as 'the most savage island in the Solomons' (91), Mauki appears as a 'lamb' alongside the European traders and blackbirders described in the tale, and Bunster's death thus appears as recompense for the years of abuse Mauki has suffered (95).

London's intriguing short story 'The Red One' (1918) offers a more subtle exploration of European degeneration, focusing on the physical and moral decline of a British naturalist (Bassett) who visits the Solomon Islands. Bassett disembarks from a blackbirding ship for a few hours' specimen collecting on Guadalcanal, but is lured into the jungle by a tantalizing sound which eventually proves to be the death of him. Thrashing his way into the mosquito-ridden interior with the help of a Melanesian guide, Bassett finds the source of the sound—a massive, hollow, resonant red metal sphere—and is desperate to be the first European to brings news of it back to 'civilization' (2003: 28). He is prevented, however, by the depredations of malaria—which debilitate him almost to the point of death—and by the machinations of 'ape-like, man-eating and head-hunting savages' (27) who eventually behead Bassett during a sacrificial ritual held in the vicinity of the mysterious sphere, which they worship as 'The Red One'. There is a moral as well as physical aspect to Bassett's ignominious fate: in order to view 'The Red One' in the first place, Bassett agrees to a sexual encounter with Balatta, an 'unthinkably disgusting bushwoman' with 'dirt-crusted shoulders' and 'rancid oily and kinky hair' who repays him by guiding him to the sacred site (19). Bassett's coupling with Balatta falls within a familiar Western discursive paradigm, representing miscegenation as a means by which the Western subject loses his/her individuality and enters a realm of bestial sexual excess and death (Spurr 1993: 182). It is significant that in documenting the moment of physical contact, the narrator describes Balatta's reaction in animalistic terms ('[she] mowed and gibbered and squealed little, queer, pig-like gurgly noises of delight' (19)): this paradigm of the bestial and sexually aggressive Melanesian is the inverse of the Romantic image of the neo-Grecian, passive, sexually yielding Polynesian.

There are clear echoes of Joseph Conrad's novella *Heart of Darkness* (1899) in London's narrative—Bassett, like Kurtz, finds 'horror' in the interior, which is populated by putatively frenzied natives emitting a babble of 'uncouth sounds' (London 2003: 12; Conrad 1973: 27)—but London's story also references another, more local degeneration narrative: Robert Louis Stevenson's *The Beach of Falesá* (1892). Stevenson's novella, which predates Conrad's *Heart of Darkness* by several years, is set on an unidentified Polynesian island and is narrated by Wiltshire, an English trader who takes over a store owned by his trading company. Wiltshire is denied custom, however, when Case, a rival trader, tricks him into marrying a local woman (Uma) who has been placed under taboo, thereby frightening off prospective customers. Case himself secures the loyalty of locals by establishing a den of 'horrors'—located in the centre of the bush—that plays upon their 'superstitions', and Wiltshire is only able to break the deadlock when he penetrates the 'heart of darkness', exposes the fraud, and kills Case. Case is clearly a representative of the imperialist greed and opportunism which Conrad was to explore in *Heart of Darkness*, but Stevenson offers a more direct prototype for Conrad's Kurtz in the form of Case's partner Randall, a retired captain who is now an ageing alcoholic, 'squatting on the floor native fashion', his eyes 'set with drink' and his 'fat and pale' body 'crawled over by flies' to which he seems oblivious (1996: 8). Randall is among the most physically degenerate of Stevenson's 'South Seas' Europeans, but other narratives such as *The Wrecker* (1892) and *The Ebb-Tide* (1893–4) feature further characters in the mould of Case: avaricious, unprincipled, and prepared to kill rival compatriots for financial gain. In this story, as in many of London's narratives, the regressive 'savagery' of Europeans is represented as more horrifying than the putative natural 'barbarity' of the natives.

The mercantile objectives of many of London and Stevenson's white men are represented as the root of their degeneracy, but in a range of other Western texts focused on the Pacific, a comparable set of associations cluster around the figure of the beachcomber, the 'renegade white man' who has abandoned European civilization altogether to take up residence in the tropics. Yet beachcombers themselves made significant contributions to the Pacific archive: Herman Melville himself was—albeit temporarily—a beachcomber, and the writings of other beachcombers such as William Diaper, William Mariner, and Samuel Patterson also provided source material for subsequent adventure fiction set in the Pacific region (V. Smith 1998: 18–52).

2.2.3 Pacific anthropology

A final branch of European discourse selected for discussion here is the discipline of social anthropology. While only representing a small proportion of the world's total population, Pacific Islanders, and particularly Melanesians, have formed the focus of a disproportionately large body of anthropological scholarship which has accumulated since the late nineteenth century. At a time when anthropologists were beginning to test the implications of Charles Darwin's theories of evolution for the empirical study of human societies, the 'remote' Pacific (sections of which remained unexplored by Europeans) was seen as an ideal laboratory in which such research could be conducted (Denoon *et al.* 2000: 20). Much of this research was concentrated within Melanesia—of great interest to anthropologists due to its social and linguistic diversity—and the published works of these anthropologists often reproduced familiar colonial discursive paradigms in which Polynesian cultures were 'romanticized' and Melanesians 'denigrated' (Hau'ofa 1975: 286).

A number of Indigenous Pacific writers have engaged critically with Pacific anthropological discourse. Notable among these writers is Epeli Hau'ofa, who himself trained as an anthropologist and has satirized Western ethnographers in a range of his fiction and non-fiction writings. In his 1975 essay 'Anthropology and Pacific Islanders', he critiques the way in which twentieth-century Western anthropologists such as Marshall Sahlins have reinscribed 'evolutionary' social models in which Melanesians are considered less 'advanced' than Polynesians. Hau'ofa's 1987 comic novel *Kisses in the Nederends* is in part a satirical response to British anthropologist Mary Douglas's *Purity and Danger* (1966), a text which produces a similar dialectical model in which Western cultures are viewed as more socially refined than non-Western societies. Hau'ofa's novel, which functions in part as ethnographic satire, explores various ways in which to transcend these oppositional (and denigratory) paradigms (see Keown 2005: 69–78).

Where Hau'ofa has critiqued Western anthropology in Melanesia, a number of other Polynesian writers—in particular, the Samoan writers Albert Wendt, Sia Figiel, and Noumea Simi—have produced counter-discursive responses to the work of the American anthropologist Margaret Mead. Mead undertook fieldwork in American Samoa in the 1920s in order to test contemporary anthropological theories about the role of nature (biology) versus nurture (socialization) upon the formation of the human psyche. Like her mentor Franz Boas, Mead believed that socialization, not heredity, was the primary determinant of human behaviour, and she undertook nine months' fieldwork in Ta'u (part of the Manu'a archipelago; see Map 2.2) in 1925 in order to compare the effects of differing social conditions upon the psychological development of teenage girls. In *Coming of Age in*

Map 2.2 The Samoan archipelago

Samoa (1928), the book which documented her findings, Mead argued that the 'general casualness' of Samoan society, where 'love and hate, jealousy and revenge, sorrow and bereavement, are all matters of weeks' and where casual pre-marital sex is accepted and encouraged as a 'natural, pleasurable' activity (1943: 162), ensured that Samoan adolescents experienced none of the transitional difficulties which American teenagers endured as they emerged into adulthood. Mead's text offers an 'Orientalist' vision of Pacific Island life, reinscribing Romantic myths about the merits of the 'prelapsarian' Pacific over the social complexities and corruptions of the 'West' (see Keown 2005: 19–23). Parts of the text (such as the opening of Chapter 2) read more like a romantic novel than an ethnographic treatise, encapsulating the rhetorical complexity and generic hybridity that scholars such as Elleke Boehmer have recognized as a central feature of much colonial discourse (Boehmer 2005: 5).

In the 1980s, Mead's theories were eventually discredited by the New Zealand-born anthropologist Derek Freeman, who had undertaken more than forty years of fieldwork both within and outside Samoa. Freeman's 1983 study *Margaret Mead and Samoa: The Making and Unmaking of an Anthropological Myth*, and his later book *The Fateful Hoaxing of Margaret Mead* (1998), systematically analysed and rejected Mead's major claims about Samoan social practices, not least her argument that Samoan society is sexually permissive.

The 'Mead–Freeman controversy' has been indexed in the work of a variety of Indigenous Samoan writers. Albert Wendt, for example, has undercut Mead's paradisical view of Samoan life in a range of his early writing (see Keown 2005: 19–28), and he offers a satirical fictional response to the Mead–Freeman legacy in his more recent novel *The Mango's Kiss* (2003), which features an American anthropologist, Freemeade, whose name conflates those of his famous 'scholarly' counterparts. Ironically, given Mead and Freeman's focus upon heterosexuality, Freemeade is a homosexual who initiates relations with local fa'afafine (trans-sexuals or transvestites) while undertaking fieldwork in a Samoan village.

Wendt's compatriot Sia Figiel also offers a series of playful jibes about Mead and Freeman: her first novel *Where We Once Belonged* (1996a), for example, includes a schoolgirl account of the Mead–Freeman debate as a petty argument about whether Samoan girls '[do] "it" a lot', as well as an episode in which two Samoan transsexuals are named after Derek Freeman (Figiel 1996a: 204, 68). Figiel's novel, however, also offers a more serious response to Mead's legacy in particular, offering a contrasting vision of Samoan adolescence as a traumatic 'coming of age' in which female chastity is enforced through verbal and physical abuse and the threat of public humiliation (see Keown 2005: 46–8).

Samoan poet Noumea Simi offers a similarly polemical response to the Mead–Freeman legacy in 'What Are We?', where the speaker urges Freeman to 'Leave us alone' and exhorts fellow Samoans to take over the task of representing themselves rather than allowing 'naive academics / and slit-minded brainwashers' to speak for them (Wendt (ed.) 1995a: 284). Simi's poem, like the work of Figiel and Wendt, is situated within a broader, ongoing debate about the discursive tyranny of Western representations of Pacific peoples. This debate entered a new phase following the publication of Paul Theroux's pseudo-anthropological travel narrative *The Happy Isles of Oceania* (1992), which reinvoked a wide range of 'noble' and 'ignoble' savage stereotypes garnered from the European discursive archive (see Edmond 1997 and Va'ai 1999). The perpetuation of Western anthropological 'myths' in texts such as Theroux's has galvanized ensuing literary satires such as Vilsoni Hereniko and Teresia Teaiwa's *Last Virgin in Paradise* (1993), a play in which a young, Mead-esque female anthropologist relentlessly questions young Pacific Islanders about their sexuality.

2.3 Settler fictions in Aotearoa/New Zealand

This final section of the chapter is focused specifically on the exploration, settlement, and colonization of Aotearoa/New Zealand, investigating literary representations of cross-cultural contact between Māori and Pākehā (European) New Zealanders, exploring the growing sense of national 'belonging' as expressed in twentieth-century Pākehā literature and other forms of self-representation, and ending with a brief overview of Pākehā women's writing.

2.3.1 'Something nobody counted on': representations of first contact in Aotearoa/New Zealand.

Throughout the late nineteenth century, and for much of the twentieth, Pākehā schoolchildren were commonly indoctrinated with triumphalist accounts of the European 'discovery' and settlement of New Zealand, from the initial forays made by Abel Tasman in the 1640s (discussed below), through Captain James Cook's 'heroic' exploits in the late eighteenth century, to the influx of benevolent missionaries and plucky pioneers from Britain in the early decades of the nineteenth century. Early issues of the New Zealand *School Journal* (established in 1907 to meet the need for locally produced school textbooks) contained essays situating Cook alongside other British maritime 'heroes' such as Lord Nelson, interweaving accounts of Cook's New Zealand adventures with narratives of British imperial consolidation in other colonies such as India and Canada.

To some degree, these settler myths held popular currency well into the closing decades of the twentieth century, but in the 1980s, during the lead-up to the 1990 sesquicentenary of the British annexation of New Zealand, a range of revisionist historical scholarship and historiographical fiction emerged, re-evaluating Aotearoa/New Zealand's colonial past from new, and often anticolonial, perspectives. Landmark historical studies such as Claudia Orange's *The Treaty of Waitangi* (1987) and James Belich's *The New Zealand Wars and the Interpretation of Racial Conflict* (1986), and historiographical novels such as Witi Ihimaera's *The Matriarch* (1986) and C. K. Stead's *The Singing Whakapapa* (1994) offered radical reassessments of the complexities of cross-cultural contact and martial conflict between

Māori and Pākeha, exposing and attempting to transcend the over-simplifications and lacunae in established accounts of the colonial dialectic. This section of the chapter explores literary representations and reinterpretations of events in Aotearoa/New Zealand's colonial history, focusing upon the work of two writers produced at key historical moments: the period immediately preceding the sesquicentenary (when Witi Ihimaera's historiographical novel *The Matriarch* was published), and the 1940 centenary celebrations of settler nationalism (as explored in the work of Pākehā poet Allen Curnow).

Literary reassessments of the 'discovery' of Aotearoa: Curnow and Ihimaera As was the case in many other parts of the Pacific, early encounters between Europeans and Māori in Aotearoa/New Zealand were often marked by misunderstanding and mutual hostility. When Dutchman Abel Tasman and his crew visited Golden Bay (known to local Māori as Taitapu) in 1642, Māori interpreted a trumpet call from the Europeans as a formal challenge and killed four crew members before Tasman retreated, dubbing the area 'Murderer's Bay' (see Map 2.3). Tasman's account of the incident conferred upon Māori a reputation as fierce warriors, and the stereotype was further consolidated when the French explorer Marion du Fresne and fifteen crewmen were killed at the Bay of Islands in 1772, following an inadvertent breach of tapu (Salmond 1991: 382–95; Edmond 1997: 223). When Cook visited New Zealand in 1769, he established comparatively good relations with Māori, but his first contact with Māori at Poverty Bay in 1769 was also marked by bloodshed: in this case, Māori were killed after Cook's crew misinterpreted Māori ceremonial protocol as hostility (King 2003: 105; Fischer 2005a: 116).

These misunderstandings and bloody skirmishes inspired a series of 'revisionist' poems produced by Pākehā poet Allen Curnow in the early 1940s. These poems emerged in the immediate aftermath of the 1940 celebrations marking the centenary of the signing of the Treaty of Waitangi (discussed below), which had marked the British annexation of Aotearoa and the 'birth' of New Zealand as a British settler colony. The celebrations witnessed the consolidation of a cultural and literary nationalism that had been fomenting throughout the 1930s, as writers, intellectuals, and politicians sought to foster and promote a sense of New Zealand's cultural independence from the imperial 'mother country'. As Stuart Murray notes, however, despite the 'smooth

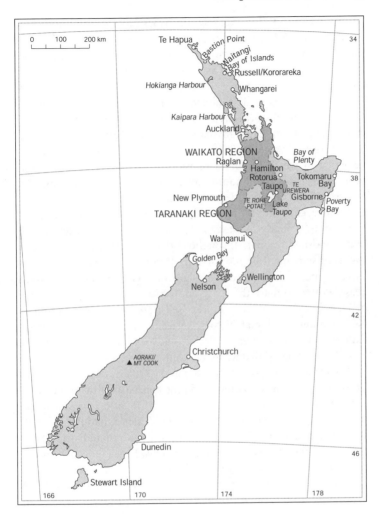

Map 2.3 Aotearoa/New Zealand

nature' of the political rhetoric that accompanied the Centennial celebrations, the poetry of Allen Curnow and other writers of the period expressed a more ambivalent attitude to the county's 'emerging nationhood' (1998: 41). Reacting against jingoistic expressions of national 'belonging' circulated among Pākehā, Curnow's 1941 poem

'House and Land', for example, describes New Zealand as 'a land of settlers / With never a soul at home', while 'The Skeleton of the Great Moa in the Canterbury Museum, Christchurch' (1943) uses the extinct moa bird as a metaphor for the precariousness and potential impermance of settler claims on the new country. Two other poems, 'The Unhistoric Story' (1941) and 'Landfall in Unknown Seas' (1943), probe at the very foundations of settler identity, challenging triumphalist myths surrounding Tasman's and Cook's 'discoveries' in Aotearoa/New Zealand. 'The Unhistoric Story', the very title of which implies a revisionist account of New Zealand's past, emphasizes the random violence and misunderstandings that accompanied Tasman and Cook's forays into Aotearoa's waters, and each stanza ends with the repeated mantra 'It was something different, something / Nobody counted on' (Curnow 1990: 94). Images of death and bloodshed resonate throughout the poem, puncturing utopian myths of settlement by representing European incursions as violent assaults upon the new land and its inhabitants. 'Landfall in Unknown Seas', written to mark the 300th anniversary of Tasman's 'discovery' of New Zealand, similarly mocks 'self-important celebration[s]' of New Zealand's colonial history, instead—and invoking Tasman's experiences as a sobering reminder—advocating an attentiveness to '[the] stain of blood that writes an island story' (1990: 105).

Where Curnow's poems emerged in the wake of centenary celebrations of New Zealand 'nationhood', the approach of the sesquicentenary in 1990 offered another opportunity for historians and writers to reflect upon founding myths of New Zealand 'national' identity. By this point, Māori writers such as Witi Ihimaera and Patricia Grace had joined the literary milieu, offering new, Indigenous perspectives on Aotearoa's colonial history. Witi Ihimaera's epic novel *The Matriarch* (1986), for example, emerged as a polemical attack upon Pākehā historical accounts of New Zealand's colonial history, revisiting and reinterpreting key aspects of cross-cultural conflict from what he termed a 'Māori perspective'. Significantly, Ihimaera describes Māori historiography as a highly subjective discourse which varies from tribe to tribe and is informed 'by the holistic frameworks of the unreal as well as the real' (1991: 53–4). In keeping with this perspective, the novel establishes a repeating pattern in which putatively established historical 'facts' recorded in dominant (Pākehā) accounts of New Zealand history are followed by 'Māori' perspectives, which often draw upon Māori mythology and cosmogony as counterdiscursive sources of historical knowledge. The novel also features a multiplicity of narrative perspectives: the voice of the dominant first-person narrator, Tamatea, frequently alternates with the voices of various historical figures—Māori and Pākehā—and with the voice of an omniscient narrator, who frequently offers vehement denunciations of Pākehā historical and discursive 'offences' against Māori.

Many of these discursive interrogations are focused upon key historical moments of contact (and conflict) between Europeans and Māori. Early in the narrative, for example, the omniscient narrator challenges dominant, triumphalist versions of Cook's 1769 landfall at Poverty Bay as a founding settler myth. The narrator reminds readers of the bloodshed that accompanied this first moment of contact, arguing that the putative 'glorious birth of the nation has the taste of bitter almonds when one remembers that six Maoris died so that a flag could be raised' (1988: 37). Here, Ihimaera's counter-history actually draws upon established facts verified by Pākehā historians (see King 2003: 103), but in many other cases—and particularly in its discussion of the 'land wars' that raged between settlers and Māori in the 1860s (see below)—the novel presents putatively 'verbatim' quotations from Pākehā historians which have in fact been edited by Ihimaera in order to emphasize or amplify Pākehā injustices against Māori. Ihimaera's techniques earned him charges of plagiarism and misrepresentation by Pākehā critics (Williams 1990: 130; Stead 2002: 335–6), but given his own comments on the subjectivity of historical discourse, and the political agenda underpinning the novel, it is hardly surprising that Ihimaera's text—which is, after all, historiographical *fiction*—is 'creative' in its representation of Aotearoa/New Zealand's colonial history.

2.3.2 *The Treaty of Waitangi and the annexation of Aotearoa/New Zealand: the context*

In its investigation of Pākehā colonial injustices against Māori, Ihimaera's narrative returns repeatedly to the 1840 signing of the Treaty of Waitangi, a founding document which formalized the British annexation of New Zealand. Before analysing Ihimaera's text in more detail, it is worth exploring the historical 'context' within which the narrative is grounded, as such details are relevant not only to a reading of Ihimaera's text, but also to the work of other Māori writers such as Patricia Grace and Alan Duff.

In the early decades of the nineteenth century, which witnessed the arrival of increasing numbers of European missionaries and traders in Aotearoa/New Zealand, the British government remained reluctant to press any imperial claims upon this 'remote' South Pacific country. The government's hand was forced, however, by the successes of the New Zealand Company, a colonization scheme, founded in 1837 by Englishman Edward Gibbon Wakefield, which transported large numbers of Britons to planned settlements throughout Aotearoa/New Zealand. The venture was threatened by a developing French interest in colonizing Aotearoa/New Zealand, and pressure from settlers and from missionaries (who were concerned about the welfare of Māori) persuaded the British government to annex the country in 1840. William Hobson was sent by the Colonial Office to negotiate a treaty with Māori chiefs in which they would cede sovereignty to the British monarch and channel all further sales of land through representatives of the Crown. In exchange, Māori would be guaranteed full proprietorship over their remaining lands, and would enjoy the same rights and privileges as all British subjects, protected by the Crown (Fischer 2005a: 124). The Treaty was first signed at Waitangi (in the Bay of Islands) by 45 Māori chiefs on 6 February 1840, and a number of other copies of the Treaty were circulated and signed at various other locations throughout the country. Those Māori who signed the Treaty of Waitangi were unaware, however, of the fact that there were significant differences between the English- and Māori-language versions of the Treaty 'text'. The Māori-language version guaranteed Māori tino rangatiratanga (full chiefly authority) over their lands, villages, and treasures (taonga), whereas the English-language version promised them only 'full exclusive and undisturbed possession' of their lands, estates, forests, and fisheries. Further, where the English-language version stipulated that Māori were ceding sovereignty to the Queen of England, the Māori version translated 'sovereignty' as 'kāwanatanga', which meant 'governorship' and thus appeared to Māori to guarantee custodianship rather than absolute sovereignty to the British monarchy (King 2003: 160; McKenzie 1999: 77–130). The five hundred Māori who eventually signed the Treaty were therefore effectively misled, particularly as the British government subsequently recognized only the English-language version. Further, the land sale terms outlined in the Treaty were repeatedly breached, particularly by the New Zealand Company, which frequently failed to identify the true owners of lands it purchased and ignored Māori disputes over proprietorial rights (Fischer 2005a: 125). Increasing numbers of European settlers arrived throughout the 1850s, outnumbering the Māori population by 1858, and accelerating settler demand for land was matched by increasing reluctance among Māori to sell. A series of ensuing disputes culminated in the North Island 'land wars' which raged between Māori, settlers, and government throughout the 1860s. Further skirmishes took place throughout the 1870s, and a final peace agreement was not made until 1881.

When the wars were over, Chief Justice Prendergast ruled that the Treaty of Waitangi was 'a simple nullity'—a stance maintained by the New Zealand government until the establishment of the Waitangi Tribunal in 1975—and large tracts of prime Māori land, some belonging to 'kūpapa' or 'loyal' tribes who had fought on the side of the Crown, were confiscated and sold to colonists. Further expropriation occurred in the wake of the Native Land Act of 1862, which legalized all land sales between Māori and colonists throughout Aotearoa/New Zealand. By the 1870s, when Māori military resistance to colonization had virtually collapsed, most remaining land was in European hands, and by 1890 the few remaining pockets of Māori land were located mainly in isolated Māori rural communities in the North Island (Fischer 2005a: 127–8).

As sociologist David Pearson points out, the wars of the 1860s were pivotal, shifting the balance of power from imperial control to settler interests, and transmuting earlier attempts at the 'peaceful and voluntary incorporation of Māori subjects [into] their forced marginalisation' (2001: 37). By the 1890s the land wars, and various introduced European diseases, had reduced the Māori population to its nadir (around 42,000), and these population figures, coupled with the influence of neo-Darwinist theories of extinction, encouraged a widespread belief that the Māori race would not last beyond the early twentieth century. This attitude persisted even after the 1901 census revealed that the Māori population was rising, and as late as 1919 the Minister of Health reported that Māori 'were dying out or "being absorbed into the white population"' (Sinclair 1986: 203; Keown 2005: 132). Yet Māori military resistance during the land wars also produced some positive effects. A variety of legislation was passed in the mid-to-late 1860s aimed at bringing Māori within the same property and legal codes as settlers: a Native Land Court and Māori justice provisions were established; special English-medium schools for Māori were founded; and 1867 saw the granting of Māori male suffrage and the provision of four Māori seats in parliament. These measures clearly afforded Māori a degree of participation in the settler state and polity, and it is important to recognize that some hapū (sub-tribes) were still relatively wealthy and autonomous in the last decades of the nineteenth century, some having taken advantage of government agricultural schemes and other economic initiatives (Pearson 2001: 37–8).

The Treaty as 'text': Witi Ihimaera's The Matriarch   The Treaty and its legacy are central to Ihimaera's revisionist historiographical narrative in *The Matriarch*. Although the omniscient narrator is generally suspicious of Pākehā discursive representations of colonial history, s/he places strong emphasis on the constitutive power of the Treaty as *text*, asserting that 'you Pakeha lawyers can argue until the cows come home that the Treaty wasn't a legal document, but *we* believe it is' (1988: 73). Here, as is the case in the discussion of various other key historical moments in the book, the omniscient narrator shifts to the second person in order to implicate Pākehā readers directly in the historical injustices described in the narrative. This strategy underscores the narrator's polemical claims that abuses of the Treaty have continued through to the present day, in which Māori remain 'landless and colonised in [their] own land' (50). However, while the narrator laments the crippling effects of colonization, in keeping with other revisionist perspectives on New Zealand's colonial history which emerged in the 1980s, s/he also moves beyond 'fatal impact' models to explore Māori resistance to colonization—particularly during the wars of the 1860s—and identifies ways in which, prior to the wars, Māori took advantage of European technologies to establish flourishing agricultural businesses.

Significantly, while Ihimaera remains suspicious of Pākehā historical discourse throughout much of the novel, when discussing the resilience of Māori under colonization he often draws upon Pākehā historical records in order to provide corroborating 'evidence'. When discussing the entrepreneurial skills of Māori in Turanga/Gisborne (near Ihimaera's own birthplace, Waituhi) in the 1850s, for example, the narrator quotes directly from a letter, written in 1852 by Turanga-based missionary T. S. Grace, which praises the business 'intelligence' of his Māori charges (50). Grace's comments are represented as a verbatim transcript, complete with square brackets indicating syntactical changes (made in the interest of clarity), thus drawing attention to the complicated layering of 'fact' and 'fiction' in Ihimaera's narrative. The Reverend T. S. Grace is a 'real' historical personage who was indeed based at Turanga in the early 1850s, but *The Matriarch*, like its 1997 sequel *The Dream Swimmer* (discussed in Chapter 3), is complex in its approach to the narration of history. In many cases, factual sources are modified while fictionalized accounts are presented in 'factual' format, and Ihimaera often privileges discursive forms conventionally deemed less historically 'reliable' (including oral 'testimonies', unpublished memoirs, radio interviews, and personal communications). These strategies effectively draw attention not only to Ihimaera's views on the subjective nature of historical interpretation, but also to the potential of fiction as a means by which to call into question the univocal authority of European 'master narratives'.

Where Ihimaera's text frequently presents Pākehā and Māori accounts of New Zealand's colonial history as radically polarized, with Pākehā versions of history often targeted as unproblematically pro-empire, other revisionist historical analyses that have emerged since the 1980s have drawn attention to the *ambivalence* often evident in Pākehā colonial discourse. In 2001, for example, literary critic and historian Ken Arvidson edited a richly contextualized new edition of *The Māori King* (1864), a non-fiction tract, produced by Pākehā magistrate John Gorst, documenting the events leading up to the Imperial army's invasion of the Waikato region in 1863. The Waikato tribes had refused to sign the Treaty of Waitangi in 1840, and after tensions between Māori, settlers, and the government intensified in the 1850s, the Waikato became the base of the nationalist Māori Kingitanga (King) Movement, which elected its first monarch (Potatau Te Wherowhero) in 1857. The King movement was committed to non-violence, and had its roots in Māori nationalist land-leagues dating back to the 1830s, but the Imperial administration viewed the King's assumption of independent sovereignty as an 'act of rebellion' necessitating a military offensive (Arvidson 2001: ix). When the conflict ended in 1864, the rich lands of the Waikato were confiscated by the imperial government. Although Gorst was a representative of the colonial government, serving in the Waikato region as Resident Magistrate and Civil Commissioner for Governer George Grey between 1861 and 1863, in *The Maori King* he takes an intriguingly equivocal stance towards the invasion of the Waikato, openly criticizing what he viewed as the manipulation of the government by land-hungry colonists (169). Nevertheless, his attitude is not straightforwardly pro-Māori: his sympathy for their dispossession at the hands of the colonists is tempered by a sometimes mocking attitude towards their attempts to 'adapt' to European customs (see Arvidson 2001: xiii).

A similar ambivalence towards Māori is expressed in another colonial text of this period: F. E. Maning's autobiography *Old New Zealand* (1863). Maning was a 'Pakeha-Maori', one of a number of resident European traders who married into Māori tribes and set up businesses in concentrated areas of European settlement (such as Kororareka and the Hokianga harbour, in the North Island) in the early decades of the nineteenth century. Poised between two cultures, Maning is critical of British annexation of New Zealand and the evangelistic interventions of missionaries, but his text, which blends autobiography, history, ethnography, and satire, also invokes established racial stereotypes of Māori as cunning, cruel, and 'careless of life', thus—as Peter Gibbons notes—constructing a moral case for government military offensives against Māori during the wars of the 1860s (Gibbons 1998: 46).

2.3.3 Settler nationalism: the background

By the 1890s, when the wars were over and most Māori land was now in European hands, a developing sense of nationhood had begun to emerge among European settlers in Aotearoa/New Zealand. While the various European immigrant groups—particularly English, Scottish, Irish, and Welsh—had maintained their ethnic and national distinctiveness throughout the nineteenth century, by the 1890s the establishment of extensive road and rail networks, and the formation of a number of colony-wide institutions and associations based on British models, had helped to consolidate a notion of New Zealand as the Britain of the south (Pearson 2001: 62). The 1893 granting of female suffrage, and various national welfare reforms (including minimum wage structures, child health services, and old-age pensions) inaugurated by the Liberal government from the early 1890s, served to promote an image of New Zealand as a progressive socio-political laboratory both at home and abroad. The involvement of New Zealand troops in the South African, First, and Second World Wars, and New Zealand's increasing exports of dairy and meat products following the introduction of refrigeration, were further sources of national pride. As Mark Williams notes, the 'process of indigenization' of the settlers is marked by the evolution of the meaning of the term 'New Zealander', which referred to Māori in the early nineteenth century but was ascribed to white descendants of the settlers by the end of that century (1997: 22). In 1901, Premier Richard Seddon arranged for an ensign (depicting the Union Jack with four red stars representing the Southern Cross) used on New Zealand ships since 1869 to be adopted as the national flag, thus introducing one of the most iconic symbols of national identity (McLeod 2000: 69–70). Seddon also developed plans for New Zealand to become an imperial power in its own right, and while these plans were not fully realized, the British Government approved New Zealand's annexation of the Cook Islands and Niue in 1901, and later acquisitions included Western Samoa (in 1914) and Tokelau (in 1925).

2.3.4 New Zealand literary nationalism from the 1930s

The political nationalism developing in the late nineteenth and early twentieth centuries also gave rise to a literary nationalism, which gathered momentum in the 1930s during the leadup to the 1940 centenary celebrations (as discussed in 2.3.1). New Zealand literature of the nineteenth and early twentieth century remained heavily reliant upon British literary models, but by the 1930s, a group of painters and writers—in particular Allen Curnow, Denis Glover, and Charles Brasch, who were all associated with the Caxton Press established in Christchurch in 1936—set about establishing a distinctive local poetic tradition. These writers dismissed existing schools of New Zealand poetry, arguing that the work of their predecessors—and women poets in particular—was marked by an embarrassing colonial deference, outmoded verse forms, Georgian diction, and the 'decorative' use of native flora and fauna. Curnow, Glover, and others argued that a truly national New Zealand poetry should be realist, masculinist, and attentive to the minutiae and distinctiveness of the local environment, rather than expressing nostalgia for the British motherland (M. Williams 1997: 22–3).

In the introduction to his landmark edited collection *A Book of New Zealand Verse 1923–45* (1945), Curnow accuses established female poets such as Eileen Duggan and Robin Hyde of 'sentimental posturing' and 'escapism' in their early work in particular. In contrast, male poets such as R. A. K. Mason and Walter D'Arcy Cresswell are credited with having inaugurated New Zealand poetry's move towards 'manhood itself' by introducing a realist 'toughness' and 'technical sureness' into their work (20, 24, 27). Curnow himself made contributions to this new 'national' literary tradition, while maintaining a critical distance from jingoistic expressions of nationhood surrounding the 1940 centenary of the signing of the Treaty of Waitangi (as noted above). In 1938, Curnow's compatriot A. R. D. Fairburn had also offered a sober reflection on New Zealand culture in his poem 'Dominion', which engages with the effects of the First World War and the Depression upon (white) New Zealand's emergent sense of national identity. 'Dominion' is the first example in New Zealand of a long poem structured—like T. S. Eliot's *The Waste Land*—through a series of disparate verse fragments, and Fairburn's work, like Eliot's, bears the stamp of both British and American literary modernism. In his 1934 essay 'Some Aspects of New Zealand Art and Letters', Fairburn advocates American literature as a useful model for literary explorations of New Zealand national identity, but the style and tone of much of his poetry—like Curnow's—is more in keeping with the Auden generation in 1930s Britain (Fairburn 1934; Jackson 1998: 434). Situating Curnow's work more specifically alongside nationalist movements elsewhere in the world, Stuart Murray argues that Curnow's explorations of national identity, and his role 'as a literary public mentor', are in part the product of his interest in W. B. Yeats and Irish nationalism, as well as other 'national decolonizing movements' in Europe and the Americas (Murray 1998: 223). Within the Pacific context, on the other hand, New Zealand literary nationalists of the 1930s consciously distinguished themselves from their Australian counterparts, who were seen as heavily reliant upon outmoded British literary models (although a number of New Zealand poets published their work in the Sydney *Bulletin* during this period) (Arvidson 2003: 68). Within Aotearoa/New Zealand, the new poetic aesthetic developed by Curnow and others was matched, in the genre of prose, by the 1930s and 1940s short stories of Frank Sargeson. Sargeson's spare realism, privileging of the demotic, and 'sympathy for the "ordinary bloke"' established the 'classic form' of the New Zealand short story for at least three decades, and was not displaced until the politics of feminism and the Māori Renaissance of the 1970s began to make their mark on New Zealand literature (M. Williams 1997: 23).

2.3.5 New Zealand women writers

The masculinist bias in mid-twentieth-century constructions of New Zealand literary history clearly sidelined the contributions of women writers and poets, in spite of the fact that Aotearoa/New Zealand had become the first sovereign state to grant women the vote in 1893. It was not until the 1960s and 1970s, with the international consolidation of the women's rights movement, that serious attempts were made to reassess the contribution of women writers to the New Zealand 'literary tradition'. Robin Hyde, for example, who battled with mental illness throughout her adulthood, and whose poetry and prose was dismissed as 'chaotic', escapist, and verging on 'hysteria' by her male contemporaries, is now recognized as having made important interventions into the emergent literary nationalism of the 1930s (Curnow 1960: 57; Bertram 1953; Murray 1998: 165–7). Her semi-autobiographical novel *The Godwits Fly* (1938) offers a penetrating exploration of New Zealand society during the 1930s, revealing the way in which class divisions between Irish, English, and other immigrant groups in Wellington (Hyde's childhood home) were altered by the Depression and by international socialism. The text also explores the emergent Pākehā nationalism of the period, as the 'colonial England-hunger' expressed by older characters in the narrative (such as Augusta Hannay, mother to the central character Eliza) begins to give way to a more locally grounded cultural aesthetic. Significantly, the novel points towards changing attitudes towards Māori in Pākehā culture, marking a gradual shift away from the 'fatal impact' rhetoric which inflected nineteenth- and early twentieth-century texts such as Alfred Domett's romanticizing epic poem 'Ranolf and Amohia' (1872) or William Satchell's 1914 novel *The Greenstone Door*. Even as late as 1945, poet Charles Brasch (in 'The Silent Land') represented the new country as a conveniently empty, 'nameless' landscape awaiting the awakening touch of the (male) settler (Curnow (ed.) 1945: 149). While Hyde's novel undeniably draws upon established racial stereotypes—Māori in the narrative appear as radically 'other', or as an integral yet alien feature of the natural landscape—her book nevertheless hints at the increasing presence of Māori in urban locations, prefiguring the large-scale migration to the cities which was to take place after the Second World War (Hyde 1993: 32).

Like Robin Hyde, Katherine Mansfield (who became associated with the 'Bloomsbury' literary set in London) also wrote of her Wellington childhood: her 1922 collection *The Garden Party and Other Stories* offers a series of vignettes based upon her memories of the Wellington area in the late nineteenth century. While many of these stories are located within the bourgeois anglophile circles in which Mansfield's family moved, stories such as 'The Garden Party' and 'The Doll's House' explore the class divisions that problematized idealized myths of social inclusion which, during and beyond this period, were circulated in order to promote New Zealand as a utopian 'better Britain' (Lamb 1999). Mansfield, like Hyde, also wrote inquiringly and ambivalently about Māori: her unfinished novel *Maata* is named after a Māori girlfriend with whom she appears to have had a sexual relationship, and as Angela Smith observes, Mansfield's narrative 'Kezia and Tui' (also unpublished during her lifetime) represents a Māori female 'as both an object of desire and a double [or] aspect of the self' (2002: xiii). Mansfield's 1912 story 'How Pearl Button Was Kidnapped' also engages directly with Māori culture, detailing the adventures of a young Pākehā girl taken on an impromptu outing by Māori women passing by her house. The story draws upon established Rousseauian stereotypes—all the Māori characters are 'fat and laughing' and seem to have an abundance of food and children (2002: 22)—but as Angela Smith notes, the story resists explicit 'racial categorization', as the Māori characters are never overtly identified by their ethnicity. Instead, the women's appearances are mediated through the narrative perspective of the child, who describes them merely as 'dark women' and, in contradiction of the story's title, appears to view them as her 'liberators' (Mansfield 2002: 22; Smith 2002: xi–xii).

Many decades after the publication of Mansfield's story, Māori writer Witi Ihimaera wrote a new version entitled 'The Affectionate Kidnappers'. The story appears in his volume of stories *Dear Miss Mansfield* (1989), published to mark the centenary of Mansfield's birth. Mansfield's story ends with the arrival of a group of Pākehā policemen coming to reclaim Pearl, and Ihimaera's narrative explores what might have happened next: in the revised version, the two women have been arrested and are facing a night in prison. Where Mansfield's tale engages more obliquely with cross-cultural conflict, Ihimaera's story confronts explicitly the kinds of Pākehā prejudices about Māori 'savages' which existed during the period, offering a politicized (yet affectionate) response to Mansfield's original narrative from a Māori, 'postcolonial' point of view.

One of the most famous revisions of an earlier New Zealand narrative is, of course, Jane Campion's film *The Piano* (1993) which, in its exploration of the challenges facing colonial settler women, reworks elements of Jane Mander's 1920 novel *The Story of a New Zealand River*, and also bears traces of the memoirs of earlier women settler-writers such as Lady Barker.[3] Mander's narrative details the experiences of an Englishwoman (Alice Roland) who marries a Pākehā man, settles in an isolated timber milling settlement in the Hokianga harbour, and struggles to adapt to pioneering life, thus furnishing some of the primary elements of Campion's film diegesis. Mander's novel, like *The Piano*, also critiques the 'imposition' upon New Zealand of 'a false secularized Puritan code of respectability imported from Victorian England', and Alice Roland, like her counterpart Ada (in *The Piano*), finds an escape from puritanism in her music (L. Jones 1998: 145). In its representation of the New Zealand physical landscape (and particularly in its murky shots of the New Zealand bush), the film also draws upon other New Zealand texts such as John Mulgan's novel *Man Alone* (1939), in which a Pākehā man's solitary sojourn in the bush reinscribes the trope of the harsh, inimical, alien colonial landscape found in a wide range of nineteenth-century New Zealand, Australian, and Canadian 'settler' writing (Murray 1998: 16–17). In Campion's film, Ada is shown fighting her way through mud, dense bush, and clinging supplejack (a type of vine), and her battle against a hostile environment also echoes Katherine Mansfield's story 'The Woman at the Store' (1912), where a woman formerly 'pretty as a wax doll' (2002: 14) has been worn down not only by beatings from her husband, but also through years of battling against the 'savage spirit of the country' on an isolated rural landholding (13). This 'savage spirit' resurfaces again in Janet Frame's 1966 novel *A State of Siege*, in which Malfred Signal, a retired art teacher in search of solitude, is found dead after taking up residence in an isolated bach (shack) on the (fictional) island of Karemoana. Just before her death, Malfred is terrorized throughout the night by a persistent knocking on the door by an unidentified intruder, and her death appears to have occurred after someone throws a stone wrapped in newspaper through her window. Throughout the ordeal, however, it is not clear whether the assailant is a human agent or some kind of embodiment of the landscape itself: the persistent knocking takes place during a violent storm, and when the window breaks, it is the wind that 'leap[s] through the ragged gap', 'enter[s] the room', and '[whistles] through the house', as though it is an elemental rather than human force that oppresses Malfred (1966: 244).

As Marc Delrez points out, the question of whether Janet Frame can be considered a 'postcolonial' writer is a vexed one, as her writing engages with existential and philosophical issues which are not primarily connected with race and cultural identity (2002: xii). Like the Caxton school, however, Frame does nevertheless explore forms of representation and perception which might transcend literary and cultural models 'imported' from Europe and America. Her autobiographies, for example, recount the way in which she gradually broke free of British literary models (particularly those associated with Romantic poetry), developing an aesthetic more attuned to the work of fellow New Zealand writers such as Frank Sargeson, while her 1988 novel *The Carpathians* critiques the effects of American cultural imperialism in a New Zealand still insecure about its own 'national' identity. In *The Carpathians*, Frame also engages more specifically with the relationship between Māori and Pākehā New Zealanders, contrasting the social cohesion among Māori in the wake of the Māori Renaissance with crass appropriations of Indigenous culture by Pākehā anxious to establish a sense of national distinctiveness. Frame's explorations of Pākehā cultural 'schizophrenia' and various forms of social marginalization have emerged in part from her years spent in mental hospitals after being misdiagnosed as schizophrenic, but as Delrez rightly points out, it is reductive to suggest that marginality is the defining feature of her writing; rather, she works towards an 'aesthetics of cultural rapprochement and relationship' that moves beyond dialectical social models (2002: xii). Such an argument helps to explain Frame's discomfort at being branded a feminist icon following the release of Jane Campion's film adaptation of her autobiographies in 1990. As Ruth Brown points out, in the wake of the success of Campion's *An Angel at My Table* (1990), a number of feminist critics reinscribed Frame's work within an established model of the circumscription of mentally ill women, positing 'institutionalisation and shock treatment as metaphors for the social control of women' and celebrating Frame's status as a 'Suffering Female Artist' (Brown 2003: 131; King 2001: 465).

While the politics of gender are not central to Frame's work, Frame does nevertheless engage with the social marginalization of women in her writing: her 1957 novel *Owls Do Cry*, like Mansfield's short story 'Daughters of the Late Colonel' (1921), explores the circumscription of women within patriarchal social paradigms, while her autobiographies, like Hyde's *The Godwits Fly*, document the debilitating physical and psychological effects of domestic servitude upon working class women. Frame's work, like Hyde's and Mansfield's, therefore offers an important counterbalance to the masculinist bias of the Caxton school. Feminist analyses of her work are also part of a more general reappraisal of New Zealand women's writing which emerged from the radical shift in New Zealand literary culture that took place in the 1970s and 1980s.

Where this chapter has focused primarily upon European representations of the Pacific, the remaining chapters in this book explore the Indigenous literatures of the Pacific. The origins and emergence of 'postcolonial' Pacific literature are investigated in Chapter 4, and Chapters 5 and 6 elaborate upon some of the stylistic and thematic aspects of Pacific literatures produced from the 1970s to the first decade of the new millennium. Chapter 3, however, extends the historical trajectory established in the first two sections of this chapter (which focused on the late eighteenth and nineteenth centuries), investigating various forms of Indigenous political and discursive resistance to colonial rule in the early-to-mid twentieth century, and ending with an exploration of the symbolic resonance of warfare and 'warriorhood' in a range of contemporary Māori literature.

3

Warfare and Westernization: Narratives of Conflict, Resistance, and Social Change

> *Ka tuwhera te tāwaha o te riri, kāore e titiro ki te ao mārama*
> *(When the gates of war have been opened, no man observes the*
> *light of reason)*
>
> (Māori proverb)

> Let our ancestor's
> rage infest your
> intentions.
>
> Make a fist
> Hold it high.
>
> Plant the resistance
> deep.
>
> ('Imaikalani Kalahele, 'Make a Fist')

As many Pacific oral histories reveal, warfare—both against other Pacific Islanders and against European colonizing forces—has been a crucial element of Pacific socio-political organization across the centuries. Using war as both a metaphor and point of departure, this chapter investigates various forms of Indigenous Pacific political and discursive resistance that have been explored—and advanced—in the work of contemporary Pacific writers.

In investigating anticolonial resistance within the Pacific, the chapter is informed by shifting theoretical assessments of the colonial dialectic within international postcolonial scholarship. Where the work of 'first-generation' postcolonial theorists such as Edward Said, for example, has been criticized for establishing models of colonial encounter which emphasize the political and discursive *dominance* of colonizer over colonized (see Moore-Gilbert 1997: 51), later theorists such as Homi Bhabha have interpreted colonial authority and discourse as much more provisional and contested, frequently undermined by various forms of *resistance* from colonized peoples (1994).

These arguments have particular relevance to the Pacific, where social Darwinist theories on the 'fatal impact' of Europeans upon Pacific Islanders persisted well into the twentieth century, even after Indigenous populations were proven to be recovering from the ravages of disease witnessed in the nineteenth century (Sinclair 1986: 203). In recent decades, however, historians have become increasingly interested in the *resilience* of Indigenous Pacific cultures under European colonialism: the new wave of revisionist historiography that swept Aotearoa/New Zealand in the 1980s (and discussed in Chapter 2) is an example of this phenomenon. Many contemporary Indigenous writers of the Pacific have responded to these developments by revisiting and refiguring key moments of Indigenous Pacific anticolonial resistance in their work.

With these factors in view, this chapter focuses upon three distinct martial contexts, or moments of Indigenous resistance and self-assertion, which have been explored in the work of various Pacific writers. The first section of the chapter (3.1) investigates literary representations of two Indigenous sovereignty movements of the early twentieth century: the Mau nationalist movement in Western Samoa, and the Maungapōhatu religious community established by Māori prophet Rua Kenana. The second section of the chapter (3.2) discusses literary explorations of the anticolonial resistance movements that emerged in Melanesia following the outbreak of the Second World War, and also investigates a range of protest literature produced in response to Western nuclear testing in the Pacific during and beyond the Cold War. The final section of the chapter (3.3) focuses more specifically upon Māori warrior culture, investigating Māori involvement in the First, Second, and Vietnam wars, and exploring the symbolic resonance of warriorhood as a trope of Indigenous resistance and self-assertion for Māori writers and activists.

3.1 Colonial endeavours and Indigenous responses in the early twentieth century: inscribing resistance

By the beginning of the twentieth century, every island in the Pacific had been brought under the 'protection' or direct colonial rule of a European or Asian power, and was to remain so until the middle of the century, although Germany's Pacific territories were lost to various other colonial powers following the outbreak of war in 1914. Having already acquired the British portion of New Guinea in 1906, for example, Australia claimed 'German' New Guinea and the phosphate-rich island of Nauru (which had been annexed by Germany in 1888), while New Zealand claimed Western Samoa. Japan seized Germany's Micronesian territories (which Germany had acquired from Spain in 1898), initiating an intensive programme of foreign settlement paralleled only in Australia and Aotearoa/New Zealand, New Caledonia, and Hawai'i. By the end of the Second World War, however, Japan had lost its Micronesian territories (including the Marshall Islands, Palau, and the Northern Marianas) to the US, which already held possession of Guam and around sixty smaller Micronesian islands used for phosphate mining or naval bases (Crocombe 2001: 419).

Apart from the transfer of Germany's colonial territories, however, the period from around 1900 until the Second World War saw forty years of relatively 'stable' colonial rule in the Pacific. The colonial administrations introduced politically centralized governments, which were a new phenomenon in the Pacific except in Tonga and Hawai'i.[1] Unsurprisingly, in the majority of cases, colonial legal and governmental structures in the Pacific were based on those of the respective colonial powers, and Pacific peoples were not commonly invited to participate in local government, yet were expected to submit to the laws and authority of the colonizers, and in many cases to pay taxes. Many Pacific Islanders did not submit willingly to these impositions, and as we will see, in some parts of the Pacific, substantial resistance movements developed well in advance of the decolonization period following the Second World War.

Discussed below are literary representations of two particular examples of Indigenous resistance to colonial 'rule' during the early decades of the twentieth century. The first is the Mau independence movement, which emerged in Western Samoa during the 1920s, and has been referenced extensively in the work of Western Samoan writer Albert Wendt and American Samoan playwright John Kneubuhl. The second case study focuses upon the Maungapōhatu religious community, established in 1907 by Rua Kenana, Māori prophet and leader of the syncretic Ringatū faith. The Maungapōhatu community, though viewed as subversive by the Pākehā authorities, was not founded primarily as a gesture of anticolonial defiance, but as we will see, in Witi Ihimaera's historiographical novel *The Dream Swimmer* (1997), Rua Kenana is recast as the founding father of a Māori nationalist ethos which Ihimaera traces right through to contemporary times.

3.1.1 Colonial rule and Indigenous resistance in the Samoas: the Mau

In investigating fictional explorations of the Samoan Mau movement, it seems appropriate to begin with the work of Albert Wendt, Samoa's most prolific and influential writer. Much of Wendt's work has engaged directly with the history of colonialism in the Pacific, particularly within his country of birth. However, Wendt has cautioned against reading the work of postcolonial writers—including himself—as documentary guides to 'Third World' cultures and histories, particularly given the singular and transformative power of the individual literary imagination. As he puts it in 'Towards a New Oceania', '[i]n the final instance, our countries, cultures, nations, planets are what we imagine them to be. One human being's reality is another's fiction' (1976a: 49). As we will see in Chapters 5 and 6, Wendt's writing shows ample evidence of this process at work: he reshapes elements of Polynesian mythology into his own unique cosmological vision(s), and experiments with various 'postmodernist' literary techniques such as metafiction and parody. However, throughout his career Wendt has also maintained a keen interest in the particularities of Samoan pre- and post-colonial history, repeatedly returning, in his fiction, to pivotal historical events such as the arrival of the London Missionary Society in the 1830s, the devastating influenza pandemic of 1918, and the circumstances surrounding Samoan independence in 1962. In novels such as *Leaves of the Banyan Tree* (1979) and *The Mango's Kiss* (2003a), and in a range of his short fiction and poetry, Wendt uses these historical events as a framework across which he weaves intricate fictional sagas of intergenerational conflict and social change. One particular historical phenomenon which is referenced in a wide range of his fiction is the Mau independence movement, which emerged in Samoa in the 1920s.

Significantly, Wendt's own grandfather was a member of the Mau, and Wendt himself completed a thesis on the Mau movement at Victoria University in Wellington, where he graduated with a Masters degree in history in 1965.[2] References to the Mau appear in a wide range of his fiction: one of the characters in his picaresque short story 'Pint-Size Devil on a Thoroughbred' (1974), for example, is a member of the Mau (46), and in his 1979 novel *Leaves of the Banyan Tree*, a reference is made to Black Saturday, a crisis (which took place in 1929) that resulted in the deaths of several Mau members (1979: 299). *Leaves of the Banyan Tree*, like much of Wendt's early fiction and poetry, focuses primarily on twentieth-century and post-independence Samoan history, situating the Mau movement within its immediate historical context, but in his 2003 novel *The Mango's Kiss*, Wendt returns to an earlier period of Samoan history, spanning the 1880s through to the 1920s (when the Mau movement was established). The majority of the characters and events in the novel are entirely fictional, but Wendt carefully grounds his narrative in its historical context, making specific references to some of the key events which took place during this transitional period of Samoan colonial history. A brief overview of these events is presented below as a background to the literary analysis which follows.

The colonization of Samoa and the emergence of the Mau: the context
The Samoan archipelago did not come under colonial jurisdiction until the very end of the nineteenth century. Trade networks were established in Samoa from the early nineteenth century, and European missionaries arrived in the islands from the 1830s, but it was not until the latter half of the nineteenth century that Europeans began settling in Samoa in larger numbers. In 1856, the German company Johann Godeffroy und Sohn established itself in Apia (the capital city of what was to become Western Samoa) on the island of Upolu, inaugurating a new era of trade in the Pacific. As Stephen Fischer observes, prior to the arrival of Godeffroy und Sohn, Pacific trade had generally been 'ephemeral, haphazard and individualistic', but the German company established the copra trade on a much larger scale than before, co-ordinating a vast network of island suppliers

within and beyond Samoa (2005*a*: 142–3). By 1864 the company had purchased several thousand acres of land on Upolu, bringing in wage labourers from China and Melanesia to work on its newly established plantations. The company's successes helped transform Apia into one of the main commercial centres in the Pacific, and increasing numbers of Europeans and Americans settled there from the 1860s (Fischer 2005*a*: 143). Although Indigenous Samoans were generally resistant to the encroachment of Europeans, a series of divisive feuds that raged among various Samoan political factions throughout the nineteenth century prevented them from presenting a united front against the foreigners. Large numbers of German, British, and American settlers purchased land in Samoa in the early 1870s, and the three colonial powers began to compete for political control of the islands. Eventually, Germany and the US partitioned Samoa between them in 1899. Germany took possession of the western half (including Upolu, Savai'i and surrounding islands), while the US took the eastern portion, which included Tutuila (where the deep-water port of Pago Pago was located), Aunu'u, and (in 1904) the Manu'a islands (comprising Ofu and Olosega) to the east. Britain renounced its claims to Samoa in exchange for German concessions on the Solomon Islands and Tonga, over which British protectorates were established (Fischer 2005*a*: 145–6; 182).

Western Samoa, which (in 1962) became the first Pacific Island territory to gain its independence, is an intriguing case study to consider in terms of Indigenous resistance to colonial rule. The German administration (1899–1914) adopted a broadly humanitarian stance in Samoa, supporting German enterprise but also preventing white settlers from purchasing more land, thereby protecting Samoans from the levels of material dispossession witnessed in other German territories such as New Guinea (Fischer 2005*a*: 184). When the New Zealand administration took over in 1914, it made a positive start by placing the highly productive German plantations under local government control (a situation which remains to this day), thus preventing foreign investors from exploiting Samoa's wealth. On the whole, however, the New Zealand administration proved authoritarian and inept. One of its most catastrophic errors was to allow the SS *Talune* to dock at Apia in November 1918 with no quarantine restrictions, in spite of the fact that the world was being swept by the devastating Spanish influenza pandemic. Some passengers on board the *Talune* carried the virus, which then spread rapidly through the islands, killing an estimated one-fifth of the Samoan population (Meleisea 1987: 129). Widespread anger at the influenza crisis was subsequently compounded by the paternalistic attitude of the New Zealand administration, which, in the 1920s and 1930s, was run largely by men of military background who were generally authoritarian and often had a poor understanding of Samoan political structures. Cross-cultural relations deteriorated further in 1922 with the passing of the Samoan Offenders Ordinance, which gave New Zealand administrators power to banish 'disruptive' Samoans from their villages without trial, and the right to deprive matai (titled leaders) of their honorific titles[3] (Hempenstall and Rutherford 1984: 33–4; 36).

In response to these and other repressive colonial measures, the Indigenous Samoan independence organization 'O le Mau' was founded in 1926, taking as its motto the slogan 'Samoa mo Samoa' (Samoa for Samoans), and initiating a campaign of systematic non-violent resistance and non-compliance with government institutions and regulations (Firth 1997a: 259). The New Zealand administration attempted to crush the movement, sending large numbers of Mau members into exile, and events reached a crisis point on 28 December 1929 ('Black Saturday'), when police opened fire on a crowd taking part in a peaceful march, killing eight Samoans and mortally wounding three others in the process. This act of violence failed to suppress the Mau movement, and in 1936, New Zealand's newly-elected Labour government eventually recognized the Mau as a legitimate political movement, making the first steps towards granting Samoan independence, which eventually came almost three decades later (Fischer 2005a: 187).

Literary explorations of the Mau: Albert Wendt and John Kneubuhl
As explained above, Albert Wendt's *The Mango's Kiss* (2003) offers one of the most extended fictional explorations of the historical circumstances that contributed to the emergence of the Mau. The narrative investigates key events which took place during this transitional period—including the consolidation of German economic interests; partition; the New Zealand takeover; the influenza pandemic; and the Mau movement—through the fictional saga of an extended Samoan family living on the island of Savai'i. Characteristically, Wendt is careful not to imply that the social changes taking place in colonial Samoa were entirely negative: the processes of Christianization and

'Westernization', for example, are represented not in terms of the 'fatal impact' of Europeans, but more as a process of negotiation between two cultures. However, the ineptitude of the New Zealand administration, and in particular the mismanagement of the 1918 influenza pandemic, is identified explicitly as a trigger for the emergence of the Mau movement: one member asserts, for example, that he is 'fighting for . . . all the people killed in the New Zealand-introduced epidemic' (448). Wendt's fictional medium allows him to explore, imaginatively, what it might have been like to live through the epidemic, and these descriptions are graphic as well as poignant: the skins of the victims turn blue, and as the bodies pile up, dogs begin to feed upon the corpses (315). At one level, these fictional details of the human costs of the epidemic serve to underscore the moral case for the emergence of the Mau, but Wendt's narrative also explores the views of Samoans who opposed the movement: later sections of the novel, for example, explore the deteriorating relationship between a Samoan woman and her half-European husband who become irreconcilably divided in their attitudes towards the efficacy of the Mau. Wendt's characters, though fictional, are delineated with great sensitivity, resulting in an intricate embroidery of interpersonal relationships which give imaginative life to the historical events that underpin the narrative.

Where Wendt situates the emergence of the Mau within its broader historical context, American Samoan playwright John Kneubuhl takes a more microscopic view in his 1997 play *Think of a Garden*, set in American Samoa in 1929. The action of the play is focused upon the days immediately preceding and following Black Saturday, dramatizing the impact of the event upon an American Samoan family (the Krebers) with strong family connections in Western Samoa. The play (written shortly before Kneubuhl's death) is partly autobiographical: its central character, David Kreber, is in many ways a version of the young Kneubuhl, born to a Samoan mother and American father whose differing cultural backgrounds and expectations cause(d) him great emotional instability and confusion. Kneubuhl/Kreber's reflections on his childhood are filtered through a choric figure, 'The Writer', who appears at strategic moments in the play to comment on his younger self (David Kreber), and on the events that unfolded in 1929, when the Krebers became embroiled in the Black Saturday crisis. David Kreber's mother Lu'isa is a distant cousin of Tupua Tamasese Lealofi III, a Mau member who was killed on Black Saturday after returning from exile in Aotearoa/New Zealand, and Kreber's American father Frank travels to Apia to investigate the events surrounding Tamasese's death.

Many Samoans and Europeans believe that the New Zealand administration gave a false account of the events of Black Saturday, and Kneubuhl's play endorses this view. The play is strongly politicized and highly critical of the New Zealand administration: Lu'isa describes the New Zealand bureaucrats as 'heartless' (1997: 31), while her brother Lilo is furious about the fact that 'arrogantly tyrannical' New Zealand commissioners have exiled over two hundred Western Samoans since the mid-1920s (19). When Tamasese is shot, 'The Writer' first relates New Zealand Commissioner Allen's 'official' account of events—in which Tamasese was allegedly hit accidentally when police fired over the 'rioters'' heads (49)—but then reveals that 'no one' believed Allen's story, and that his father Frank went to Apia to find out the truth. Frank reports that Tamasese and other members of the Mau were deliberately 'murdered' by a team of expert sharpshooters 'brought in specially from New Zealand' some days before the event (73).

Kneubuhl's play, which has been performed in Pago Pago, Auckland, Wellington, and Honolulu, is a devastating critique of New Zealand's mismanagement of Western Samoa after the 1914 takeover, but it is significant that little mention is made of the reaction of the American Samoan administration to these events. Many 'eastern' or American Samoans became involved in the Mau movement, and sympathetic protests mounted in American Samoa were met with the violent imposition of martial law by the US naval administration (Lee and Salas (eds.) 1999: 107). However, given that Kneubuhl's play is a fictional dramatization of the events of 1929, it is not surprising that he should choose to omit those historical details which might complicate or dilute the play's polemical attack upon the ineptitude of the New Zealand administration.

3.1.2 Māori resistance to Pākehā political hegemony: Rua Kenana and the Ringatū faith

This section focuses upon a rather different form of resistance to colonial rule: the emergence of Māori millennialist movements, and in particular the syncretic Ringatū faith, in Aotearoa/New Zealand. The section begins with an overview of the circumstances surrounding the emergence of Māori millennialist movements, and then investigates the way in which Witi Ihimaera's novel *The Dream Swimmer* (1997) repositions Rua Kenana, leader of the Ringatū in the early decades of the twentieth century, as the founder of a Māori nationalist ethos.

Māori millennialism and the Ringatū: the historical background
While the popularity of social Darwinist 'fatal impact' rhetoric led to exaggerated reports of the susceptibility of Pacific Islanders to introduced European diseases (see Chapter 2), it is nevertheless the case that from the 1840s onwards, concern about the decline of the Māori population through introduced diseases was a contributing factor in the emergence of various syncretic religious movements of the nineteenth and early twentieth centuries. Noting that Pākehā appeared comparatively immune to the introduced diseases, many Māori began to believe that the power of the Christian god was greater than the mana of the Māori gods, and could therefore protect Māori against these new illnesses if they adopted the new faith, or at least abandoned their ancient beliefs and established a new religious order. These attitudes, and the conflicts over land and sovereignty which began to develop in the mid-nineteenth century, gave rise to various syncretic religions which equated Māori with the exiled tribes of Israel, combining Māori and Old Testament traditions of prophecy by predicting that Māori would one day regain sovereignty over their 'promised land' (Binney 1996: 154). In this sense, there was an anticolonial element to these new religious movements: they were not straightforward assimilations of Christian doctrine, but rather looked forward to a time when Māori could reclaim their lands from the invading Pākehā.

The Ringatū faith—established by prophet and healer Te Kooti Arikirangi Te Turuki (of the Rongowhakaata tribe) in the 1880s—subscribed to these principles, drawing a direct parallel between the colonial oppression of the Māori and the persecution of the Israelites in Egypt. Te Kooti experienced his first visions after being imprisoned for espionage (without trial, and on questionable evidence) on the island of Wharekauri (one of the Chatham Islands) in 1866. In July 1868, Te Kooti and a group of followers escaped back to the mainland by capturing a supply ship, and their relentless pursuit by colonial forces triggered Te Kooti's decision to engage in guerilla warfare against the Pākehā. This war, in which Te Kooti and his followers shuttled back and forth between the Urewera mountains (inland from Gisborne) and Te Rohe Pōtae (the realm of the Māori King, west of Lake Taupo), lasted until 1872, when Te Kooti was finally granted sanctuary in Te Rohe Pōtae. In 1873, Te Kooti adopted the Māori King Tawhaio's doctrine of pacifism, and eventually made his peace with the colonial government, obtaining a formal pardon some ten years prior to his death in 1893.

Before he died, Te Kooti predicted the emergence of a successor, the Mihaia Hou (new messiah), who would redeem the 'promised land' for Māori. In 1905, the Tūhoe prophet Rua Kenana Hepetipa was eventually recognized as Te Kooti's successor after experiencing his first vision at Maungapōhatu in the Urewera mountains. Here, Rua Kenana arranged for the establishment of a religious community, known as Hiruharama Hou—the New Jerusalem—in 1907 (Binney et al. 1979: 15; Keown 2005: 139). Rua Kenana and his followers were committed to the Ringatū doctrine of peace established by Te Kooti, and ironically, this stance led to major conflict with the government following the outbreak of the First World War. Rua Kenana and his followers refused to volunteer for service in the armed forces, and the government, already suspicious of Rua Kenana's activities as a healer and prophet, construed this behaviour as seditious. Refusing to volunteer was not illegal, so when an armed police expedition assaulted Maungapōhatu on 2 April 1916, it was ostensibly to arrest Rua for illegal grog dealing. Rua was tried for sedition but was imprisoned merely for earlier 'morally resisting arrest', and was finally released in 1918. He returned to Maungapōhatu, remaining as leader of the Ringatū faith until his death in 1937 (Binney 1996: 179–80).

Māori millennialism and anticolonialism: the case of Witi Ihimaera's The Dream Swimmer   As explained in Chapter 2, the 1980s witnessed the emergence of a range of revisionist perspectives on Aotearoa/New Zealand's colonial history, and Māori writer Witi Ihimaera offered a fictional contribution to the debate with the publication of his 1986 historiographical novel *The Matriarch*, followed in 1997 by a sequel, *The Dream Swimmer*. Both novels explore Māori millennialism as a form of resistance against Pākehā colonial authority, offering fictional dramatizations of the lives of Te Kooti and Rua Kenana. Ihimaera's revisionist historiographical agenda in *The Matriarch* includes a radical reassessment of dominant Pākehā accounts of Te Kooti—one of Ihimaera's own ancestors—as a ruthless guerilla warrior, instead representing him as an heroic leader committed to Māori socio-political emancipation. Similar objectives underpin *The Dream Swimmer*, which refigures Rua Kenana—treated as a renegade by the Pākehā legal establishment—as a Māori nationalist icon. Significantly, in his author's note at the beginning of the book, Ihimaera names various historical sources consulted during the writing of the book, identifying Judith Binney, Gillian Chaplin, and Craig Wallace's *Mihaia* (1979)—a biography of Rua Kenana—as one of the main sources of information on the Ringatū prophet. In consulting this text, it becomes apparent that—as was the case in *The Matriarch*—Ihimaera has used his source material selectively, emphasizing particular events and downplaying others in order to underscore Rua's putatively nationalist objectives (Keown 2005: 140).

In constructing Rua as a radical nationalist committed to the expulsion of the Pākehā, for example, Ihimaera omits aspects of his philosophy that communicated his desire for bicultural accord. He represents Rua's community at Maungapōhatu as a 'bastion of Maoridom against the Pakeha', and Rua himself as separatist committed to 'Maori nationalism' (1997: 138). Yet Binney *et al.* argue that after speaking with the Premier Sir Joseph Ward in 1908, Rua was reported to have abandoned his plans for a separate Māori government, adopting the maxim 'Kotahi te ture mō ngā Iwi e Rua ('one law for both peoples'), which suggested a commitment to a bicultural rather than separatist vision (Binney *et al.* 1979: 37–8). Where Ihimaera (using portentous biblical rhetoric) represents Rua as a charismatic leader representing the interests of all Māori, striving 'to gather the Children of Israel and bring them as one nation in the lands upon the mountains of Israel' (147), Binney *et al.* argue that Rua's interests were primarily restricted to his own tribe, the Tūhoe, and that there was considerable and widespread resistance to Rua's activities among other Māori. However, as outlined in Chapter 2, Ihimaera has argued that he is governed by a relativist approach to historiography, maintaining that Māori interpretations of history have less to do with agreed, universalized 'facts' than with individual or tribal perspectives on historical events. Indeed, as a writer of fiction, Ihimaera is under no obligation to adhere strictly to 'received' accounts of historical events, and in its blend of fact and fantasy, the novel advances the double agenda which critic Stuart Murray locates at the core of postcolonial nationalist discourses:

The need to write history is one that unites both postcoloniality and national-ism. The former wishes to correct the false image created by the warped logic of the colonial process. The latter seeks to provide mythologies to strengthen the sense of a collective self. Clearly, the two can, and do, combine.

(Murray 1997: 10)

Considered in these terms, Ihimaera's novel clearly demonstrates the way in which postcolonial writing can refigure and transform historical events in order to challenge dominant narratives of colo-nial history. Rua Kenana's religious community at Maungapōhatu was, demonstrably, an example of Indigenous anticolonial resistance, in that it represented a refusal to assimilate to the sociopolitical and religious structures of the dominant Pākehā culture. Howev-er, Ihimaera's novel amplifies this resistance in order to recast Rua as a nationalist figurehead for *all* Māori, and he places him in a genealogy of Māori leaders leading up to the present day. Citing various political developments of the 1990s, including the financial settlement of various tribal land claims against the Crown, Ihimaera reinvokes the millennialist rhetoric of Rua Kenana and Te Kooti by anticipating the imminent achievement of Māori sovereignty as the century draws to its end. However, Ihimaera argues that this objective will be achieved not by charismatic individuals such as the millennialist leaders of days gone by, but rather by the 'col-lective energy' of the Māori people, who will 'take the iwi into the promised land of Canaan' (1997: 417). In this sense, the novel becomes a rallying cry for contemporary Māori, demonstrating the way in which postcolonial literatures can anticipate—and even seek actively to advance—Indigenous self-determination by appealing to communitarian values.

3.2 War in the Pacific

Moving beyond the earlier twentieth-century contexts discussed above, this section of the chapter discusses literary representations of anticolonial resistance movements that emerged during the Second World War and the Cold War. The first four sub-sections below are focused on the Melanesian anticolonial and millennialist movements that emerged during the Second World War, while the final four investigate Indigenous political and literary responses to nuclear testing in the Pacific during and beyond the Cold War.

3.2.1 The Second World War: the historical context

One of the most cataclysmic events of the twentieth century was the advent of the Second World War, which brought many Pacific Islanders (and particularly Melanesians) into contact with western cultures and commodities for the first time. War broke out in the Pacific in December 1941 when Japan mounted a devastating surprise attack upon the US fleet at Pearl Harbour, Hawai'i, subsequently capturing a range of other US military bases in Guam and the Philippines, and routing British forces in Hong Kong, Singapore, and Malaya. These attacks were made partly in retaliation for sanctions taken against Japan by the US, Britain, and the Netherlands, who froze Japanese financial assets and prevented Japan from purchasing oil (essential to its military operations) after Japan joined the Axis powers and occupied French Indochina (Vietnam) in 1940. By this time, Japan had already fortified the Micronesian territories it had seized from Germany during the First World War, and therefore had an ideal staging post from which to capture the oil-rich Dutch East Indies (Indonesia), and to expand further into the Pacific in pursuit of its imperialist ambitions.

As Stewart Firth points out, the Pacific War can be visualized as a sudden thrust outwards by Japan from Micronesia for the first half-year, extending control south and south-east, over Guam, the Gilbert Islands (Kiribati), New Guinea, and parts of the Solomons. Until May 1942 the Japanese encountered no effective resistance, and occupied not only most of south-east Asia but also the Gilbert Islands, the Solomons, Australian New Guinea, and parts of Papua. Japan was poised to capture Port Moresby (in Australian New Guinea) by sea, but in early May, they were turned back from a seaborne invasion of central Papua by carriers and aircraft of the US fleet in the Battle of the Coral Sea (see Map 3.1). A month later, at the Battle of Midway, the Americans repelled the combined Japanese Fleet under Admiral Yamamoto and retained a vital submarine refuelling base at Midway

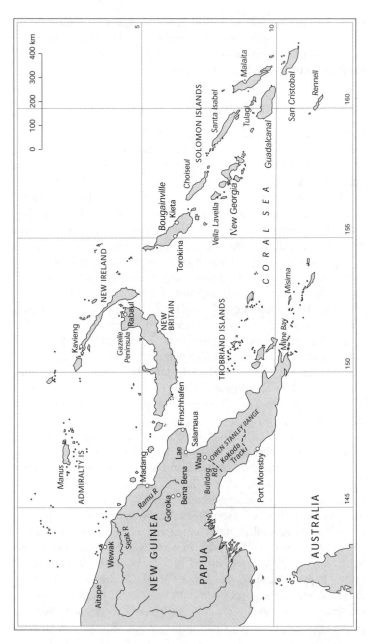

Map 3.1 Papua New Guinea, Bougainville, and the Solomon Islands

Atoll, north-west of Hawai'i. For a short time Japan continued to gain territory, including the phosphate-rich islands of Nauru and Banaba (one of the Kiribati islands) in August 1942, but thereafter Japan gradually lost its ground to the Americans, who reclaimed Allied territories on their way north and north-west towards Japan, and had also seized all of Japan's Micronesian territories by the end of the war (Firth 1997*b*: 296).

Many Pacific Islanders became directly involved in the Pacific war as labourers and members of the armed forces. The most concentrated and prolonged combat took place in Papua New Guinea and the Solomon Islands, where thousands of Papuans and New Guineans, and hundreds of Solomon Islanders, served as combatants, agricultural labourers, and carriers of supplies and wounded troops. The involvement of these Islanders in the war was to transform their relationships to colonial administrators, and to trigger the emergence of a number of anticolonial and millennialist movements.

One of the major catalysts in this process was the contact between Melanesians and American soldiers, whose friendliness and generosity caused Melanesians to reassess their relationship to their colonial administrators. (The Solomon Islands had been under British administration since 1893, and Papua and New Guinea had been partitioned between Britain and Germany respectively in 1884, with Australia eventually taking over both territories: Papua in 1905 and New Guinea in 1914.) The thousands of American troops who arrived in Papua New Guinea and the Solomons during the war treated Melanesians very differently from what they had been accustomed to from British and Australian administrators: they frequently invited Melanesians to share their food, and paid generously for souvenirs and other goods supplied by local people. Further, many Melanesians were amazed by the fact that black American soldiers appeared to have a relationship of equality with the white Americans, a situation which threw into relief their own subordination by colonial forces, and made them less inclined to return to their former positions after the war ended. These transformative events, which have been referenced extensively in Melanesian oral histories, have also been explored in a range of Melanesian literary texts. Discussed below are two key examples: a novel by Papua New Guinean writer Vincent Eri, and a dramatic adaptation of the autobiography of Solomon Islander Jonathan Fifi'i.

3.2.2 *Literary explorations of war and resistance: Vincent Eri and Jonathan Fifi'i*

One of the most extended fictional explorations of the war, including its transformative effects upon relationships between Melanesians and colonial administrators, appears in *The Crocodile* (1970), a novel by Papua New Guinean writer Vincent Eri. Set in the village of Moveave in the Gulf District of Papua (where Eri himself was born in 1936), the narrative is a *bildungsroman* focused on the experiences of Hoiri Sevese, whose life is transformed when he and other members of his village are forced to become carriers for the Australian New Guinea Administrative Unit (ANGAU) during the Second World War. The narrative—one of a number of nationalist literary texts published in advance of Papua New Guinean independence in 1975 (see Chapter 4)—posits the events of the war as a trigger for the emergence of substantial anticolonial feeling among Indigenous Papua New Guineans. In particular, Eri dramatizes the growing resentment felt by Papua New Guineans towards Australian colonial administrators, contrasting the imperious behaviour of ANGAU officials with the generosity and respect shown to Melanesians by the Americans. After one of Hoiri's companions receives ten pounds from a black American soldier in payment for a carved mask, for example, he offers a withering denunciation of the tight-fisted Australians, who would never pay a Melanesian such a handsome sum, and would be more likely to punish carriers with 'a stinging cane across the arse-hole for stealing a miserable tin of fish' (160). The mid-section of the novel offers a merciless caricature of Australian colonial authority in the form of Mr Smith, a pompous ANGAU patrol officer who screams insults at his undernourished native labourers while stuffing himself with roast chicken and imbibing liberal quantities of rum.

In addition to these fictional embellishments, the novel also includes factual references which point towards the enduring significance of the war within Papua New Guinean oral histories. Chapter 7, for example, ends with a direct transcript of a protest song, 'sung to this day', which contends that the 'white man' has 'forced' Papua New Guineans to fight in the war 'against our wishes' (157). As Lamont Lindstrom and Geoffrey White point out, in oral societies such as those in rural Papua New Guinea and the Solomon Islands, many war songs—including anticolonial protest songs—have been preserved to this day alongside older, more traditional songs and chants, thus indexing the enduring importance of the war experience to present-day 'social identities, relations, and claims' (1993: 193). The subversive nature of the song Eri chooses to reference in his novel is significant, not only underscoring the anticolonial agenda which drives the fictional narrative, but also reinscribing the events of the war within the contemporary context of anticolonial nationalism in 1970s Papua New Guinea.

Another significant literary exploration of the transformative experiences of the war appears in Julian Treadaway's *Fifi'i* (2002), a dramatization of events described in the autobiography of Solomon Islander Jonathan Fifi'i. Fifi'i (who grew up on the island of Malaita) fought with the Americans in the Solomon Islands during the war, and his experiences were recorded and transcribed by anthropologist Roger Keesing, and published under the title *From Pig-theft to Parliament: My Life between Two Worlds* (1989). Significantly, Fifi'i's autobiography offers a detailed account of the way in which the relationships that developed between Solomon Islanders and African-American soldiers ultimately served to undermine British colonial authority, and these social dynamics are foregrounded in the play. One scene, for example, dramatizes a conversation between Fifi'i and Solomon, one of the African American soldiers, who compares the treatment of Melanesians by the British to the former treatment of African slaves in America, and exhorts Fifi'i and his compatriots to resist British domination after the war ends through organized protest ('You have to struggle') (74). The dialogue in the play, though based closely on conversations recorded in Fifi'i's autobiography, has been simplified in order to make the play accessible to schoolchildren, but Fifi'i's anticolonial sentiments remain undiluted, and he appears throughout the play as a choric figure, making explicit his anger towards the British:

[They] tried their best to keep us from getting any ideas or acquiring any possessions that would make us think that we were human beings, not natives whose place was to serve and work for white people. Older men on Malaita are still angry about what they did to this very day.

(75)

Later sections of the play explore the involvement of Fifi'i and his peers in the Malaitan post-war independence movement 'Ma'asina Rule', one of the most effective anticolonial resistance movements to emerge in Melanesia during this period. Like the members of the Samoan Mau, proponents of the Maʻasina Rule movement were committed to non-violent protest, and they brought the British administration to a standstill by refusing to pay taxes or to work for the government or white plantation owners, instead advocating self-rule under local chiefs. Maʻasina, a word with cognates in various Malaitan languages, denotes the relationship between people in the same family, and thus encapsulated the sense of collaboration that united members of the organization, maximizing its disruptive impact upon colonial rule. In south Malaita, the movement had become sufficiently organized to collect a head tax and reinstate a version of customary law by 1946, and as it spread through the eastern and central Solomons in 1946 and 1947, the British arrested leaders on Malaita, Guadalcanal, and San Cristobal, imprisoning hundreds of islanders who refused to pay taxes. Fifiʻi was one of those prisoners, but the final sections of the play look beyond his personal experiences to the wider significance and successes of the movement, which persuaded the British to grant Solomon Islanders more political autonomy, medical treatment and education, and finally, independence in 1978 (Firth 1997b: 318). The play celebrates these achievements, but also ends didactically, as Fifiʻi exhorts the audience not to forget what the members of the Maʻasina movement fought for, particularly given the neocolonial discourse of economic 'development' that has spread throughout the Pacific in the post-independence period.

3.2.3 *Melanesian 'Cargo Cults': the context*

Another consequence of Melanesian involvement in the Second World War was the emergence of a number of Melanesian millennialist movements, popularly known as 'cargo cults'. These movements drew upon Melanesian religious beliefs in order to account for, and emulate, the material wealth that Westerners—and particularly the American military—brought with them to the Pacific. In many cases, they also represented a form of anticolonial resistance.

Melanesian religions have a number of central precepts in common: people live not as isolated individuals but as members of a community of people and spirits, with generations of ancestors providing models of conduct for the community. Living people achieve the 'good life' by cultivating the right relations with the appropriate humans and spirits, and are rewarded with high social status and material wealth. When large numbers of Europeans arrived in Melanesia during the war, traditional aspirations for material reward, dissatisfaction with colonial rule, and introduced Christian doctrines of prophecy and deliverance combined to create the social conditions in which the millennialist movements were to flourish.

For example, when Americans arrived in Melanesia in huge numbers during the Second World War, they brought with them material wealth and new technologies which they shared generously with Melanesians, thus appearing to fulfil aspects of the millennial aspirations outlined above. When British and Australian colonial officials confiscated Melanesian goods acquired from the Americans after the war ended, attempting to force Melanesians back into slave-labour conditions on colonial plantations, many Melanesians were no longer prepared to submit to colonial authority, believing that the administrators were robbing them of their rightful rewards. After the war ended and the Americans left, taking much of their 'cargo' with them, many Melanesians believed that the 'ancestors' would return at some point, bringing material goods and deliverance from colonial forces (Firth 1997b: 316). In many cases, cult followers performed various rituals (such as prayer sessions, ritual cleansing, and drilling) in anticipation of deliverance, while in others, pigs were killed and gardens left untended in the expectation that there would be an abundance of food in the new world that was yet to come (Hempenstall and Rutherford 1984: 142).

3.2.4 Literary explorations of the cargo cults: Kama Kerpi and Earnest Mararunga

Like the Samoan Mau movement, the Melanesian cargo cults did not (as a rule) espouse anticolonial violence, but the disruptions they caused to colonial administrations have inspired a range of literature produced by Western writers such as Randolph Stow, whose novel *Visitants* (1979) depicts a Papuan community in which an outbreak of millennialist fervour provokes mass hysteria, vandalism, and murder. Stow's sensationalist account differs significantly from the more circumspect meditations upon millennialism in the work of Indigenous Papua New Guinean writers such as Kama Kerpi and Earnest Mararunga. Kama Kerpi's short story 'Cargo' (1975), for example, explores cargo cult doctrine through the naïve perspectives of two young schoolboys. In Kerpi's story, it is the Catholic church that is represented as preventing villagers (in an unspecified part of Papua New Guinea) from acquiring cargo. The schoolboys, whose names (Abram and Cain) have ironic biblical resonance, discuss how they might go about thwarting the church, and Cain resolves that he will ask his grandfather, who died a year ago, to help him. The two boys decide that they must use Catholic icons and rituals to achieve their objective, so they conduct an impromptu ceremony in the local church, setting a page from the Bible on fire, distributing holy water, drinking sacramental wine, and asking God to 'let the riches pass on to the rightful owners' (Wendt (ed.) 1980: 149). Such an approach is in keeping with many Melanesian millennialist movements, which involved the emulation of European activities that were believed to bring the coveted cargo (Hempenstall and Rutherford 1984: 121). By focusing his narrative on the experiences of children, however, Kerpi imbues these events with a certain amount of comic irony, as it is clear the boys do not fully understand the political significance of what they are doing. Yet the behaviour of these young characters also points towards the genuinely subversive qualities of the millennialist movements: when Kerpi's story ends, the two boys are still awaiting an answer to their prayers, but significantly, the narrative concludes with them joining forces with two other village boys also seeking cargo. This alliance encapsulates the spirit of collaboration which characterized many of the millennialist movements, thereby increasing their effectiveness as a protest against colonial authority.

Where Kerpi's story represents cargo cults as a means of Indigenous unification, 'The Load of Firewood' (1974), a short story by Earnest Mararunga, explores the potentially divisive effects of the post-war Melanesian millennialist movements. The narrator of the story describes an argument between two Papua New Guinean men who offer conflicting advice on how to obtain the white man's cargo. The younger man advocates Western education as a route to success, while the older (named Karipan) believes that the destruction of village gardens and domestic animals will convince the ancestors to reward the villagers with the white man's cargo. The narrator, who was himself a young man when the debate took place, chooses the route of 'progress' offered by the younger advocate, and like other 'postcolonial' narratives of colonial incursion (such as Chinua Achebe's *Things Fall Apart* (1958) and Ngugi's *The River Between* (1965)), Mararunga's story thus explores the ways in which colonialism creates internecine (and inter-generational) conflict among Indigenous peoples. In this case, the narrator is able to comment on the events with the benefit of hindsight: his adult 'narrating self' looks back upon the experiences of his younger self twenty years earlier, ridiculing the naiveties of those fellow villagers taken in by 'the rogue Karipan' (Wendt (ed.) 1980: 189–90). The conclusion of the story, however, is ambiguous: the narrator had originally decided to get educated in order to 'liberate' his people from superstition, but the ending reveals that he never returned to his village, and offers no clue as to what he has gained from his experiences. This inconclusive ending to the tale implies that in rejecting the traditions of village life, the narrator may have lost more than he imagined in his decision to follow the ways of the white man.

3.2.5 The Cold War and nuclear testing in the Pacific

The Second World War clearly effected dramatic changes in Pacific—particularly Melanesian—sociopolitical structures, but after the combat ended, a new phase of military incursion began, as various Western nations began testing nuclear weapons in the Pacific. Nuclear and other weapons testing in the Pacific has served as another catalyst for Indigenous Pacific political and discursive resistance against Western incursion, this time with specific reference to its effects upon the environment.

Many Indigenous Pacific oral traditions and cosmologies record complex interrelationships between Pacific Islanders and the natural environment. Polynesian religions, for example, feature 'departmental' gods who protect and inhabit particular realms of the natural world, and the spirits of the dead are, in many cases, believed to dwell within the bodies of particular birds or animals, or within other living entities such as trees. Environmental conservationism has been central to many Pacific subsistence economies for centuries, with intricate rituals and protocol (surrounding activities such as fishing and hunting) which have served to protect the fragile ecosystems upon which Pacific Islanders have depended for their survival. These traditions have played a significant role in the emergence of a wide range of Indigenous Pacific protest literature produced in response to US and French weapons testing in the Pacific since the end of the Second World War.

Britain also conducted intermittent nuclear tests in the Pacific between 1952 and 1968 (see Map 3.2), but French and US testing was much more extensive and damaging both to the environment and to the health of Indigenous Pacific Islanders. The sections below outline some of the political and literary protests which accompanied US and French military testing in the Pacific between 1946 and 1996.

3.2.6 US Cold War politics in Micronesia and Hawai'i: the background

The Cold War was a diplomatic standoff in which the US and its Western allies attempted to prevent the spread of communism from Russia into Eastern Europe, the Asia-Pacific, and South America. In order to establish 'loyal outposts' from which to head off potential communist advances from Russia and China, and to draw fire from the US mainland in the event of war, the US established 'forward bases' stretching across the Pacific from Hawai'i through Kwajalein (in the Marshall Islands group), to Guam and on to the Philippines (Dibblin 1988: 194). Throughout the Cold War—which effectively ended with the collapse of communism in Eastern Europe in the late 1980s—US and Russian warships and submarines armed with nuclear warheads patrolled the Pacific, and US nuclear weapons were stockpiled in Hawai'i and Guam (Crocombe 2001: 587).

From 1946, the United States Atomic Energy Commission ran a series of nuclear tests in Micronesia in order to establish whether continental detonations would endanger US public health and safety, and there is speculation that US forces may have intentionally left Micronesians at unsafe distances from the testing sites in order to document the effects of radiation on humans (Crocombe 1995: 212). During a series of tests in 1954, for example, a hydrogen bomb code-named BRAVO was detonated on Bikini (in the Marshall Islands group), and following a change in wind direction, the people of Rongelap, an island 300 kilometres east of the test site, were exposed to radioactive fallout (see Map 3.3). The Americans did not evacuate the islanders until the morning of the third day after the blast,

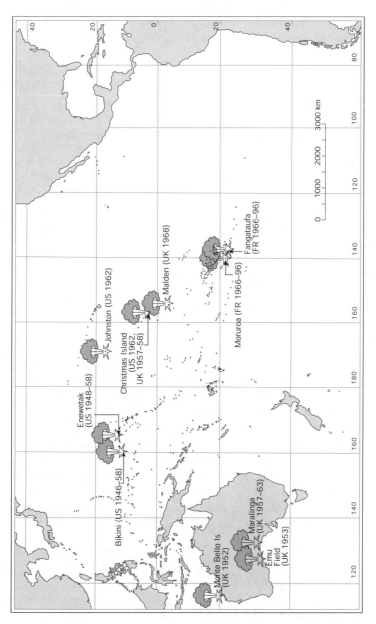

Map 3.2 Nuclear test sites in the Pacific

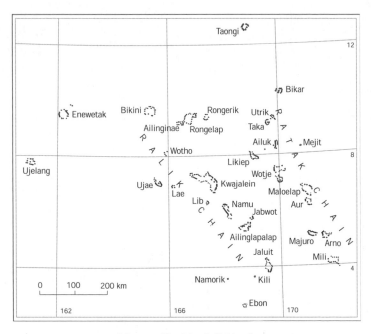

Map 3.3 The Marshall Islands

while islanders on Utrik Atoll further east, which was also exposed to fallout, were not evacuated until the fourth day. The extensive radiation injuries (such as vomiting, diarrhoea, and burns) sustained by the islanders were carefully documented by US researchers, and many islanders suffered long-term health problems (such as cancer, paralysis, and birth defects in children born to irradiated mothers). The official US argument was that the wind direction had changed unexpectedly, but many Marshallese believe they were deliberately exposed to fallout so the United States could establish the effects of radiation on humans over an extended period of time (Firth and Von Strokirch 1997: 328–30; Crocombe 1995: 212–23).

Indigenous literary responses to nuclear testing: Hone Tuwhare and Cite Morei The BRAVO bombing brought the affected Marshallese (around 11,000 in number) to world attention (Firth and Von Strokirch 1997: 329), and eyewitness reports from Rongelap residents, who initially mistook the detonating bomb for a sunrise (dubbing the incident ('the day of two suns'), may have helped to inspire Māori poet Hone Tuwhare's renowned anti-nuclear poem 'No Ordinary Sun' (1958). In the poem, Tuwhare imagines the impact of nuclear fallout upon a tree (a potent symbol of growth, endurance, and renewal), describing the flash of the nuclear bomb detonation as 'no gallant monsoon's flash' or 'dashing trade wind's blast', but rather a devastating force that will kill the tree and all the natural life forms that surround it (1994: 28). Tuwhare's imagery is apocalyptic: the bomb has razed the environment and drained it of colour and fertility; all that remains are the 'shadowless' mountains, 'white' plains, and the 'drab' sea floor (28). Tuwhare's condemnation of human despoliation of the natural world is redolent of the work of Romantic poets such as William Wordsworth and William Blake, positing nuclear testing in the Pacific as a disastrous new chapter in the history of industrialization (see also Arvidson 1993: 26). However, the poem can also be considered within the context of Māori cosmology, in which aspects of the environment are believed to be protected and embodied by individual deities. Trees fall within the domain of Tāne, god of the forest, while the earth in which they grow is the body of Papatūānuku, the earth mother. An attack upon the environment therefore represents a desecration of the body of Papatūānuku, and in this respect Tuwhare's poem can be situated alongside the work of other Māori writers such as Patricia Grace, whose short story 'Journey' (1980) describes the incursions of earth-moving machines as deep, bleeding incisions carved into the body of the earth mother.

By the time public opposition to nuclear testing in the Pacific became widespread in the 1970s, the US had already shifted its nuclear tests to Nevada and New Mexico, but it still retains military bases throughout Micronesia, and maintains an intercontinental ballistic missile testing range at Kwajalein to this day (Crocombe 2001: 429). Indigenous Pacific writers were still expressing their opposition to US nuclear and other military activity in Micronesia as late as 1992, when a range of anti-nuclear poetry and prose was published in the anthology *Te Rau Maire [The Fern Leaf]: Poems and Stories of the Pacific*. Notable among these texts is Cite Morei's poem 'Belau Be Brave', which emerged in response to a political standoff over military issues which took place between the Palau people and the US government in the early 1990s (prior to Palau's independence in 1994). The US had been putting enormous pressure on Palau (also known as Belau) to abandon its anti-nuclear stance (encoded in Palau's 1979 constitution), and to provide more land for military purposes, in exchange for aid. Morei exhorts her compatriots not to sell their 'seas' and 'soul / For everlasting food stamps', and asks a rhetorical question of the Americans and of the French, who were testing at Moruroa at the time: 'is not Bikini enough? / Mururoa, Hiroshima? Nagasaki?' (Crocombe *et al.* (eds.) 1992: 4). The form of Morei's poem, which is broken up into irregular, often ragged verse paragraphs, encapsulates her frustration, but also conveys a steely resolve, with repeated imperatives urging her people to 'be brave' and 'survive'. Palau's anti-nuclear movement is represented as just one more chapter in a long history of Indigenous Palauan resistance against Western incursion, whether it be from 'beachcombers' and 'traders' with their foreign 'diseases', or from modern-day Americans with their deadly weapons of war.

3.2.7 US military testing in Hawai'i: the Kaho'olawe campaign

Like parts of Micronesia, the US state of Hawai'i also remains heavily militarized to this day: nearly thirty percent of the land on O'ahu, the most populous island on which Hawai'i's capital Honolulu is located, is still controlled by the US military. Six hundred thousand acres of Hawai'ian land were commandeered during the Second World War, and hundreds of acres of Native Trust lands were taken during the Vietnam War for military operations (Trask 1999a: 68). By the mid-1970s, however, a substantial native Hawai'ian protest movement had developed in opposition to the continued exploitation of Hawai'ian land for military purposes, and in 1976, these concerns became focused on the island of Kaho'olawe. Located off the southwest coast of Maui (see Map 2.1), Kaho'olawe is a site of traditional Hawai'ian religious worship that had been used as a US military bombing target since 1941. A grassroots organization called the Protect Kaho'olawe 'Ohana ('Ohana means 'family' or 'clan group') was formed in 1976 with the aim of halting US military activity on the island. The organization carried out a series of 'illegal' occupations of Kaho'olawe in 1976 and 1977, arguing that the despoliation of the island through bombing and unregulated animal grazing contravened the native Hawai'ian land use ethic known as mālama 'āina, or 'protect the land' (Trask 1999a: 68). In 1980, the 'Ohana secured a Consent Decree that gave Hawai'ians access to Kaho'olawe for religious, cultural, educational, and scientific activities, and in 1981 the entire island was placed on the National Register of Historic Places. Military operations finally ceased on the island in 1990, and in 1994, the title of the island was returned to the people of Hawai'i. Soil conservation and revegetation programmes have been instituted, Hawai'ian religious sites have been rededicated, and the island is now used for a variety of religious and other cultural activities.

Throughout the Kaho'olawe campaign, a number of Hawai'ian writers expressed their opposition to US military occupation of the island. In 1984, for example, *Ho'i Ho'i Hou*, an anthology of poetry and prose dedicated to Hawai'ian environmental activists George Helm and Kimo Mitchell, was published as a special issue of the Hawai'i-based literary journal *Bamboo Ridge*. Helm and Mitchell had 'disappeared' in 1977 while engaged in a protest occupation of Kaho'olawe, but many believed that they had been murdered, and the journal issue therefore includes a variety of elegiac tributes to Helm and Mitchell, as well as a range of lyric poems lamenting the continuing desecration of the island. In 1985, another special issue of *Bamboo Ridge*, entitled *Mālama: Hawaiian Land and Water*, was published, described by editor Dana Naone Hall as a 'companion volume' to *Ho'i Ho'i Hou* (1985: 3). As its title suggests, Hall's anthology celebrates the cultural significance of Hawai'ian natural resources, and several essays and poems in the collection make direct reference to the Kaho'olawe campaign, drawing upon Polynesian environmental conservationism and cosmologies in their opposition to the bombing. The anthology offers a rich combination of poetics and politics: lyrical and anthropomorphic representations of Kaho'olawe as a lost relative appear alongside historic petitions protesting against the alienation of Hawai'ian land during the mid-nineteenth century, when the great 'Māhele' division of 1848–50 eradicated the traditional system of communal land tenure and allowed large tracts of land to fall into the hands of Euro-American investors. The inclusion of this historical material locates the Kaho'olawe campaign within a broader context of anticolonial protest against the exploitation of Hawai'i's natural environment.

A further tribute to the Kaho'olawe campaign emerged in 1994, when a special issue of the Pacific journal *Mānoa* was produced partly in order to celebrate the return of Kaho'olawe to the Hawai'ian people.

The issue includes a photographic portrait, two essays, and a narrative poem, composed in Hawai'ian by Pualani Kanaka'ole Kanahele and performed at 'healing ceremonies' that took place in August 1992. The poem, printed in Hawai'ian with an English translation, is epic in scope, tracing the history of the island from its mythological origins to the present day. Kanahele's description of the reclamation ceremony as 'the day of sovereignty' situates the event within the wider context of the Hawai'ian Indigenous civil rights movement, suggesting that the return of Kaho'olawe has heralded a new era of self-assertion for the Hawai'ian people (Kaho'olawe Island Reserve Commission 1995: 22).

3.2.8 French nuclear activity in the Pacific: the context

While US military activity in the Pacific has clearly remained a prominent issue in Pacific Islands writing into the new millennium, France was the only Western power still undertaking nuclear tests in the Pacific in the last decade of the twentieth century. When Algeria gained its independence from France in 1962, France was forced to cease nuclear testing in what is now the Algerian Sahara, and chose French Polynesia as its new testing site, establishing facilities on two atolls in the Tuamotu Island group: Fangataufa and Moruroa (known in French as Mururoa). In May 1966, the Centre d'Experimentation du Pacifique (CEP) began testing on Moruroa in spite of robust local opposition, promising that bombs would only be exploded when winds were blowing towards the south, where there were no inhabited islands (Dibblin 1988: 202). Testing was to continue in the Tuamotu group for the next thirty years. For the first decade, France conducted atmospheric tests, in spite of the fact that the United States, Britain, and the Soviet Union had already signed a Partial Test Ban Treaty (in 1963) and had agreed to move their tests underground to reduce environmental pollution. As international protest against nuclear testing escalated in the 1970s, France finally abandoned atmospheric testing in 1975, first testing below the coral atoll and then under the lagoon, primarily in Moruroa. These tests caused immense environmental damage, creating cracks in the reef from which radioactive waste leaked into the ocean, and in 1981, severe storms caused plutonium residues from the atmospheric tests to traverse the Moruroa lagoon (Firth and Von Strokirch 1997: 347).

As knowledge of the adverse impact of French and American nuclear tests became more widely publicized in the 1970s, increasing numbers of newly independent Pacific island nations expressed their opposition to the tests. In 1985, the South Pacific Forum (a regional organization founded in 1971) drafted a South Pacific Nuclear-Free Zone Treaty which was signed by Forum countries in 1986, though the US refused to subscribe to the document (Firth and Von Strokirch 1997: 343; 325). 1985 was also the year in which the Greenpeace flagship *Rainbow Warrior*, which was about to travel to Moruroa to disrupt French nuclear tests, was bombed and sunk in Auckland Harbour by government-sponsored French saboteurs, provoking widespread international condemnation (Dibblin 1988: 69). In 1987, the New Zealand government instituted a strict ban on nuclear-powered or nuclear-armed ships visiting New Zealand ports, leading to New Zealand's partial exclusion from the ANZUS pact, which had been formed between New Zealand, Australia, and the US in 1951 in order to maintain security in each nation's 'sphere of influence' within the Pacific.

French nuclear testing in the Pacific also precipitated substantial protests within French Polynesia itself—riots and demonstrations occurred throughout the thirty-year testing period, for example—but France was able to maintain its operations largely by creating aid dependency within the region. In the early 1960s, the economy in French Polynesia was depressed, and the CEP brought prosperity through massive investment in infrastructure, customs revenue, local expenditure, and employment. However, these measures could not prevent the emergence of a wide variety of Indigenous protest literature that emerged in French Polynesia and New Caledonia throughout the nuclear testing period.

Indigenous literary responses to French nuclear testing: Chantal Spitz and Déwé Gorodé   One of the earliest collections of anti-nuclear poetry to emerge from French Polynesia was a 1982 special trilingual issue of the Fiji-based literary journal *Mana*, featuring the work of Ma'ohi (Indigenous) poets Hubert Brémond, Henri Hiro, and Charles Manutahi. Henri Hiro became directly involved in the Ma'ohi anti-nuclear movement from the 1970s, organizing various protest demonstrations against testing in Moruroa, and many of his poems in the *Mana* issue lament the fact that the economic dependency brought about by French military investment in Polynesia has caused many Ma'ohi to become 'idle', abandoning traditional subsistence activities such as fishing and the cultivation of crops (Crocombe (ed.) 1982: 59). Many of Hiro's poems, like those of Brémond and Manutahi, are redolent of French Romanticism in their emphasis on the 'fatal impact' of French military incursion upon Ma'ohi traditions and the natural environment, but others make direct appeals to various Tahitian deities connected with the natural environment, urging them to rise from their 'torpor' and reinvigorate Ma'ohi culture (65). The anthology is thus suspended between two phases of Pacific literary and political consciousness, on the one hand lamenting the apparently irreparable environmental and cultural 'damage' caused by colonization, and on the other, anticipating a time when Ma'ohi will be able to rise up and reclaim their lands and traditions. Throughout the collection, the widespread references to the natural world and its associated deities also serve as a specific reminder of the animistic beliefs that underpin Polynesian environmental conservationism.

Perhaps the most extended literary critique of French military activity in the Pacific has been offered by Ma'ohi writer Chantal Spitz, whose 1991 novel *L'île des Rêves Écrasés* ('The Island of Crushed Dreams') traces three generations of Ma'ohi living on the fictional island of Ruahine, site of a French military testing base. The novel contains direct authorial criticisms of Western incursion into the Pacific, and the sociopolitical changes in Ruahine closely resemble those which took place in Tahiti following the beginning of nuclear testing in the 1960s: trade deficits, widespread crime, and growing social inequalities. Spitz also laments the degradation of the environment through nuclear testing, and at one point the land itself appeals directly to the Ma'ohi people, urging them not to allow the military to 'kill you and turn you into / A new [people] without soul or land' (Spitz 1991: 23; trans. Nicole 1999: 279). Like Hiro, Brémond, and Manutahi, Spitz also, therefore, anchors her polemical attack upon French military imperialism firmly within Polynesian spiritual beliefs in the sanctity of the natural environment.

Indigenous writers of New Caledonia, another of France's colonies, have also expressed their resistance to French nuclear testing within the Pacific. Most prominent among these is writer, poet, and political activist Dewé Gorodé, who herself became directly involved in the Nuclear Free Pacific Movement (now known as the Nuclear Free and

Independent Pacific organization) (Brown 2004: xvi). Gorodé has produced a range of protest literature focused upon French nuclear testing, and while much of this writing is in French, her poem 'Wave-Song'—written in 1974 while the French were still conducting atmospheric tests—has been published in *Sharing as Custom Provides* (2004*a*), an anthology of Gorodé's poetry in English translation. Gorodé's poem, like the work of her French Polynesian counterparts, focuses upon the environmental damage caused by French nuclear testing. The poem was written from Camp-Est prison in Noumea—where Gorodé had been incarcerated for her involvement with protest demonstrations associated with the Kanaky independence movement (see Chapter 4)—and in dramatizing Gorodé's sense of entrapment, it establishes a contrast between the sere, sun-baked exercise yard and the cool plentitude of the sea beyond the prison walls. The 'wave-song' is a 'lullaby' which soothes the poet's 'watchful' spirit, but it also carries the voices of the oppressed, and news of 'the huge white mushroom cloud / infecting the sky over Mururoa' (2004*a*: 43). While the poem is, in many ways, a lament, it ends triumphantly as Gorodé posits the restless movement of the waves as a symbol of the endurance and resilience of Pacific peoples, whose strength and resolve will '[carry them] forward / in dignity' (Gorodé 2004*a*: 43). Gorodé's writing, and her political involvements, are discussed in more detail in Chapter 4.

3.3 Māori warrior culture

This final section of the chapter focuses more specifically on fictional explorations of Māori involvement in various twentieth-century military conflicts, including the First, Second, and Vietnam War(s). As outlined in Chapter 2, from the early days of European incursion into the Pacific, New Zealand Māori gained a reputation as a fierce warrior culture, and this stereotype was consolidated when Māori inflicted a series of humiliating defeats upon colonial troops during the 'land wars' of the 1860s and 1870s. Māori involvement in various 'international' wars of the twentieth century, however, emerged less as an expression of anticolonial resistance than as a manifestation of pride in a long-established Māori warrior tradition. This had much to do with the fact that Māori who took part in these wars were fighting alongside, rather than against, the Pākehā (European New Zealanders). As we will see, the achievements of Māori combatants, particularly in the Second World War, have been memorialized in Māori oral histories, and have also served as a source of inspiration for various Māori writers of the late twentieth century. Māori 'warriorhood' has also been invoked by contemporary Māori activists and cultural historians as a metaphor for processes of anticolonial resistance which continue to this day, given that many Māori view themselves as still 'colonized' within their own land.

3.3.1 Māori involvement in the First and Second World Wars

The First World War witnessed an ideological clash between Māori who wished to volunteer for service, and those who opposed fighting on behalf of a government that had failed to honour its obligations under the Treaty of Waitangi. The Te Arawa tribe of the Bay of Plenty, which had fought on the side of the government in the wars of the 1860s, was the first to volunteer its services when war broke out in 1914, while the Waikato tribes—whose lands had been unjustly confiscated by the colonial government—refused to volunteer, in spite of pressure from Māori leaders such as MP Sir Maui Pomare (Gardiner 1992: 22; Walker 2004: 181). As historian Wira Gardiner points out, the determination of the Māori members of parliament—who included Pomare, Apirana Ngata, Te Rangi Hiroa (Sir Peter Buck), and Taare Parata—to involve Māori in the war effort can be viewed as part of a general resurgence in Māori culture that took place at the beginning of the twentieth century. After the devastations of war, disease, and dispossession visited upon Māori during the late nineteenth century, the first decade of the twentieth century witnessed the emergence of a young, dynamic group of Māori leaders, educated within the Pākehā system and dedicated to eradicating Māori health problems, raising education levels, and gaining equal status for Māori. With the outbreak of the First World War, Apirana Ngata, who became the first Māori university graduate in 1893 and entered Parliament in 1905, succeeded in raising a Māori contingent, which became known as Te-Hokowhitu-a-Tū (the army of Tūmatauenga, Māori god of war), and saw action in Gallipoli with the Australian and New Zealand (ANZAC) soldiers. In 1917, the force was reconstituted as the New Zealand (Māori) Pioneer Battalion, and was sent to work on communication trenches and defence lines on the Western Front (Gardiner 1992: 13, 21).

To a people with established skills in hand-held weaponry, this relegation to a labouring role was demeaning, and the embarrassment it caused is referenced briefly in Māori playwright Hone Kouka's *Ngā Tāngata Toa* (1994). The play is set in 1919, shortly after the end of the war, and opens with the return of war veteran Taneatua and his fellow Māori soldiers, who have served with the Pioneer Battalion in Europe. The soldiers are welcomed as war heroes (the 'tāngata toa' indexed in the play's title), but one woman reassures her husband (who did not go to war and is jealous of Taneatua's 'heroic' status) by arguing that Taneatua was merely a 'ditch digger' whose most illustrious act was 'to dig holes for the Pakeha soldiers' tutae [excrement]' (Kouka 1994: 17, 33).

The Second World War witnessed a much more prominent role for Māori combat soldiers. At the instigation of Apirana Ngata and other Māori leaders, the government agreed in October 1939 to raise an all-Māori battalion, which became the 28th battalion of the New Zealand army. Leaving Aotearoa/New Zealand in May 1940, the battalion saw action in Greece, Crete, North Africa, and Italy. These soldiers gained a reputation for bravery and skill in close-quarter combat (particularly with bayonets), and many participants received decorations: Commander Arapeta Awatere, for example, received the Military Cross and the Distinguished Service Order, while Lieutenant Te Moana-Nui-a-Kiwa Ngarimu of Ruatoria was posthumously awarded the Victoria Cross. Several commanders of the Battalion (including Charles Bennett, Arapeta Awatere, and James Henare) subsequently became important leaders in peacetime, developing projects to improve the socioeconomic position of Māori in the post-war period.

The involvement of Māori in the Second World War, and in other twentieth-century conflicts such as the Vietnam War, has inspired a number of creative works produced by Māori writers. Patricia Grace's 2004 novel *Tu*, for example, is centrally focused on the activities of the Māori Battalion in the Second World War. The novel explores the war diaries of a fictional Māori Battalion soldier Te-Hokowhitu-a-Tu, whose name commemorates his father's membership of the Māori Pioneer Battalion during the First World War. While the adventures of Tu and his brothers and fellow soldiers Pita and Rangi are fictional,

Grace's account of their involvement with the Battalion is based on meticulous research into the various phases of conflict during the war, incorporating historical detail from J. F. Cody's *28th (Maori) Battalion* (1956), the official army history of the Battalion, and Wira Gardiner's *Te Mura o te Ahi [The Blazing of the Fire]: The Story of the Maori Battalion* (1992). Grace also draws upon private memoirs and mementoes of the war kept by Battalion veterans, including her own father. She attributes the close combat and tactical skills exhibited by the Battalion in part to the Māori 'warrior' heritage: Tu's skills with the bayonet, for example, are traced back to lessons in handling the taiaha (a traditional hand held weapon) that he received from his uncle.[4] Similarly, during the protracted campaign to displace the Germans at Cassino in Italy, two of Tu's fellow soldiers inscribe their faces with 'traditional' moko (tattoo) patterns and strike poses commonly assumed during performances of pre-combat haka (including widened eyes, protruding tongue, and exaggerated hand gestures). The 'tattooed' soldiers are unaware of the full semiotic significance of their markings, but Tu, again trained by his uncle, knows that traditionally, each marking recorded details of the wearer's birth, lineage, social status, expertise, and achievements (Grace 2004: 190–1; see also Keown 2005: 185). From Tu's point of view, the markings imbue the soldiers with the status of warrior chiefs, and one of them, Gary, heroically sacrifices himself by creating a diversion to save the lives of his comrades (193). After the war ends, however, Tu is critical of the reasons why many Māori went to war—some urged by elders to draw on their warrior heritage and 'demonstrate pride of race', and others in the hope that it would make Māori socially equal to the Pākehā—and he asks whether, given that the war 'has left our small nation beheaded, disabled, debilitated', the price has been 'too high' (Grace 2004: 278–9).

Where Grace's *Tu* is based partly on the experiences of her own father during the Second World War, in 2001 Cook Islands-born writer Alistair Campbell published *Maori Battalion*, a poetry collection dedicated to the memory of his brother Stuart, one of a number of Pacific Islanders who joined the 'D' division of the Māori Battalion. The collection is divided into four sections, exploring the four main theatres of war in chronological order. The sequence is carefully researched, again drawing on Cody and Gardiner, but Campbell (like Grace) interweaves fact and fiction, reconstructing various phases of combat from the imagined perspectives of Māori soldiers. In 'Tohi' (reprinted in Albert Wendt's 2003 anthology *Whetu Moana*), Campbell represents bayonet combat as a continuation of the Māori warrior tradition, noting that while Māori no longer perform tohi (purification ceremonies) as they did in previous centuries, the rituals are still undertaken in the 'heart and guts' of the Māori soldier. Campbell imagines the soldiers inspired by Tūmatauenga, and speculates about what would have happened to the enemy in the days of cannibalism 'when kaitangata [consumption of human flesh] was the warrior's just reward' (Wendt *et al.* (eds.) 2003: 34). Campbell's text, like Grace's, is just one of a considerable number of creative and non-fiction publications on Māori war achievements that emerged at the dawn of the new millennium.

3.3.2 *Māori soldiers in Vietnam: Hone Tuwhare, Witi Ihimaera, and John Broughton*

Where the involvement of Māori troops in the two world wars has been a source of pride for many Māori, the Vietnam war has left a rather different legacy. During and after the Second World War, New Zealand's defence programme became more closely linked to the US and Australia rather than Britain, in the interests of regulating security within the Pacific region. When the United States asked New Zealand for a contribution to its war against communist forces in Vietnam, the incumbent National government agreed, subscribing to the 'domino theory' which held that if communism was allowed to take root in South Vietnam, it would soon spread to other Pacific nations and pose a threat to 'Western' democracies in the region. The Labour opposition party, however, did not support New Zealand involvement in the war, arguing that the conflict in Vietnam was a civil war, and nationwide protests were mounted against New Zealand's involvement in Vietnam (between 1964 and 1972) by a substantial proportion of the New Zealand public (King 2003: 453–4).

In addition to the general public, a number of New Zealand writers also expressed their opposition to the war. One of the most prominent of these was poet Hone Tuwhare, who included several anti-war poems in his 1972 collection *Sapwood and Milk*. Notable among these is 'Speak to Me, Brother', in which a Māori opposed to the Vietnam War 'speaks to' a fellow Māori who is about to begin his tour of duty. Only the objector's voice is heard in the poem, as he 'repeats' the soldier's justifications for conscription and then good-naturedly but pointedly demolishes them. The argument that the Vietcong represent a threat to New Zealand security is dismissed as paranoia; the claim that New Zealand is helping to defend 'the "Free World"' is condemned as intolerant dogma; and the belief that New Zealand military assistance is vital to the Americans is dismissed with the withering comment 'Fuck-sake man: they can BUY and SELL us' (Thieme (ed.) 1996: 610). The speaker also draws an implicit link between Māori respect for the land, and the 'big feeling' the 'rice farmers' in Vietnam have for their own native soil, thus implying a spiritual affiliation between the two cultures. The poem's juxtaposition of the vulnerable Vietnamese and the powerful Americans suggests that the slaying of Vietnamese by Māori troops would be an act of bad faith, given that both cultures have already suffered colonial military oppression—Māori under the British, and the Vietnamese under the French and now the Americans.

Witi Ihimaera's novel *The Uncle's Story* (2000*a*), a substantial section of which is set during the Vietnam war, also explores the ethical problems facing Māori soldiers in Vietnam. Michael Mahana, the narrator of the novel, is given the diary of his uncle Sam, who volunteered for service in the Vietnam war under pressure from his father Arapeta, a war hero who received a Military Cross after serving as a commander with the Māori Battalion in the Second World War (34). Michael's own father boasts of Arapeta's bravery, arguing that he 'relied on the warrior blood of his ancestors—their intelligence, their cunning and their ability to lead—to get him through' (15). During a farewell ceremony for Sam and two fellow Māori soldiers, George and Turei, Arapeta himself speaks at length about the achievements of the Māori Battalion, and then situates the young men's enlistment for Vietnam within an illustrious history of Māori warriorhood, arguing that the three men are 'carrying on the tradition of their forebears' (42).

However, Arapeta's triumphalist send-off does not prepare Sam and his companions for the complexities and horrors of the war in Vietnam. Because it is very difficult to distinguish between the non-communist Vietnamese and the Vietcong, the soldiers often end up killing the people they are meant to protect, and Sam himself becomes confused about where his loyalties lie when he meets an elderly Vietcong supporter who reminds him of his own deceased grand-aunt. Further, although Sam and George (having lost Turei) are given a hero's welcome at their marae when they finally return home, unlike the Māori Battalion veterans, they receive a hostile reception outside their immediate community, 'humiliated' by protest groups, receiving no formal recognition from the government, and some of them dying as a result of exposure to chemicals in Vietnam (187).

The effects of a toxic chemical called 'Agent Orange', used by the Americans to defoliate areas of jungle in South Vietnam, are dramatized in *Michael James Manaia* (1991/1994), a play by John Broughton which focuses on the experiences of a Māori Vietnam veteran. The two-act play, first performed in 1991, takes the form of an extended monologue by the title character, an experienced soldier who reminisces about his service in Malaya and Vietnam. Like Arapeta in Ihimaera's *The Uncle's Story*, Manaia's father fought in the Māori Battalion during the Second World War, and Manaia's enlistment for service in Malaya and Vietnam initially appears as a continuation of a 'proud' tradition of Māori warriorhood. Where the Battalion heroes have enjoyed an enduring reputation for bravery, however, Manaia reveals at the end of the play that his exposure to Agent Orange has left him with a legacy of ill-health and personal loss. After the war ended, it was proven that Agent Orange was a cancer-causing agent which also precipitated 'birth defects, still births and miscarriages' (97), and when Manaia marries and attempts to start a family back in Aotearoa/New Zealand, his wife has four miscarriages before finally giving birth to a severely deformed child. The play closes with the chilling implication that Manaia, unable to face raising a disabled child, kills his own baby.

3.3.3 *The Māori warrior as cultural symbol: Alan Duff and Ranginui Walker*

The trope of the Māori warrior was disseminated to a wide international audience with the release of Lee Tamahori's *Once Were Warriors* (1994), a film based on Alan Duff's novel (of the same name) published in 1990. Duff's writing offers an ambivalent response to the 'Māori warrior' legacy, and his comments on violence within the contemporary Māori community are at times contradictory. In his 1999 autobiography *Out of the Mist and Steam*, for example, he suggests that Māori have a natural predilection for violence, claiming that his 'Māori warrior genes' have helped him overcome many male assailants over the years (207). His 1998 novel *Both Sides of the Moon* offers graphic, visceral representations of precolonial warfare as the putative foundation of modern Māori violence, resonating with Heretaunga Pat Baker's sensationalist accounts of Māori martial cruelty in his earlier novel *Behind the Tattooed Face* (1975, see also Heim 1998: 15–18). On the other hand, Duff has also recognized that much violent behaviour is socially-determined, targeting domestic violence as a repetitive and destructive cycle within working-class Māori society (1999: 158; Keown 2005: 172).

Through a variety of narrative perspectives rendered in free indirect discourse, *Once Were Warriors* explores both sides of this 'nature–nurture' debate, acknowledging (for example) that poverty and race-related social divisions have contributed to violent crime and abuse among working-class Māori, but also positing an innate Māori 'warriorhood' which has endured throughout Aotearoa/New Zealand's colonial and postcolonial history. This warrior ethic, Duff implies, has been altered (though not eradicated) by the processes of colonization and urbanization: traditional inter-tribal warfare has been replaced by fighting between gangs (a new kind of ritualized violence), but also by other forms of violence including wife-beating, sexual abuse, and drunken brawling.

Through the ruminations of Beth Heke, one of the central characters in the novel, Duff suggests that gang warfare is a debased and corrupted form of warriorhood. When Beth's son Nig joins a local gang called the Brown Fists, for example, the spurious nature of his warrior identity is revealed when he receives a facial tattoo that reproduces a traditional Māori moko design but is applied through modern needle-prick techniques, rather than being carved into the skin with a traditional chisel (Duff 1994: 189; Keown 2005: 186).

In Lee Tamahori's film adaptation of Duff's novel, however, scriptwriter Riwia Brown radically alters this dynamic: in contrast to Duff's 'filthy' and debased delinquents, the gang members in the film are represented as well-toned, shiny-leather-clad modern warriors. The original gang name ('The Brown Fists') has been changed to 'Toa Aotearoa', which translates literally as 'warriors/champions of Aotearoa', suggesting a return to a traditional (and collective) Māori warrior ethic that presents a positive contrast to the destructive muscularity of Jake's wife-beating generation of Māori men (Keown 2005: 175–88). After leaving her abusive husband, Beth herself becomes a female 'warrior' (in both novel and film versions of *Once Were Warriors*), as she develops—and imparts to other Māori—the confidence to break the cycle of poverty and violence that has crippled many of her people for generations. In this respect, her character advances Duff's own 'self-help' philosophy: he has argued that while Māori have suffered injustices at the hands of the Pākehā, they must find the inner strength—the warrior fighting spirit—that will enable them to rise above the socio-economic deprivation that afflicts many contemporary Māori (Duff 1993, 1999).

While Duff has offended many of his peers by arguing that Māori should stop 'blaming' Pākehā for their social problems, his claim for an enduring 'warrior' ethic in Māori society is shared by other contemporary Māori commentators such as Ranginui Walker, whose historical study *Ka Whawhai Tonu Matou: Struggle Without End* (1990/2004) documents the Māori struggle for self-determination. The title of the book was inspired by a famous statement made by warrior-chief Rewi Maniapoto, who repelled three assaults by imperial troops on Orakau Pa (a fortified village) in the Waikato in 1864. Rewi Maniapoto is reputed to have addressed Major William Gilbert Mair with the defiant words 'E hoa, ka whawhai tonu ahau ki a koe ake, ake, ake' (Friend, I shall continue to fight you for ever and ever), and Walker selected Maniapoto's manifesto as an iconic expression of the anticolonial sentiments he describes in his book (King 2003: 215–16). Tellingly, in a 1994 review of Tamahori's *Once Were Warriors*, Walker describes the film as a positive, empowering representation of Māori warriorhood in contrast to Duff's novel, which (Walker claims) posits Māori combative abilities as 'a genetic flaw' (1994: 134–5). Walker himself, however, has also been accused of stereotyping in his discussion of Māori warriorhood: in a review of Walker's *Ka Whawhai Tonu Matou*, Paul Moon argues that Walker's representation of Māori as a warrior people, witnessed (for example) in his claim that that the Māori battalion 'rekindled the fighting spirit of a warrior race' (Walker 2004: 240) reinforces colonial stereotypes of which Walker is highly critical elsewhere in his book (Moon 1996: n.p.).

While it is undeniable that modern celebrations of Māori warriorhood do resonate (to some degree) with colonial stereotypes, this does not negate the potency of warriorhood as a metaphor for socio-political activism among contemporary Māori. Rewi Maniapoto's battle-cry, and the motif of warriorhood, have remained a source of inspiration for generations of Māori activists, particularly since the Māori Renaissance of the 1970s (see Chapter 4). One of the most famous Māori activist groups to emerge in the 1970s was 'Ngā Tamatoa' ('the young warriors'), and the phrase 'ka whawhai tonu matou ake, ake, ake' has been invoked by countless Māori activists since that period. In a speech delivered in 2003, Māori MP John Tamihere advocated a 'warriors not whingers' approach to improving the socio-economic position of contemporary Māori, and Māori film-maker Merata Mita selected the name 'Patu' (denoting a Māori war-club) for her 1983 documentary film about Māori involvement in protests against the 1981 Springbok rugby tour of New Zealand. The tour took place while South Africa was still under apartheid, and Mita's film encodes Māori warfare as a symbol of political resistance against racism, not only within South Africa, but also within Aotearoa/New Zealand itself. In this and other contexts, the motif of Māori warriorhood is invoked as much in the service of ideological 'battles' as martial struggles, and it remains an important source of political motivation and self-esteem among contemporary Māori. The drive for Māori self-determination is discussed further in Chapter 4, which also outlines the main 'centres' from which Indigenous Pacific literature has emerged during the 1970s and beyond.

4

The 1970s and Beyond: The Emergence of the 'New' Pacific Literatures in English

Colonialism, by shattering the world of the traditional artist, also broke open the way for a new type of artist who is not bound by traditional styles and attitudes and conventions, who explores his own individuality, experiments freely and expresses his own values and ideas, his own mana unfettered by accepted convention.

(Albert Wendt, 'Don't Generalise about the South Pacific')

The canoe is afloat . . . confidence is growing. . . . [T]he rich cargoes of individual talent from every part of the Pacific [are being carried] to every other part, both within and beyond the island shores.

(Marjorie Tuainekore Crocombe, editor's introduction to *Mana Annual of Creative Writing*, 1974)

'Self-expression is a prerequisite of self-respect.' So argued Albert Wendt in 'Towards a New Oceania' (1976*a*), one of the first critical analyses of the emerging field of Indigenous Pacific literatures in English. Wendt's statement encapsulated the counterdiscursive objectives of many 'first-generation' Pacific writers of the 1970s, whose work was centrally concerned with developing an Indigenous literary aesthetic and debunking Western 'myths' about Pacific peoples. This chapter explores the work of many of these early Pacific writers, but also looks beyond the 1970s in order to investigate the stylistic and conceptual shifts that have taken place in the decades following the polemical 'first wave' of Indigenous writing.

However, rather than generalize about the region as a whole, this chapter focuses upon six particular 'centres' of literary activity in the Pacific, each characterized by its own unique historical and political circumstances. These 'centres' include Papua New Guinea; Fiji and the USP nations; Hawai'i and the 'American' Pacific (including American Samoa and Micronesia); the Francophone Pacific (including French Polynesia/Tahiti Nui, Wallis and Futuna, New Caledonia, and parts of Vanuatu); Hispanophone Easter Island/Rapa Nui; and Aotearoa/New Zealand (see Subramani 1992: x–xi). Evidently, some of these groupings of nations (in particular, the 'American', Francophone, and Hispanophone categories) are constituted by their shared experience of colonization under a particular European or American imperial 'power', and much of the counterdiscursive writing from these groups is inflected by these relationships. However, the remaining three 'centres' of literary activity are characterized by different sociopolitical circumstances. Māori writing of Aotearoa/New Zealand is considered as a distinct category on its own, inflected by its unique relationship with the Pākehā (European) settler culture, whose continuing presence in Aotearoa denies Māori 'postcolonial' status. The Indigenous literatures of Papua New Guinea and some of the USP nations, on the other hand, emerged largely as a consequence of the establishment of local universities in Papua New Guinea and Fiji (in the late 1960s) in preparation for independence. Relatively speaking, Papua New Guinea and some of the USP nations have lower literacy rates and publishing resources in comparison to the other literary 'centres' discussed in this chapter, and to this day, many writers from these countries are still closely linked to—and often work within—these universities, which provide vital resources and support networks for Pacific writers and scholars.

It is worth acknowledging, at this point, that the sheer volume and diversity of creative writing from which these six literary profiles have been constructed has necessitated a synoptic and inevitably partial approach to these various literary contexts. Much of the discussion focuses upon the more polemical or anticolonial aspects of Pacific writing, but where possible, the chapter also investigates the ways in which these literatures are located in Indigenous Pacific linguistic and mythopoeic traditions, preparing the ground for the more detailed stylistic analyses which appear in Chapter 5.

Before embarking on a discussion of these six literary groupings, it is worth making a few preliminary remarks about the origins of Pacific literature as a 'textual' corpus. Although 'postcolonial' Pacific literatures emerged during and beyond the decolonizing period of the 1960s and 1970s, these texts can be situated within a Pacific *literary* (as opposed to oral) tradition that dates back to the early nineteenth century, when European missionaries first developed orthographies for Indigenous Pacific languages (see Chapter 5). The missionaries taught Pacific Island peoples to read and write, first in their own vernaculars and then in English, primarily in order to disseminate the Bible and other Christian tracts. Once literate, Pacific Islanders began to produce written texts of their own: along with mission-inspired publications, other forms of Indigenous writing that emerged during the nineteenth and early twentieth centuries included biographies, autobiographies, family histories, and genealogies. The missionaries generally discouraged Pacific Islanders from writing fiction, however, and it wasn't until 1960 that the first Indigenous Pacific novel—*Makutu*, by Cook Islander Tom Davis and his wife Lydia—was published. Because the novel did not break significantly with the modes and conventions of European 'Pacific' literature—as it took the form of a realist adventure story narrated by an English doctor—it is generally viewed as a precursor, rather than forerunner, of the anticolonial Indigenous Pacific literature which emerged towards the end of the 1960s (Subramani 1992: 14). By this time, Māori writers and 'Western-educated' Pacific Islanders (such as Albert Wendt) had already begun publishing individual creative works in metropolitan literary journals, magazines, and newspapers, and Māori poet Hone Tuwhare had published his first poetry collection (*No Ordinary Sun*) as early as 1964. However, the first major phase of Indigenous literary efflorescence was to begin in Papua New Guinea, where the establishment of a national university in 1966 brought substantial numbers of Indigenous Pacific writers together for the first time.

4.1 Papua New Guinea

The first wave of Indigenous creative writing in Papua New Guinea began in 1967 when Ulli Beier—who had already been a catalyst in the development of contemporary Indigenous literature and art in

Nigeria during the 1950s and 1960s—began teaching a creative writing course at the university of Papua New Guinea (UPNG). Throughout the 1970s, Beier published a wide range of his students' work in literary anthologies targeted primarily towards 'Western' readers in Australia and the US, but he also established his own local poetry imprint, *Papua Pocket Poets*, and founded Papua New Guinea's first literary journal, *Kovave* (1969–74). In his teaching, Beier exposed his students to a wide variety of African literatures, and a range of Papua New Guinean literature published during the 1960s and 1970s deploys the pseudo-ethnographic realism evident in texts such as Chinua Achebe's *Things Fall Apart* (1958). As Beier reveals, many Papua New Guinean writers of this period identified closely with the 'cultural anxieties and political issues' explored in African writing, and various African writers, including Taban Lo Liyong (from Uganda) and Wole Soyinka (from Nigeria), visited the UPNG campus in these early years (2005: 138).

A wide selection of poetry and prose published in *Kovave* was later reprinted in *Lali* (1980), Albert Wendt's first edited collection of Pacific writing. Much of this material took the form of polemical attacks upon colonial political and discursive hegemony, expressing a cultural nationalist aesthetic that developed in advance of Papua New Guinea's independence from Australia (in 1975). One of the most assertively anticolonial writers of this period is John Kasaipwalova, whose poem 'Reluctant Flame'—first published in 1971 and reprinted in *Lali*—achieved wide international acclaim. Kasaipwalova was a committed proponent of the 'Black Power' movement that flourished at UPNG in the late 1960s and early 1970s, and his poem draws inspiration from black civil rights struggles in the US and South Africa. Written in blank verse, and divided into irregular verse-paragraphs studded with expletives and scatological imagery, Kasaipwalova's poem is explosively anticolonial, establishing a series of binary oppositions contrasting the cultural 'chill' of colonialism with the blazing 'heat' of political and discursive resistance. Setting the poem's political agenda within an international context, Kasaipwalova asserts that the 'flame' of Papua New Guinean nationalism can draw 'fuel' from the struggles of colonized 'brother[s]' in Africa and the US, and he also associates the Papua New Guinean nationalist movement with the guerilla tactics used by the Vietcong in the Vietnam war (Wendt (ed.) 1980: 195). Kasaipwalova's advocacy of violence as a means by which to eject the colonial forces echoes the work of Martiniquan psychiatrist Frantz Fanon, whose sympathy for the Algerian independence movement prompted him to publish the influential anticolonial text *The Wretched of the Earth* (1961/1963), itself adopted as a manifesto by black civil rights activists such as Malcolm X and Steve Biko (Young 2001: 280). Kasaipwalova's interest in international black civil rights movements was shared by other Papua New Guinean writers such as Russell Soaba, whose first novel *Wanpis* (1977) focuses on a group of students who become involved in the Black Power movement at UPNG. On the other hand, Kasaipwalova's emphasis on the subversive power of *rhetoric*, exercised as he exchanges his 'bush knife for the pen' (193), resonates with other anticolonial poems of the period such as Kumalau Tawali's 'The Bush Kanaka Speaks' (1970). 'Kanaka' is a pidgin word derived from the term for 'man' or 'person' in various Polynesian languages, and it was adopted by Europeans as a derogatory colonial label for Indigenous peoples throughout the Pacific. In his poem, Tawali effects a linguistic transformation, reclaiming the word 'kanaka' and stripping it of its negative associations, so that it becomes a symbol of native self-assertion rather than colonial circumscription. The poem, an angry rejection of colonial stereotypes about 'ignorant' and 'dirty' natives, thus resonates with the Indian critic Gayatri Spivak's famous essay 'Can the Subaltern Speak?' (1988): Tawali's 'subaltern' emerges from the prison house of colonial discourse and redefines his material conditions and aspirations on his own terms (Wendt (ed.) 1980: 199–200).

It has been argued that much of the momentum in Papua New Guinean creative writing came from the drive for independence, and that the literary movement lost impetus in the immediate post-independence period (Krauth 1993; Winduo 1990). Many previously active writers such as Kumulau Tawali, Leo Hannett, John Kasaipwalova, and John Waiko became heavily involved in other political and cultural projects after independence, and Beier himself, undeniably a driving force behind the Papua New Guinean literary movement, was away at the University of Ife in Nigeria from 1971–4. There were few periodical publishing outlets in the latter part of the 1970s, but a few established writers (such as Paulias Matane and Russell Soaba) published single-authored books during this period.

In the 1980s, a further phase of literary activity began in Papua New Guinea with the establishment of the literary magazines *Ondobondo*,

Bikmaus, *Sope*, and *The PNG Writer*, in which a new generation of authors (such as Nora Vagi Brash, Steven Winduo, Sorariba Nash, and John Kolia) published their work. Much of this material is not readily available outside Papua New Guinea, but some has been reprinted in *Nuanua* (1995*a*), Wendt's second anthology of Pacific literature. Some of these works, like those published in *Lali*, focus on the deleterious effects of colonialism upon Papua New Guinean cultural practices, but others take up more recognizably post-independence issues such as urbanization, Westernization, and the socio-economic imbalances caused by the emergence of new political élites. Nora Vagi Brash's lyric poem 'Mass Media, Mass Mania', for example, targets consumer capitalism as a new and damaging 'religion' in Papua New Guinea, invoking the repetition of words, sounds, and syntactic structures often used in consumer product advertising to create a sense of monotonous inevitability about the spread of consumerism in modern Papua New Guinea. In the first stanza, a list of junk foods is followed by an alliterative inventory of undesirable side-effects ('Toothache, decoy, decay'), while later sections of the poem morph advertising jingles into grim statements of mental and social decay ('Whiter wash . . . brain wash'). The poem ends with the ambiguous phrase 'SOLD OUT', which not only indexes the constant consumer demand for products, but also implies that Westernization causes Indigenous peoples to 'sell out' on their traditional values and cultural practices (Wendt (ed.) 1995*a*: 178). Joyce Kumbeli's lyric poem 'Caught Up' explores similar issues, describing a Papua New Guinean who purchases raffle tickets compulsively in the hope of winning money to spend on consumer products (211), while Loujaya Kouza's lyric poem 'The Expatriate' introduces a man whose contact with Western cultures has rendered him too proud to accept offers of 'traditional' food and drink from his compatriots (210). Jack Lahui's story 'We Are Tukes' offers a more nuanced exploration of cultural syncretism, focusing on two young men who are partial to cigarettes and beer but still adhere to the oral and spiritual traditions of their home village, Porebada. During a drinking session, one of the boys offers a formulaic recitation of his genealogy, indexing the continuing importance of oral traditions to Papua New Guinean peoples.

Oral traditions have also been kept alive in the large number of unpublished dramatic works and radio plays produced in Papua New Guinea since independence (Stella 1999: 228). Many of the dramatic performances by Papua New Guinea's numerous theatre groups have been direct adaptations of myths, legends, and folklore, blending oral tradition and Western poetics: Kasaipwalova's folk opera *Sail the Midnight Sun*, which references Papua New Guinean fertility myths, is an example of this type of syncretic drama (see Wendt (ed.) 1995*a*: 180–99). Nora Vagi Brash is perhaps the best-known among the small group of playwrights who have published their work, and many of her plays explore the effects of modernization and urbanization upon Papua New Guinean peoples. Her play 'Which Way, Big Man?', arguably the best-known of her dramatic works, offers a comi-satirical analysis of post-independence urban élites which resonates with the work of Polynesian writers such as Albert Wendt and Epeli Hau'ofa. First performed by Papua New Guinea's National Theatre Company in 1976, 'Which Way, Big Man?' centres on a party given by a pretentious Papua New Guinean public servant and his wife, whose names—'Gou Haia' and 'Sinob Haia'—point towards their pecuniary and social aspirations. The party is organized to celebrate Gou Haia's promotion to the office of 'Director of National Identity', but festivities come to an abrupt end after a university student accuses the Haias and their associates of corruption, at which point Sinob enters into a drunken brawl with her husband's typist. Brash's play is redolent of Polynesian comic theatre traditions (see Chapter 6), in which biting social criticism is offered under the veil of humour. Further, like the work of many other Pacific writers (see Chapter 5), it is also centrally concerned with the politics of language: Gou's and Sinob's social pretensions are underscored by their refusal to speak Tok Pisin, the local lingua franca, and much of the comedy of the play is enacted in the clash of registers between English—the language of the urban élites—and pidgin, often used by rural and 'menial' characters in order to ridicule the snobbish Haias.

The 1990s and beyond have witnessed the emergence of an increasing number of Papua New Guinean female authors. Nigerian academic Adeola James ran a workshop for Pacific women writers at UPNG in 1992, and many of these authors published their work in James's edited collection *PNG Women Writers: An Anthology* (1996). Much of the material in the anthology—which includes poetry, prose, drama, and interviews with selected authors—is polemical, striking out against the circumscription of women under (neo)colonialism and patriarchy, and criticizing corruption among post-independence political élites. Other works, however, such as the lyric poems 'Song of the Winds' (by Nora Vagi Brash) and 'Avala' (by Fa'afo N. Patrick), posit the 'spiritual' and material connections between Papua New Guineans and the natural environment as sources of cultural continuity. These poems resonate with the verse of Steven Winduo, whose poetry collections *Lomo'ha I am, in Spirit's Voice I Call* (1991) and *Hembemba: Rivers of the Forest* (2000) link the vicissitudes of human life with the rhythms and life-cycles of the natural world. Where many Polynesian writers have invoked the natural world as a positive source of energy and empowerment, however, Winduo's work—like that of other contemporary PNG poets such as Peggy Iruru and Sally-Ann Bagita—often deploys natural imagery to advance what Rob Wilson has called 'an ancestral sublime vision of dark seeing' (2002: 509), identifying destructive elemental forces as metaphors for human existential anguish. Winduo is one of the few contemporary Papua New Guinean writers to have achieved international recognition in recent years; as he has pointed out, there is still relatively little support for creative writers in Papua New Guinea (Wood 2006: 87). Since the 1990s, however, UPNG has once again begun to take an active role in publishing the work of Papua New Guinean writers, launching the literary journal *Savannah Flames* in 1992, and establishing the Melanesian and Pacific Studies Centre (MAPS), which is committed to publishing works by writers throughout Melanesia.

4.2 Fiji and the University of the South Pacific

The University of the South Pacific (USP), which opened in Fiji in 1968, became the second locus of Indigenous literary efflorescence in the Pacific. Significantly, the South Pacific Creative Arts Society (SPCAS), formed at USP in 1972, was directly inspired by the outpouring of creative writing from Papua New Guinea in the late 1960s and early 1970s, and Marjorie Crocombe, inaugural editor of the SPCAS journal *Mana* (established in 1973), had studied creative writing with Beier at UPNG. USP soon became the locus of a lively new anglophone creative writing movement, particularly from 1974, when Albert Wendt began teaching creative writing at the university. The SPCAS developed its own imprint, Mana Publications, and various students, academics, and other creative writers in Fiji—such as Jo Nacola (from Fiji), Vilsoni

Hereniko (Rotuma), Sano Malifa and Momoe Von Reiche (Samoa), and Makiuti Tongia (Cook Islands)—published book-length works throughout the 1970s. Many of the best-known writers and critics of the contemporary Pacific—including Epeli Hau'ofa, Satendra Nandan, Subramani, Konai Helu Thaman, and Albert Wendt—have been connected with USP at some point in their careers, and Wendt's first two anthologies of Pacific writing, *Lali* and *Nuanua*, are almost exclusively focused on writers from Fiji and other nations served by the USP.[1]

Rather than attempt to summarize the enormous body of writing that has emerged from the USP region, this section of the chapter focuses upon a series of political crises—the military coups of 1987 and 2000—that have had a profound effect upon the cultural and literary dynamics of Fiji and the USP. In the 1970s, the activities of the SPCAS were closely connected with larger political philosophies of the period, particularly the ideology of the 'Pacific Way'. Proponents of this movement sought to unite Pacific Islanders ideologically against the 'colonial powers', emphasizing cultural commonalities between Pacific peoples and celebrating putatively 'Pacific' values (such as communalism, reciprocity, and love and respect for the land and other people) (Va'ai 1999: 33–5). The USP, which brought together students from various different Pacific Island nations, seemed the ideal laboratory in which to foster these principles, and the SPCAS, like other USP-based arts organizations, actively promoted the 'unity-in-diversity' model throughout the 1970s. However, the idealist regionalism of the 'Pacific Way' ideology was eroded during the 1980s, when, following the decolonization of the majority of the USP states, Pacific Island politics became more introspective and parochial. Much Pacific literature of this period—including the work of Albert Wendt and Epeli Hau'ofa—began to focus more closely upon neocolonialism and the emergence of post-independence politico-social élites within particular national contexts (see Chapter 6). In 1987, the myth of pan-Pacific tolerance, cooperation, and non-violence was shattered when Fijian nationalists staged two military coups, radically altering the intercultural politics of the Pacific and bringing Fiji's post-colonial political problems to world attention.

The legacy of indenture and the Fiji coups: the context   The Fiji coups had their origins in inter-ethnic conflict between Indigenous Fijians and the descendants of the indentured Indian labourers who were transported to Fiji to work on colonial sugar plantations from the late nineteenth century. To orient readers unfamiliar with this context, this section of the chapter outlines some of the main historical trends and developments that have inflected Fiji's unique socio-political milieu, before going on to examine literary responses to the Fiji coups.

Fiji ceded itself to Britain in 1874 to circumvent threats of an invasion from Tonga, and between 1879 and 1916 (shortly before indenture was abolished in 1920), some sixty thousand Indian labourers were transported to Fiji, most of them to work on the sugar estates of the Colonial Sugar Refining Company (CSR) of Australia. Indenture was secured with the signing of an agreement—which came to be known by the phonetic approximation 'girmit' by the workers or 'girmitiyas'—that specified the conditions of work, pay, accommodation, and provision of basic facilities (Lal 2004: 6). The indenture period was normally five years, after which labourers could work for a further five years to earn their passage back to India (I. C. Campbell 1989: 175–6). There were some benefits to the indenture system in Fiji: for many girmitiyas, living conditions were better than they had been in India, and caste divisions were less rigidly enforced as people from different backgrounds had to work and live close together in 'coolie lines' (V. Mishra 1977: 396; Lal 2004: 12). However, labouring conditions were hard and remuneration—based on the amount of work an individual completed—was often poor, meaning that many labourers could not afford to return to India even if they wished to do so (Lal 2004: 13). From the 1880s, free settlements were established by ex-indentured labourers who earned a living from agriculture and various trades, and free migrants, primarily from Gujarat, began arriving from 1904, eventually dominating trade and commerce in the Indo-Fijian community (Lal 2004: 22–3).

Although Indo-Fijians have played a major role in Fiji's business sector, their socio-economic aspirations have been held in check by land tenure laws established in colonial Fiji. Mindful of the damaging effects of Indigenous land alienation in other colonies such as Hawai'i, the British colonial authorities decided to protect Indigenous Fijian landholdings, and to this day, over 80 per cent of Fijian land remains in Indigenous ownership, with Indians largely dependent upon the granting of leases by the owners (Nandan 2000:

22). The protectionist policies of the colonial government served to segregate Indians and Indigenous Fijians, ensuring that the two cultures have lived almost completely separate existences, maintaining discrete educational, religious, and other community institutions to this day (Lal 2004: 24; Campbell 1989: 175–6).

By the time Fiji gained its independence in 1970, these cultural schisms had become entrenched, and Indigenous Fijians—who had become outnumbered by Indo-Fijians after the Second World War—feared that Indo-Fijians would attempt to take control of their lands and resources once Britain had withdrawn. However, the early years of independence saw a period of relative stability under the governance of the Alliance Party (led by Indigenous Fijian Ratu Sir Kamisese Mara), which protected the interests of Fiji's 'ruling class' of chiefs as well as Europeans and wealthy Indians. In 1987, however, the Indigenous Fijian-dominated leadership was replaced with a multi-ethnic coalition led by Dr Timoci Bavadra, an Indigenous Fijian supported by the Indo-Fijian community. Bavadra's government comprised comparatively equal numbers of Indian and Indigenous Fijian members, but less than a month after he came to power, Bavadra was forcibly removed during a military coup led by Lieutenant Colonel Sitiveni Rabuka, who claimed to be acting on behalf of Indigenous Fijians concerned about racial discrimination. After a period of unsuccessful negotiations, a second coup was staged in September 1987, after which Fiji was declared a republic, and Governor-General Ratu Sir Penaia Ganilau (an Indigenous Fijian) was appointed President with Ratu Sir Kamisese Mara as Prime Minister. A new constitution (implemented in 1990) severely disadvantaged Indo-Fijians, reserving most political offices for Indigenous Fijians. After some years of negotiation, the 1997 constitution reopened the Prime Ministerial position to citizens of all ethnicities, but tensions rose again in May 1999, when a multi-racial coalition led by Mahendra Chaudhry—Fiji's first Indian Prime Minister—came to power. In 2000, Fijian nationalist George Speight (of mixed Fijian and European descent) led another military coup that removed Chaudhry from office, and although Speight was eventually arrested and the suspended constitution reinstated, when democratic elections took place once again in 2002, the interim Prime Minister Laisenia Qarase defeated Chaudhry, ensuring the continuing dominance of Indigenous Fijians in the highest offices of government.

These events have undeniably had a catastrophic effect on relations between Indians and Indigenous Fijians, and have also inspired a wide range of Fijian literature exploring the cross-cultural conflict surrounding the coups. As Subramani observes, since independence both races have regarded themselves as 'victims', the Indigenous Fijians owning most of the land and in control of government but socio-economically dispossessed, and the Indians, though 'visibly in control of the commerce in towns and cities', owning only two per cent of the land and haunted by the legacy of indenture (1995: 36). The coups in 1987 and 2000 further deepened these inter-racial schisms, giving the lie to the vision of Fiji as a multicultural paradise marketed to tourists with the phrase 'Fiji: the way the world should be', and causing thousands of skilled Indo-Fijians to leave the country (L. Thomas 2001: 118).

With these factors in mind, the next two sections investigate the ways in which cross-cultural conflict between Indigenous Fijians and Indians has inflected the work of various writers in Fiji, beginning with Indo-Fijian literature focused upon the legacy of indenture, and then examining Indo-Fijian and Indigenous literary responses to the coups themselves.

Literary explorations of indenture: Subramani and Satendra Nandan
The legacy of indenture, and the divisions between Indigenous Fijians and Indians, have inspired a range of literature produced by Indo-Fijian writers in the post-independence period. One of the most sustained literary explorations of indenture appears in *The Fantasy Eaters* (1988), a collection of stories by Subramani. In stories such as 'Sautu' and 'Marigolds' (reprinted in *Lali*) and 'Tell Me Where the Train Goes' (reprinted in *Nuanua*), Subramani explores what Indo-Fijian scholar Vijay Mishra has termed the 'girmit ideology'. According to Mishra, this 'ideology' conceptualizes the experience of indenture as akin to a 'failed millennial quest', in which the harsh realities of life on the Fijian plantations (and in the coolie lines) shattered labourers' 'dreams' of a 'promised land' in which they would 'escape from the degrading realities of Indian life' (1977: 395). This sense of disappointment and dispossession haunts a range of Subramani's stories. 'Sautu', for example, set in a squalid village established by ex-indentured labourers, describes the mental deterioration of Dhanpat, an elderly villager worn down by his impoverished existence

and the demoralizing weight of his girmit heritage. 'Marigolds', on the other hand, is narrated by a neurotic Indo-Fijian schoolteacher conscious that his Fijian compatriots view him as 'a member of the desperate, money-grubbing fraternity' of urbanized Indo-Fijians (1988: 43). The schoolteacher feels trapped by his girmit heritage, observing that '[t]here is no alternative life: a hundred years of history on these islands has resulted in wilderness and distress' (45). 'Tell Me Where the Train Goes' returns to the actual experience of indenture, depicting a community of Indo-Fijian sugarcane labourers working on a plantation overseen by a bullying 'Sahib', Mr Pepper. In this story, related by an anonymous omniscient narrator but often focalized through the consciousness of various members of the community, the coolie lines ('twenty-odd rusty corrugated iron and timber hutments') are described as a 'nightmarish world' where 'shipwrecked ... refugees from a depressed subcontinent' are 'brutalised by ghetto life' (Wendt (ed.) 1995a: 115, 116, 119). Significantly, the shipwreck metaphor not only implies that the labourers are now trapped in Fiji with no chance of escape to the mother country, but also indexes an historical disaster which took place in the early years of indenture.

The catastrophe occurred on 11 May 1884, when the ship *Syria*, which was bringing girmitiyas to Fiji, was wrecked on Nasilai reef, resulting in the deaths of many of the passengers (V. Mishra 1992: 4). Allusions to the shipwreck of the *Syria* appear not only in Subramani's writing, but also in the work of Indo-Fijian writer Satendra Nandan, who visited the site of the wreck and viewed it as a key symbol of the dispossession of Indo-Fijians (Nandan 1991: 160). In his 1991 novel *The Wounded Sea*, Nandan describes the 1987 coup as a re-enactment of the *Syria* shipwreck (1991: 161), while the speaker in his poem 'The Ghost' implies that the 'voices from *syria*' will haunt Indo-Fijians in perpetuity (1985: 54). The poem describes the speaker's meeting with a girmitiya's 'ghost' who compares the experience of indenture with the period of exile suffered by Rama, hero of the Hindu epic the *Rāmāyana* (see Chapter 5). The 'ghost' implies that while Rama was able eventually to return from exile to the kingdom of Ayodhya, Indo-Fijians, trapped in Fiji, have been forced to construct their own imaginary Ayodhya(s), taking refuge in the Hindu philosophies and sacred texts that constitute the girmitiyas' only remaining link with the homeland (1985: 53).

Vijay Mishra has argued that such strategies of identification are central to the putatively flawed logic of the 'girmit ideology'. He asserts that nostalgic links with the cultural traditions of India, coupled with suspicion of Indigenous Fijians (shored up by the separatist policies of the British colonial authorities), have doomed the Indo-Fijian 'fragment' to sociopolitical failure, preventing meaningful dialogue between Indians and Indigenous Fijians and ultimately helping to precipitate the 1987 coups (1992: 2–3; see also Mishra 1977). Mishra's comments resonate with the work of Trinidadian writer V. S. Naipaul, who has identified similar strategies of identification among the descendants of Indian indentured labourers in Trinidad. In his 2001 Nobel Prize lecture, for example, Naipaul argued that Trinidad's immigrant Indian community failed to come to terms with the complexities of Trinidad's multicultural history because '[h]alf of us . . . were pretending . . . [or] perhaps only feeling . . . that we had brought a kind of India with us, which we could . . . unroll like a carpet on the flat land' (2001: n.p.). Closer to home, Mishra's arguments have been referenced in Mohit Prasad's poem 'Girmit Centre', which playfully satirizes the way in which girmitiya experience has been appropriated by academic scholars philosophizing about 'diasporic identities' (2001: 71).

Literary explorations of the Fiji coups: Satendra Nandan and Sudesh Mishra As outlined above, the events of 1987 and 2000 have also inspired a range of writing responding directly to the coups themselves. Indo-Fijian writer Satendra Nandan, for, example, who was a Labour MP and Minister for Health and Social Welfare in Bavadra's 1987 Coalition Government, has written extensively about the coups and their effects on the Indo-Fijian community. In the fourth section of his semi-autobiographical novel *The Wounded Sea* (1991)—the first novel to be published by an Indo-Fijian—Nandan reconstructs the events of the 1987 coups, including the arrest and detention of Bavadra and his cabinet during the first coup, and Nandan's eventual departure into exile in Australia after the second coup. Nandan has also explored the events and effects of the coups in a range of his non-fiction writings, including the book-length works *Fiji: Paradise in Pieces* (2000) and *Requiem for a Rainbow: A Fijian Indian Story* (2001).

Indo-Fijian poet Sudesh Mishra has also produced a range of writing in response to the coups. He was a contributor to Arlene Griffen's edited anthology *With Heart and Nerve and Sinew: Post-Coup Writing from Fiji*, originally published in 1990 to commemorate the death of Dr Bavadra, and reissued in a revised, expanded edition in 1997. In 'Elegy', Mishra salutes Bavadra as the hope of his people, 'Noah to our Ark', and marvels at his 'humility / Amid all the vainglory' (Griffen (ed.) 1997*a*: 82–3). Bavadra died of cancer, but many now view him as a martyr felled by the traumatic events of 1987, and Mishra's biblical rhetoric contributes to the mythologization of Bavadra as a messianic figure. In 'Detainee II', Mishra salutes USP lecturer Som Prakash, who was arrested and detained for two weeks in 1988 after criticizing a recently published biography of Colonel Rabuka. Mishra's poem describes Prakash's interrogation under a naked light bulb, which becomes a metaphor for the prisoner's tortured consciousness: the bulb 'perspires' while Prakash's 'mind's tungsten is burnt' as he is accused of being 'a Security Risk, a threat / To the Republic' (84).

In his 2002 poetry and prose collection *Diaspora and the Difficult Art of Dying*, Mishra focuses more closely upon the aftermath of the coups, offering lyrical meditations upon the new post-coup Indian diasporic communities that have developed within the 'Western' countries that border the Pacific. Mishra explores the condition of exile at a stylistic as well as thematic level: as he explains in his preface, the collection, like the 'diasporic consciousness', is founded upon 'discontinuities . . . shifts and breaks', eschewing regularities of form and metre. Many of the poems in the collection are in free verse with irregular line breaks, and several explore a range of disparate geographical locations which are nevertheless 'linked' within the memory of the poet. The final piece in the collection is a stream of consciousness monologue redolent of the work of modernist writers such as James Joyce and Virginia Woolf. Its sparsely punctuated, peripatetic prose encapsulates the ragged dispersal of Indo-Fijians who 'lifted clear off the ground and wafted across the reefs to lands of their new diaspora, america and canada and aotearoa and australia' (2002: 78). Mishra himself is a member of the new diaspora, describing himself as a 'stateless' wanderer 'looking for the resolute world / In a word that is no more' (41), and while the collection is in part a lament for the social upheaval caused by the coups, it also celebrates the creative opportunities produced by the exilic experience. Mishra's work thus intersects with the writing of various other postcolonial Indian emigrés, recalling both the pessimism of V. S. Naipaul, and the more celebratory writings of Homi Bhabha and Salman Rushdie.

Indigenous literary responses to the coups: Vilsoni Hereniko and Larry Thomas   When the coups of 1987 and 2000 took place, many Indigenous peoples of the Pacific expressed support for the Indigenous Fijian cause on the grounds of a common 'First Peoples' status asserted against the claims of 'colonizing' or 'immigrant' cultures. However, a number of Indigenous writers within and beyond Fiji have produced literary works which seek to narrow the cultural gap opened by these catastrophic events.

Playwright Vilsoni Hereniko, for example, offers an allegorical response to the 1987 coups in his play *The Monster* (1987/1989). Hereniko was born in Rotuma (a Polynesian island north of Fiji), but he was teaching drama and theatre at USP during the 1987 coups, and *The Monster*, first performed in October 1987, allegorizes inter-racial disharmony in the immediate aftermath of these events. As Ian Gaskell points out, *The Monster* was performed at a highly sensitive time when 'any commentary on political events necessitated circumspection' (2001: 6), and Hereniko was able to escape censure by reworking the events of the coup into an allegorical, post-apocalyptic fantasy. Most of the action of the play centres on Ta and Rua,[2] two Beckettian beggars who speak of a huge conflict involving gunfire, and who struggle for ownership of a basket full of food and other items necessary for survival. In the original 1987 performance, Hereniko cast Ta as an Indigenous Fijian and Rua as a Fiji Indian, thus alluding to the inter-racial conflicts which precipitated the coups. Ta and Rua's struggle is finally resolved at the end of the play, when—after a monster tries to gain control of the basket—Ta and Rua finally join forces, defeating the creature and sharing the contents of the basket between them. Hereniko has described the end of the play as 'contrived and didactic', but argues that the positive ending 'seemed necessary particularly when the situation in Fiji seemed hopeless' (Hereniko 2001: 89). In this respect, *The Monster* resonates with Hereniko's earlier realist drama *Sera's Choice* (1986), which anticipates the 1987 coups in its exploration of a deteriorating relationship between an Indian man (Anil) and Fijian woman (Sera). Like *The Monster*, *Sera's Choice* ends optimistically as Anil begins to take an interest in Sera's cultural practices and values, suggesting a movement towards racial harmony rather than interethnic division.

Playwright Larry Thomas, of mixed Fijian and European ancestry, offers a more direct response to the coups in his 1997 play *To Let*

You Know (published in 2002). Thomas grew up in Raiwaqa, an ethnically diverse working-class district of Suva, and many of his plays focus upon the dispossessed urban dwellers known as the kai loma or 'other': part-Europeans and other mixed race peoples who have become 'socially, economically and politically marginalized' in the wake of increasing ethnic fundamentalism in Fiji (Gaskell 2001: 6). In *To Let You Know*, Thomas explores the aftermath of the 1987 coups in a multimedia performance that includes music, dance, dialogue, and video clips. While the various characters in the play stand as symbolic representatives of various ethnic groups in Fiji, the 'realities' of Fiji's economic and inter-racial problems are underscored through the inclusion of audio-visual documentary material, including video clips of 'talking heads' discussing inter-racial tensions, and slides of impoverished and neglected children.

While the play therefore enlists 'factual' material in order to emphasize the severity of Fiji's inter-racial schisms, Thomas, like Hereniko, also uses the creative medium of drama in order to project a resolution of cross-cultural conflict. Hope for reconciliation is offered symbolically in a series of choreographed dance sequences featuring a Fijian man and an Indian woman, whose cultural differences are at first reinforced by the fact that they dance to the beat of 'different drums': the Fijian man's instrument is a lali (a wooden gong used throughout the Pacific), while the Indian woman moves to the rhythm of an Indian tabla (pair of drums). Eventually, however, the dancers begin to 'borrow' movements and motifs from each other, ending, as Ian Gaskell notes, 'by performing the same dance, a new one that harmoniously blends elements of both cultures' and suggests a future 'redolent with possibility and hope' (2002: iv–v). This hope was to some degree dashed by the Speight coup of 2000, which Thomas went on to investigate in his 2002 video documentary *A Race for Rights*. Thomas, who appears at the beginning of the video, is careful not to influence the viewer with ideologically charged voice-overs, instead leaving representatives of Fiji's various ethnic communities to present their own, often conflicting, versions of events. The documentary, like many of Thomas's plays, thus explores Fiji's interethnic complexities from a multiplicity of perspectives.

The coups have clearly had an enormous impact on Fijian politics and literature since the late 1980s, but these events have not put an end to the creative dialogue between Indian, Indigenous Fijian, and other writers within and beyond Fiji. In 1995, for example, the 'Niu Waves' writers' collective was formed at USP with the aim of bringing together writers from throughout the Pacific, and in 2001 the organization released its first publication, *Niu Waves: Contemporary Writing from Oceania* (edited by Robert Nicole). The anthology features the work of Indo-Fijians *and* Indigenous Fijians, as well as material by other writers from Tonga, Rotuma, the Solomon Islands, and Kiribati, thus reviving the literary regionalism which flourished at USP prior to the coups. The *Niu Waves* anthology was funded by the Oceania Centre for Arts and Culture and the Pacific Writing Forum, both founded at USP in 1997 in order to foster literature, art, dance, and other creative works produced by Pacific Islanders from a range of ethnic backgrounds (see Chapter 6).

4.3 Hawai'i and the 'American Pacific'

This section of the chapter focuses upon the literatures of three Pacific nations—Hawai'i, Guam, and American Samoa—united by their experience of American imperialism. All three countries were annexed by the US in 1898, but where Guam and American Samoa have been relatively sparsely populated by Americans, Hawai'i became an American settler colony, with disastrous consequences for Indigenous Hawai'ians. During the early decades of the nineteenth century, thousands of Hawai'ians were killed by diseases introduced by Europeans, and after the Māhele land division of 1848–50 (see Chapter 3), increasing numbers of Euro-American investors established plantations on former native Hawai'ian land, also bringing tens of thousands of Asian indentured labourers into the country. By the time native Hawai'ians were outnumbered by immigrants in the 1880s, US residents in Hawai'i were making increasingly clamorous demands for American annexation, and after the Hawai'ian reigning monarch Queen Lili'uokalani was deposed in a businessman's coup (backed by the US navy) in 1893, it was only a matter of time before Hawai'i would become an American colony.

When considering Indigenous Hawai'ian literature as a textual corpus, it is important not to overlook the substantial archive of nineteenth-century anticolonial writing, much of which protests against the alienation of Hawai'ian land and political sovereignty.[3]

However, it was not until after Hawai'i became the fiftieth US state in 1959, and particularly after the native Hawai'ian nationalist movement gathered momentum in the 1970s, that a substantial Indigenous creative writing movement began to develop.

John Dominis Holt, of mixed Polynesian and European ancestry, was the first Indigenous Hawai'ian writer to publish a significant corpus of creative writing in English. His acclaimed novel *Waimea Summer* (1976) explores class dynamics and racial tensions among contemporary Hawai'ians, and he has produced a number of other literary works, including a play and a long poem focused on the 1893 overthrow of the Hawai'ian monarchy. His 1964 essay, 'On Being Hawaiian', is an important precursor of the Hawai'ian sovereignty movement, taking the form of a nationalist manifesto in which Holt situates Hawai'ian claims to recognition and self-determination alongside those of African Americans and American Indians (Holt 1964: 9).

The 1960s and early 1970s also saw the emergence of a generation of younger Hawai'ian writers (such as Dana Naone Hall, Joseph P. Balaz, and Wayne Kaumuali'i Westlake) who began publishing in small-press literary magazines. The writers of this period did not, as a rule, engage explicitly with Indigenous identity politics—instead experimenting with various poetic forms including concrete poetry and the haiku—but during the 1980s, a new wave of polemical writing emerged, energized by the burgeoning native Hawai'ian sovereignty movement.

Some of the key tenets of the movement included the protection and revitalization of the Hawai'ian language and various sacred sites; a renewed interest in traditional practices such as taro farming; and growing demands for native Hawai'ian self-determination. The movement also triggered a revival of Hawai'ian oral literature and performance arts, including hula (dances often accompanied by sung poetry), oli (chants), and mele (songs) (Trask 1999c: 170). In response to these developments, writers of the 1980s (such as Haunani Kay-Trask, 'Imaikalani Kalahele and Māhealani Kamau'u) began to draw more extensively upon Hawai'ian words, phrases, and place names, also making more specific 'appeals for collective consciousness' in keeping with the political objectives of the native sovereignty movement (Hamasaki 1993: 201). Some of these writers became directly involved in the sovereignty movement:

Haunani-Kay Trask, for example, is a founding member of Ka Lāhui Hawai'i, the largest native sovereignty organization in Hawai'i. Trask's seminal collection of political writings—*From a Native Daughter* (1993/9)—has been published by the University of Hawai'i Press, which also distributes the work of Trask and other leading Pacific writers in its 'Talanoa: Pacific Literature' series (launched in 1994).

The centrality of sovereignty politics to contemporary native Hawai'ian literature is clearly evident in a range of Hawai'ian poetry published in *Whetu Moana* (2003), the first of Wendt's Pacific literary anthologies to include work by Hawai'ian writers. Joe Balaz's well known poem 'Moe'uhane' ['Dream'] (1984), for example, offers a subtle assertion of native Hawai'ian sovereignty politics in the speaker's enumeration of his/her daily rituals—such as fishing and the cultivation of crops—which connect with ancestral cultural practices. The poem at first appears to imply that contemporary Hawai'ians have lost connection with their traditions, as the speaker claims that s/he cannot 'go back' to the 'ways of the past'. By the end of the poem, however, this heritage is asserted as an unbroken line of continuity: the reason the speaker cannot 'go back' is because s/he 'never left' (Wendt *et al.* (eds.) 2003: 6).

Also published in *Whetu Moana* is a range of political verse drawn from 'Imaikalani Kalahele's self-illustrated book of poems *Kalahele* (2002), which engages more explicitly with the native Hawai'ian sovereignty movement. 'Make a fist', for example, links the cultivation of political resistance with the growing of crops, urging Hawai'ians to '[p]lant the resistance deep' and ending with repeated imperatives in Hawai'ian instructing activists to 'Kanu' (plant) and 'ho'oulu' (grow, foster) the sovereignty movement (Wendt *et al.* (eds.) 2003: 89). Kalahele's poem 'Rise Up' also promotes political activism, instructing Hawai'ians to transcend 'colonial thinking' and muster a collective strength encapsulated in the communal ritual of drinking 'awa (an intoxicating but non-alcoholic drink made from the roots of the pepper plant). Again the poem ends with Hawai'ian imperatives, 'E ala!' (wake/rise up!) and 'Kū'ē!' (resist!), implicitly linking the revival of the Hawai'ian language with other forms of native Hawai'ian self-assertion (Wendt *et al.* (eds.) 2003: 92).

A selection of polemical poems by Māhealani Kamau'u is also included in *Whetu Moana*. 'Uluhaimalama' was written in honour of

Queen Lili'uokalani on the hundredth anniversary of her birthday, and as Kamau'u explains, the name of the poem, which is also the name the queen conferred upon her garden, can be translated thus: 'as plants grow up out of the dark into the light, so shall light come to the Hawaiian nation' [*sic*]. Kamau'u presents Lili'uokalani's prophecy as a manifesto for the contemporary sovereignty movement, noting that while native Hawai'ians have endured US hegemony with 'manacled hands' and 'shackled feet', nevertheless they have 'put down roots' and 'covered the Earth', becoming '[b]old flowers for [Lili'uokalani's] crown' (Wendt *et al.* (eds.) 2003: 98–9). The biblical and pastoral imagery used in the poem thus underscores the power struggle between the US and native Hawai'ians, establishing an interplay between imagery of imprisonment (representing US hegemony) and of renewal in nature (representing the sovereignty movement).

The formal register adopted in 'Uluhaimalama' contrasts sharply with Kamau'u's use of colloquial English in her protest poem 'Host Culture'. Here, Kamau'u attacks the phrase 'host culture' as a euphemistic label for native Hawai'ians, objecting that the Americans 'act like / They was invited— / Like all these years, / We been partying / Or something' (96). The poem is full of angry rhetoric ('Nobody invited anybody— / They pulled a number on us, / Big time!'), and the speaker enumerates the socio-economic problems plaguing contemporary native Hawai'ians as a result of their loss of sovereignty. The main register used in the poem is Hawai'i Creole English, a vernacular dialect, associated with working-class non-white Hawai'ians, which is discussed further in Chapter 5 of this book.

A variety of poems by Haunani-Kay Trask, perhaps the best-known contemporary native Hawai'ian writer, also appear in *Whetu Moana*. Much of her verse is inspired by her involvement in Ka Lāhui Hawai'i, expressing her commitment to reclaiming and regenerating Hawai'ian natural resources and cultural practices. While a number of her poems (such as 'The Broken Gourd' and 'Pūowaina: Flag Day') are explicitly anticolonial, many others (such as 'Into Our Light I Will Go Forever') are lyrical celebrations of Hawai'i's fertile landscapes and the myths attached to them. As will be discussed in Chapter 5, these political and lyrical strands are brought together in a variety of poems focused on the Hawai'ian volcano goddess Pele, whose explosive power is invoked as a metaphorical means by which to combat the forces of Americanization in modern Hawai'i.

Many of the poems in Trask's two published collections, *Light in the Crevice Never Seen* (1999b) and *Night is a Sharkskin Drum* (2002) lament the effects of American and Japanese corporate tourist development upon landscapes sacred to the Hawai'ian people, drawing upon arguments she has made in *From a Native Daughter* regarding the tourist industry's 'prostitution' of Hawai'ian land and culture (1999a: 143). Some of the most vivid denunciations of the tourist industry appear in Trask's poems 'Hawai'i' and 'Waikīkī'. 'Hawai'i' contrasts tourist myths of beach paradises and voluptuous hula dancers with the realities of Hawai'i's damaged landscape, within which heiau (pre-Christian religious shrines) 'lie crushed' beneath hotel lavatory buildings, and the bones of the ancestors are exhumed to make way for new tourist developments (1999b: 36). In 'Waikīkī' Trask further explores this juxtaposition of the sacred and the profane, focusing on the tourist mecca of Waikīkī, a district of Honolulu which is among the most densely developed tourist destinations in the world. Trask establishes a contrast between pre-colonial Waikīkī, the former 'home of *ali'i* [chiefs, rulers]', and the present 'sewer center / of Hawai'i', a haven for drug traffickers, pimps, and criminal gangs, thus using scatological imagery to underscore her anger at the environmental and cultural degradation of this sacred site (140).

Trask's lament for the despoliation of Waikīkī resonates with 'Mountains in the Sea', a poem by Richard Hamasaki which similarly describes the formerly fertile landscape as a damaged, barren space dominated by 'towered cement' and industrial pollution (2000: 5). Hamasaki is of Japanese ancestry, but in this and a range of his other poems, he pays tribute to native Hawai'ian environmental conservationism. Particularly notable is his poem 'Westlake' (Hamasaki 2000: 8–11), which commemorates the involvement of native Hawai'ian activists Wayne Kaumuali'i Westlake, George Helm, and Kimo Mitchell in the campaign for the demilitarization of Kaho'olawe (discussed in Chapter 3). Hamasaki's poetry bears witness to a flourishing tradition of Asian writing within Hawai'i, and while there is not space to discuss this tradition in detail here, the work of Lois Ann Yamanaka, one of Hawai'i's best-known Asian poets, is explored in Chapter 5. The two sections below are focused upon literary developments within two further 'American' Pacific territories: American Samoa and Guam.

American Samoan literature: Caroline Sinavaiana-Gabbard and Dan Taulapapa McMullin   American Samoa, like Hawai'i, is one of the few Pacific Island territories that have yet to become independent. This is arguably due in part to the fact that American Samoa's naval administration, which ruled from 1900 to 1951, made few interventions into Samoan affairs, and traditional social structures were still largely intact by the time a civilian administration was established in 1951 (Fischer 2005a: 182). The new civilian administration gave American Samoans local autonomy through a territorial congress and senate, and many aspects of the fa'a Sāmoa (Samoan way of life) have survived.[4] Under this system, American Samoans have therefore maintained a sense of local sovereignty while also retaining the 'benefits' of US citizenship (Crocombe 2001: 432; McMullin 1999: 119).

American Samoan poet Caroline Sinavaiana-Gabbard, however, has written critically about US imperialism in 'Amerika Samoa' (an indigenized spelling of 'American Samoa'). In an autobiographical essay which introduces her poetry collection *Alchemies of Distance* (2001), Sinavaiana-Gabbard describes American Samoa as 'our occupied homeland' stifled under 'the colonial miasma of Uncle Sam', and she draws attention to the way in which imported American commodities and popular culture have intensified American Samoa's dependency on the mainland US. In 1997, Sinavaiana-Gabbard took up a teaching position in Hawai'i, and her poem 'death at the christmas fair: elegy for a fallen shopper' (reprinted in *Whetu Moana*) resonates with Trask's poetry in its condemnation of American commercial development in Hawai'i. The poem describes a working-class Hawai'ian man dying of a heart attack in Honolulu's crowded commercial centre, and Sinavaiana-Gabbard interprets the man's death as a symbol of protest against the commodification of Hawai'ian culture for 'consumptive / [American tourists] grasping / hawaiian land desecrated w / plastic / commodities' [*sic*] (184). The poem ends with Sinavaiana-Gabbard leaving the shopping area without purchasing a single product: this is a gesture made not only in 'honor' of her 'fallen' fellow Polynesian, but also as a sign of 'protest' against America's continuing economic exploitation of the Pacific (Wendt *et al.* (eds.) 2003: 183–4).

Writer, painter, and film-maker Dan Taulapapa McMullin, who was born in American Samoa but emigrated to California as a child, has also made a significant contribution to Pacific literature. Much of his work focuses on gay and lesbian identity politics, particularly those of fa'afafine (Samoan trans-sexuals or transvestites), and a range of this material will be discussed in Chapter 6. As well as exploring gay and fa'afafine sexualities, McMullin has also reflected upon American Samoa's status as a military colony. In an essay on the poetry of Henri Hiro, for example, he identifies commonalities between Tahiti and American Samoa as American military colonies (2005), and his poem 'Sinalela and the One-Eyed Fish' (2004: 19) makes reference to tourism and missile testing in American Samoa in the midst of a fantastical narrative about a gay ex-rugby player who visits the underworld after being swallowed by a 'one-eyed fish'. The poem contains obvious (homo)sexual symbolism, but it is also a syncretic blend of Western and Samoan storytelling, melding aspects of the fairy tale 'Cinderella' (Sinalela's namesake) with Samoan beliefs in the spirit world. The poem is published in McMullin's début poetry collection, *A Drag Queen Named Pipi* (2004).

The literature of Guam   The final locus of literary activity in the 'American Pacific' to be discussed here is Guam, a Micronesian island, annexed by the US in 1898, which remains an unincorporated US territory. In comparison to Hawai'i in particular, Guam features few publishing opportunities for local writers: the literary journal *Storyboard*, established in 1991, is the only regular local forum for the publication of contemporary creative writing, although Micronesian oral literature has been collected and disseminated in schools throughout Guam and the Trust Territory of the Pacific Islands. Named after an Indigenous art form from Belau (Palau) in which stories are presented visually, *Storyboard* publishes art, poetry, fiction, and non-fiction in English and other Pacific languages, particularly those of Micronesia, thus serving a similar 'regional' function as *Mana* at USP, or the UHP journals *Mānoa* and *The Contemporary Pacific* (established in 1989). Members of various US Micronesian territories have also published sporadically outside Micronesia, and a number of anticolonial poems and stories by writers from the 'American Pacific' (including Guam, the Marshall Islands, American Samoa, and Belau/Palau) were published in the 1992 literary anthology *Te Rau Maire* (ed. Crocombe *et al.*). In addition to the anticolonial material discussed in Chapter 3, this anthology includes a wide range of lyric poems and stories exploring the spiritual significance of the natural world, and celebrating the endurance into modern times of 'traditional' Micronesian cultural practices such as oratory, ritual dance, and weaving.

4.4 **The Francophone Pacific**

While anglophone literature by Indigenous Pacific Islanders has circulated widely within and beyond the Pacific since the 1970s, Indigenous francophone literatures have received very little attention outside their countries of origin, largely due to the dominance of English as a lingua franca throughout the Pacific region. Until fairly recently, very little francophone Pacific literature had been translated into English, although the 1982 trilingual Tahitian edition of *Mana* (discussed in Chapter 3) is a notable exception. This section of the chapter explores a range of creative writing (both in French and in English translation) from the French colonies of the Pacific, focusing in particular upon Tahiti Nui (French Polynesia), New Caledonia/Kanaky, and Vanuatu.

The first wave of francophone anticolonial writing in the Pacific emerged in Tahiti in the late 1960s and early 1970s, spearheaded by Ma'ohi poets Hubert Brémond, Henri Hiro, Charles Manutahi, Vaitiare, and Turo Raapoto. As Robert Nicole points out, the work of these early poets, many of whom were educated at metropolitan French universities, is clearly influenced by the prevailing nostalgia and sense of lost pastoral innocence evident in the work of 'Orientalist' French writers such as Pierre Loti (Nicole 2001: 184). Where Loti's novel *Le Mariage de Loti* (1880) invoked the fatal impact model partly to justify the French colonial presence in the Pacific, however, many of the first-generation Ma'ohi poets lament the despoliation and deterioration of Ma'ohi land and culture as a direct result of French military incursion into the Pacific (see Chapter 3). The selection of poems in the 1982 special issue of *Mana* also allude to the political agendas that drove the developing Ma'ohi nationalist movement: Brémond's 'Who am I?' anticipates a day of 'freedom' upon which Ma'ohi will decide their 'own fate' (Crocombe (ed.) 1982: 29), while Hiro's 'God of Culture' implores Oihanu (Ma'ohi god of culture and husbandry) to empower the 'new generation' and help them 'rise' and 'beat down the prohibitions' imposed by the French colonizers (Crocombe (ed.) 1982: 41–3).

A new wave of Ma'ohi writing—largely driven by three women writers, Michou Chaze, Chantal Spitz, and Vaitiare—has emerged since the 1980s, exploring the problems of identification facing Ma'ohi in contemporary French Polynesia. All three women write in French, but as Nicole observes, Chaze in particular uses a 'richly hybridized "Tahitian-French"' register which posits the indigenization of the French language as a destabilization of metropolitan French linguistic authority (Nicole 1999: 278). Vaitiare's writing has moved from an early emphasis on ethnic difference to an advocation of harmonious multiculturalism in French Polynesia, but France's enduring colonial and military presence in Tahiti Nui has ensured a steady stream of anticolonial writing, with Chantal Spitz's 1991 novel *L'île des Rêves Écrasés* (discussed in Chapter 3) as a prominent example.

In keeping with the growing interest in francophone postcolonial studies that has developed since the 1990s, a wider range of franco-phone Pacific writing is now available in English translation. 2006 saw the publication of *Vārua Tupu*, a special issue of *Mānoa* featuring Ma'ohi contemporary poetry, autobiography, and fiction in English translation, and a 2005 special issue of the *International Journal of Francophone Studies* (8.3) includes English translations of the poetry of Henri Hiro, as well as a range of criticism focused on Ma'ohi and Kanaky literature.

Among France's Pacific territories, New Caledonia/Kanaky has witnessed some of the most sustained political and discursive resistance against colonial occupation. Annexed by France in 1863, New Caledonia became a penal colony in the second half of the nine-teenth century, and after the transportation of convicts ended in 1897, many former prisoners remained in New Caledonia, along with free French migrants who established plantations and ranches from the 1850s in particular. From the 1870s, when gold, nickel, and copper deposits were discovered, further French migrants flooded into the country, and large numbers of Indigenous Melanesians were resettled on reserves and forced to work as indentured labourers. Indigenous New Caledonians presented vigorous and often violent resistance to French occupation throughout New Caledonia's colonial history, with major Melanesian uprisings in 1878 and 1917, but it was not until the 1970s that a sustained independence movement began to gath-er momentum. Melanesian nationalists called themselves 'Kanaks' and their country 'Kanaky', re-indigenizing the Polynesian word 'kanaka' (man/person), which had been adopted by colonists as a generic and often derogatory label for Indigenous Pacific Islanders (see Chapter 3).

As was the case in Hawai'i, the Kanak nationalist movement also triggered the emergence of a Kanak literary nationalism spearheaded by writers such as Déwé Gorodé, Wanir Wélépane, and Pierre Gope (Brown 2004: xvii). Most of this material is only available in French, but some has been translated into English. Gope's play *Le Dernier Crépuscule*, which explores the impact of commercial mining upon Kanak peoples, was translated into English and published as *The Last Nightfall* (2001), while in 2004, two volumes of poetry and prose by Gorodé, Kanaky's best-known contemporary creative writer, were published in English translation by Pandanus Books of Australia. These include a poetry anthology (*Sharing as Custom Provides*), and a volume of short fiction (*The Kanak Apple Season*).

Sharing as Custom Provides is a parallel edition featuring poems in the original French and in English translation, and it is notable that where Gorodé has used words from her native Paicî language, these remain untranslated in both French and English versions, though glosses are provided in the endnotes. This accords Gorodé's native language a certain primacy in the text, posing a challenge to the dominance of the two 'metropolitan' languages and underscoring the relationship between linguistic and political self-determination. As Gorodé puts it in her poem 'Word of Struggle', a term from the ancestral language can become 'the word that dares make a stand' in a 'radical poetics' which articulates 'a politics of struggle' (2004*a*: 6). These lines have particular resonance given that during her career as a schoolteacher and political activist, Gorodé has militated against the continuing dominance of French language and culture in New Caledonia. In the 1980s, for example, she helped establish the *Ecoles Populaires Kanak* (EPK), specialist schools which educated Kanak children about their own culture and in their own Kanak languages.

Gorodé is also a founding member of the Kanak independence organizations Groupe 1878 and PALIKA (Parti de Libération Kanak), and several of her poems were written in Camp-Est prison in Noumea, where Gorodé was incarcerated in 1974 and 1977 following her involvement in political protests (P. Brown 2004: xvi). In 'Behind the Walls', Gorodé expresses a sense of solidarity with oppressed Kanaks of earlier

generations who have been 'down-trodden humiliated beaten / in the
icy silence of colonial tombs' (8), while in 'Where is the Moon?', her
obscured view of the night sky from her prison cell prompts a meditation upon other aspects of the Kanak landscape which have been
occluded and obliterated by the mining industry in particular. Other
poems engage more specifically with the despoliation of Kanaky land
through urban industrial development. 'Waste Land', for example,
describes a Kanak slum settlement wreathed in smoke from the Noumea nickel factory, offering an ironic 'postcolonial' commentary upon
T. S. Eliot's critique of decayed civilization in his modernist epic poem
'The Waste Land' (1922). Another poem, 'Tropical Town', punctures
the tourist myth of New Caledonia as a Pacific paradise: Noumea's
'few coconut palms' are vastly outnumbered by concrete and iron
monoliths which serve as a reminder that 'we're in France' rather than
some prelapsarian idyll 'of long ago and times gone by' (2004a: 146).

In contrast to Tahiti Nui and Kanaky, France's other colonies (Vanuatu, and Wallis and Futuna) have produced very little anticolonial
literature, partly due to the success of French policies of assimilation
and enforced dependency in these areas (Nicole 1999: 285). However,
some of the anglophone writers anthologized in *Lali* and *Nuanua* have
engaged critically with Vanuatu's colonial history, which involved the
partition of the country between Britain and France. (A joint naval
commission was established in 1888, and a condominium government
in 1906.) Albert Leomala's poem 'New Hebrides', for example, was
written shortly before the New Hebrides became independent (and
renamed Vanuatu) in 1980. The poem appears in *Lali* in parallel English
and pidgin versions, formally figuring the cultural schizophrenia of
ni-Vanuatu (Indigenous Vanuatuan) people under the Anglo-French
condominium. The two colonial powers are described as 'two chiefs /
who are killing you', and a mischievous reference to the French as a
plague of 'frogs' appears towards the end of the poem (Wendt (ed.)
1980: 119). Grace Mera Molisa's post-independence poem 'Custom'
(1983), republished in *Nuanua*, identifies 'Franco-Britannic / life and
lingo' as a continuing neocolonial presence in Vanuatu. Using the
poem's metalinguistic focus as an opportunity for a sly pun, she
argues that Vanuatu is afflicted with a 'pandemonic / condominium
/ complex', invoking the satirical nickname for the Anglo-French
condominium—'pandemonium'—adopted by ni-Vanuatu peoples
in advance of independence (Wendt (ed.) 1995a: 391).

4.5 Easter Island/Rapa Nui: Hispanophone Pacific literature

The fifth literary 'centre' to be discussed in this chapter is Rapa Nui,[5] a Chilean territory (annexed in 1888) which is known officially by its Spanish name, Isla de Pascua (Easter Island). Situated 1900 kilometres from the nearest populated landmass (Pitcairn Island) and 3700 kilometres from the west coast of South America, Rapa Nui is one of the most isolated communities on earth. Due to its strategic location on a trading route between South America and East Asia, Rapa Nui was first used as a naval station by the Chilean administration, but from the late 1890s until the early 1950s, various Chilean sheep farming companies dominated the economy, forcing the Rapanui people onto reservations in order to 'clear' the land for grazing. Naval rule was re-established over the island in the 1950s, and apart from a brief period of civilian government from 1966–73, the island has remained under Chilean administration as an 'internal colony', though not without protest from Rapa Nui's Indigenous peoples (Fischer 2005b: 199; 250).

While Rapa Nui has not undergone an Indigenous cultural renaissance on the same scale as many other nations of the Pacific, a movement to revitalize the Rapanui language and various 'traditional' cultural practices began in the 1980s (Fischer 2005b: 258). In precolonial times, Easter Islanders wrote their language in figures (known as rongo-rongo) on wooden tablets, but this tradition had been lost, and aside from word lists, dictionaries, and grammars produced by outsiders, there was no corpus of written material in Rapanui until a preliminary orthography was developed in the early 1980s (Phelps 1985). Inaugural writers' workshops for adult Rapanui speakers were held on Easter Island in 1984 and 1985, and a number of works produced by these writers were published in Rapanui with Spanish translations in the 1986 anthology *Relatos de la Isla de Pascua/A 'Amu o Rapa Nui*, published by Andrés Bello (Santiago). Several titles by Rapanui writers have been produced by small local publishers, but these texts are not readily available outside Rapa Nui. Very little Indigenous creative writing in English exists, although a multilingual children's book by Catherine Orliac and Véronique Willemin, *Te Tumu o Rapa Nui* (in a parallel Rapanui, Spanish, English, and French edition) was published in 2005 by the Easter Island Foundation.

4.6 The Māori Renaissance and the emergence of Māori literature in English

The emergence of an anglophone Māori literary tradition—the final corpus of creative writing to be discussed in this chapter—was the product of the immense changes in Māori society that took place following the end of the Second World War. Aotearoa/New Zealand's economy was rapidly industrialized during this period, triggering a large-scale migration of Māori from small, largely rural tribal communities into the Pākehā-dominated urban centres in search of employment and education opportunities. As historian Michael King points out, in little more than a generation Māori became an 'overwhelmingly urban people': while only 11.2 per cent of Māori were urban dwellers in 1936, this rose to 25.7 per cent by 1945, and to 81 per cent by 1996 (King 2003: 473).

The process of urbanization created a number of social pressures within the Māori community. Many Māori who came to the cities during and after the Second World War were channelled into manual and unskilled labour, forming what was to become an established urban underclass vulnerable to unemployment in times of economic crisis. With Pākehā and Māori living and interacting closely for the first time, inter-racial tensions began to develop, with instances of overt discrimination against Māori in employment, housing provision, and public services (King 2003: 474–5). Urbanization also caused many Māori to lose contact with their tribal communities, leading to a decline in the observance of 'traditional' ideologies and cultural practices. A landmark language survey undertaken in the early 1970s revealed a huge reduction in the numbers of speakers of Māori as a first language: most native speakers were over thirty years of age, and only around two per cent of Māori children were growing up speaking Māori as their first language (McRae 1991: 2). As Michael King points out, the adoption of an English-only education policy in the 1860s had 'done some damage' to the transmission of the culture, but the decline accelerated significantly in the postwar period, when Māori children were urged by their families to speak English as a means of educational and social advancement (2003: 477).

These language statistics, and widespread concerns about political and socio-economic disparities between Māori and Pākehā, gave rise to a pan-Māori politico-cultural movement known as the Māori Renaissance. Throughout the 1970s, urban Māori began to establish supra-tribal Māori organizations in order to replace the traditional infrastructures of the dwindling rural communities, while political activists petitioned parliament for the establishment of courses in Māori language and culture in schools. Activist groups also advocated the concept of biculturalism in Aotearoa/New Zealand society as an alternative to government 'integration' policies, which many Māori viewed as thinly disguised variations on the colonialist policy of cultural 'assimilation' (King 2003: 482–3). In response to Māori concerns about the government's failure to honour its obligations under the Treaty of Waitangi, the Waitangi Tribunal was formed in 1975, charged with hearing Māori land claims and making recommendations to the government. In 1985, the incumbent Labour government passed the Waitangi Tribunal Amendment Act, allowing for the filing of claims dating back to 1840, when the Treaty was originally signed. While many Māori became—and remain—dissatisfied about the efficacy and legitimacy of the Tribunal, these were important measures which laid the foundations for the eventual 'settlement' of various tribal land claims negotiated between government and individual Māori iwi (tribes) in the 1990s.

In addition to triggering these various political developments, the Māori Renaissance also witnessed the emergence of a new tradition of Māori creative literature in English. During the 1950s and 1960s, some creative writing in English by Māori authors had already appeared in *Te Ao Hou*, a magazine—established by the Department of Māori Affairs—which introduced an annual literary competition for Māori writers in 1956. Authors such as J. C. Sturm, Rora Paki, Rowley Habib, Riki Erihi, Arapera Blank, Barry Mitcalfe, Harry Dansey, and Hirini/Sidney Moko Mead were regular contributors to *Te Ao Hou* in the 1950s and 1960s, as was Hone Tuwhare, whose poetry collection *No Ordinary Sun* (1964) was the first single-authored creative work to be published by a Māori writer. Tuwhare quickly became—and arguably remains—Aotearoa/New Zealand's most renowned and prolific Māori poet. Much of his early poetry is now out of print, but a range of material from various phases of his career has been anthologized in *Deep River Talk* (1993), an edition of his collected poems now published by the University of Hawai'i Press.

Throughout his career, Tuwhare has produced a variety of lyric poems celebrating the natural world, drawing upon Māori values emphasizing aroha (love) and respect for the land. From the 1970s, however, his poetry has also engaged with the politics of the Māori Renaissance and its relationship to other international movements against racial discrimination. His elegiac poem 'Martin Luther King' from his 1972 collection *Sapwood and Milk*, for example, laments King's death and praises his anti-Vietnam War stance, which Tuwhare shared (see Chapter 3). In his 1978 collection *Making a Fist of It*, Tuwhare turned his attention to the 1976 race-riots in Soweto, lamenting the cost to human life but also acknowledging the symbolic importance of these events to the anti-apartheid movement. The title poem ends, for example, with an image of a black South African girl 'standing up: beautiful' against a backdrop of upraised 'black work-hardened hands', the assertive 'fist(s)' indexed in the poem's title (1994: 125).

Tuwhare's personal involvement in the Māori Renaissance is referenced in a range of his poetry. His acclaimed poem 'Rain-maker's song for Whina' (1978), for example, celebrates the leadership of Māori activist Whina Cooper during the Māori Land March of 1975, when thousands of Māori walked from Te Hapua (in the far north of the North Island) to Wellington, the seat of government, in a protest against the continuing expropriation of Māori land. Tuwhare himself took part in the march, and in the poem he recalls Whina's rousing speeches made on various marae (ceremonial meeting places) during the journey. Tuwhare demonstrates his respect for Whina by saluting her in Māori as 'E kui' (venerable elder woman), but also characteristically mixes formal and informal registers, establishing a sense of solidarity with Whina as a fellow activist: 'I'm all-eared-in to you, baby ... *Kia ora tonu koe* [warm greetings and thanks to you]' (1994: 127).

Where Tuwhare excelled as a poet, two other Māori writers, Witi Ihimaera and Patricia Grace, became the first to publish book-length fictional works. Ihimaera's short-story collection *Pounamu, Pounamu* was published in 1972, followed by his first novel (*Tangi*) in 1973, a second novel (*Whanau*) in 1974, and a second collection of short stories, *The New Net Goes Fishing*, in 1977. Patricia Grace's collection *Waiariki and Other Stories* (1975) was the first book-length fiction publication by a Māori woman writer, and her first novel (*Mutuwhenua*) was published in 1978, followed by a second collection of short stories (*The Dream Sleepers*) in 1980.

Ihimaera and Grace's early stories—many of which were originally published in *Te Ao Hou* and other periodicals—engage with issues explored by many of the other *Te Ao Hou* authors of the 1950s and 1960s, referencing the immense social changes brought about by the post-war migration to the cities. Both Ihimaera and Grace were also centrally concerned with the politics of representation, pointing out that their writing posed a challenge to Romantic and negative stereotypes of Māori produced in Pākehā literature (Beavis 1971: 53; Grace 1978a: 80). In Grace's fiction in particular, issues of representation are closely linked with concepts of self-empowerment. In her 1975 story 'Parade', for example, a young Māori woman who is taking part in a community carnival feels uncomfortable under the Pākehā gaze, suspecting that the Pākehā are viewing the Māori participants as they would 'Animals in cages', or exhibits in museums (1994: 88). One of her elders, however, sagely informs her that 'It is your job, this. To show others who we are' (91), and the statement becomes a manifesto for Grace's own role as a Māori writer. Elsewhere in her writing, Grace links the position of the Māori writer with the social function performed by the 'traditional' Māori artist (such as the wood-carver in her 1986 novel *Potiki*): both create cultural continuity by giving artistic form to the histories and values of the Māori people (Keown 2005: 155–8).

It has often been argued—perhaps most famously by Ihimaera himself—that Māori writing of the 1960s and 1970s was nostalgic and romanticized in its representation of Māori (village) life, and that Māori writers did not engage substantially with contemporary urban life and its sociopolitical problems until the mid-1980s (Ihimaera 1982). However, a detailed examination of Ihimaera and Grace's early work does reveal an engagement with the political realities of the period. Ihimaera's story 'Clenched Fist' from his 1977 collection *The New Net Goes Fishing*, for example, focuses on a young Māori man (Api) who has adopted the rhetoric of the African-American Black Power movement in his battle against white racism. Several of Ihimaera's other early stories explore racist attitudes to Māori which developed in the post-war urbanization period: 'A Sense of Belonging' (1977) focuses on a Māori bank teller who is spurned by a racist Pākehā customer, while 'The Other Side of the Fence' (1972) features a

Pākehā man whose affection for his Māori neighbours is tempered by stereotypical views of Māori as light-fingered and conniving rascals. Early stories by Grace such as 'A Way of Talking' (1975) and 'Journey' (1980) similarly explore racial discrimination against Māori.

In its engagement with Māori socio-political issues, Grace's writing has focused in particular on two key issues foregrounded since the Māori Renaissance: the alienation of Māori land, and the decline and recent revitalization of the Māori language. Grace's engagement with Māori language issues is explored in Chapter 5, but it is worth investigating her fictional explorations of Māori land issues in some detail here. In her novels *Potiki* (1986), *Cousins* (1992), and *Baby No-Eyes* (1998) in particular, Grace provides allegorical responses to high-profile land disputes between Māori and Pākehā. In *Potiki*, for example, which describes the efforts of a Māori community to prevent Pākehā developers from purchasing their land, Grace draws upon two factual land disputes—which took place at Bastion Point and the Raglan Golf Course in the North Island—that she describes as 'legitimizing' her narrative (Keown 2000: 55; Tausky 1991: 97). Both incidents involved campaigns for the return of communal Māori land that had never legally been purchased. *Potiki* also draws upon Grace's personal involvement in land-rights politics, indexing the attempts of developers to purchase her own ancestral land at Plimmerton, near Wellington (Keown 2000a: 62–3; Tausky 1991: 98). In *Cousins* (1992), one of Grace's central characters recalls taking part in the 1975 Māori Land March, while in *Baby No-Eyes* (1998), Grace references the 1995 occupation of the Moutoa Gardens (in Wanganui), which are situated on an area of disputed territory 'purchased' from local Māori by the settler government in 1848. Her 2001 novel *Dogside Story* engages more closely with Māori environmental conservationism, focusing on a coastal Māori community's attempts to safely accommodate visitors wishing to see in the new millennium sunrise at Gisborne (on the east coast of the North Island).

In these various texts, Grace emphasizes the importance of land to Māori, not only as a material source of sustenance and subsistence, but also as a locus of personal and tribal identification. In precolonial times, Māori identity was tribal and each iwi (tribe) had its own ancestral land held in communal ownership. Pre-colonial Māori birth rites—still observed by many today—required the burial of a new-born's placenta in the earth where the child was born, and with children of high birth, a tree was planted to mark the spot. The etymology of the Māori word 'whenua'—which denotes both 'land' and 'afterbirth'—draws attention to this close relationship between body and land, which is perpetuated in death with the burial of the deceased in the same ancestral soil (Keown 2000*b*: 71). A reference to the afterbirth-burying custom is made in *Potiki*, which also draws extensively upon Māori mythological narratives focused on the land and sea. Tokowaru-i-te-marama—a young disabled boy in the novel—is based partly upon Māui, the legendary trickster and demigod who is said to have 'fished up' the North Island with a hook fashioned from his grandmother's magic jawbone. Further, Toko's grandparents Roimata and Hemi are closely associated with Ranginui and Papatūānuku, the sky-father and earth-mother whose offspring became the guardians of particular realms within the natural world (Keown 2000*b*). These mythological narratives are discussed in more detail in Chapter 5.

Ihimaera's writing, like Grace's, also explores the 'spiritual' significance of land to Māori, and a number of his novels and stories are set in Waituhi, a fictionalized version of his own home village situated on the east coast of the North Island. Ihimaera's 1986 epic novel *The Matriarch* (discussed in Chapters 2 and 3) is centrally concerned with the alienation of Māori land throughout Aotearoa/New Zealand's colonial history, and at various points in the novel, the main narrator Tamatea walks the boundaries of his ancestral land with his grandmother Artemis, who informs him that a detailed knowledge of the territory is central to his personal and tribal identity (1988: 95). *The Matriarch* represented a watershed in Ihimaera's literary career, marking a radical shift away from the biculturalist politics which inflected his earlier writing and advancing a new Māori nationalist agenda which is developed further in *The Dream Swimmer* (1997), the sequel to *The Matriarch* (Keown 2005: 127–48; see also Chapter 3). Another significant shift in Ihimaera's literary profile took place in 1995, when he published his homosexual 'coming out' novel *Nights in the Gardens of Spain*. His 2000 novel *The Uncle's Story* also explores issues of gender and sexuality, investigating the pressures facing gay and lesbian Māori in a culture which does not readily tolerate homosexuality (see Chapter 6). Ihimaera's engagement with the putative inflexibility of Māori gender roles in these novels can be traced back to his 1987 novel *The Whale Rider*, where a young woman named Pai is denied leadership of her people by a grandfather who believes only men are entitled to this role. *The Whale Rider*, and Niki Caro's 2003 film adaptation of the novel, are discussed in more detail in Chapter 6.

Another writer who has made a significant impact on the field of Māori literature is Alan Duff, whose 1990 novel *Once Were Warriors* (discussed in Chapter 3) offered a controversial new vision of urban Māori life. Written in part as a reaction against the harmonious visions of Māori–Pākehā race-relations circulated during the sesquicentennial celebrations of the signing of the Treaty of Waitangi, the novel focuses on a community of state-housed, mainly unemployed urban Māori living in a haze of beer, cigarettes, and violence. Duff claims his novel posed a challenge to the 'rose-tinted' view of rural Māori life which—he argued—characterized the work of other Māori writers such as Ihimaera and Grace, instead depicting the urban working-class Māori 'as he truly lived' (1993: viii). However, it is notable that the redemptive ending of the novel involves the return of Beth, one of the urban dispossessed, to her (rural) home marae, which is constructed as a source of cultural regeneration and spiritual energy (Keown 2005: 170–90).

This kind of dialectical opposition—in which Māori 'spirituality' and environmental protectionism are presented as positive alternatives to the putative spiritual poverty of late capitalist urban (Pākehā) society—has famously been called into question by theorists Allan Hanson and Ruth Brown. Hanson, an anthropologist, identifies the concept of 'Māoritanga' (Māoriness) as a 'culture invention' which—rather like the dialectics of Orientalism—represents Māori 'values' as the inverse of 'Pakeha failings' (1989: 894). Brown similarly criticizes the practice whereby Māori 'spirituality' or intimacy with the natural world is posited as a palliative to Pākehā capitalism, arguing that it represents a twentieth-century transmutation of English Romanticism 'in ethnic dress' (1989: 253). Brown's criticisms are directed in particular at part-Māori writer Keri Hulme, whose novel *The Bone People* (1983) won the 1985 Booker McConnell prize. Hulme's novel, like Duff's, details the devastating impact of domestic violence within Māori communities, and also describes an eventual process of redemption and reconciliation as two of the main characters (Kerewin and Joe) reconnect with their Māori spiritual heritage. Brown argues that Hulme's vision is at odds with the realities of the modern, urbanized Māori world, but as anthropologist Stephen Webster has observed, while conceptions of

Māori spirituality and harmony with the natural world have become established cultural stereotypes, this does not necessarily prove that they have no basis in reality (1998: 29; Keown 2005: 102–26).

Ihimaera, Grace, Duff, Hulme, and Tuwhare remain the best-known contemporary Māori writers, but a new generation of writers has also emerged, many of whom feature alongside established Māori writers in *Whetu Moana*, the 2003 anthology of Polynesian poetry edited by Albert Wendt, Reina Whaitiri, and Robert Sullivan. Some of these poets, such as Jacq Carter, reflect upon the political issues which emerged from the Māori Renaissance: Carter's 'At the end of our road' compares the 1977 occupation of Bastion Point with other protests mounted by Māori throughout Aotearoa/New Zealand's colonial history, while 'Aroha' laments the alienation of Māori land and looks forward to the achievement of Māori self-determination. Other poets such as Samuel Cruickshank celebrate the lives of urban Māori without anticipating a return to more 'traditional' (or purist) ways of life: in his poem 'urban iwi: tihei mauri ora!' Cruickshank imagines Māori 'bound together' by mobile phones and with the city as their marae, travelling in cars rather than canoes, and enjoying 'traditional' foods such as kūmara (sweet potato) and watercress in classy Auckland restaurants. Cruickshank does not dismiss city life as a soulless alternative to traditional rural life, but rather celebrates the mana (power) and innovation skills possessed by 'our globalised selves' (47). Many of the poems in Robert Sullivan's poetry collection *Star Waka* (1999), some of which are reprinted in *Whetu Moana*, similarly reflect upon the translation of traditional cultural concepts into the modern world. The term waka, which traditionally denoted the canoe or seafaring vessel, is used to refer to a variety of modern forms of transport including cars, aeroplanes, and space-craft.

Alongside the work of younger writers, a variety of poems by the first generation of Māori writers is also included in *Whetu Moana*: Jacqui Sturm's 'He waiata tēnei mō Parihaka' (193) recalls the deeds of the pacifist prophet Te Whiti, while Rore Hapipi's 'Ballad of the Four Maori Boys' is a satirical reflection on the social problems created by welfare dependency among young Māori men (70–1). Apirana Taylor's 'Whakapapa' (211) and 'Te Ihi' (212) assert the enduring importance of the creation myths to contemporary Māori identity, and also included is a selection of poems from Hone Tuwhare's *Shape*

Shifter (1997) and *Piggy-Back Moon* (2001), many of which celebrate the natural world. Further developments in Māori literature since the 1990s are discussed in Chapter 6 of this book, while Chapter 5 elaborates upon some of the linguistic and mythopoeic issues discussed in this chapter, offering detailed stylistic analyses of language strategies in Pacific literatures.

5

Orality, Textuality, and Memory: The Language of Pacific Literatures

These islands rising from wave's edge—
blue myth brooding in orchid,
fern and banyan, fearful gods
awaiting birth from blood clot
into stone image and chant.

(Albert Wendt, 'Inside Us the Dead')

The land and the sea and the shores . . . were our science and our
sustenance. And they are our own universe about which there are
stories of great deeds and relationships and magic and imaginings,
love and terror, heroes, heroines, villains and fools. Enough for a
lifetime of telling.

(Patricia Grace, *Potiki*)

This chapter departs from the broadly chronological focus of previous chapters in order to explore the importance of oral literary traditions to contemporary Pacific literatures. It begins with an overview of the transition from orality to print in Pacific cultures, exploring the interchange between Indigenous, colonial, and contact languages during the colonial period, and offering stylistic analyses of the ways in which Pacific writers incorporate vocabulary and grammatical features from colonial contact languages (such as Melanesian Pidgin, Hawai'i Creole English, and Fiji Hindi) into their work. The second section of the chapter examines the ways in which vocabulary, grammatical features, and oral narrative patterns from *Indigenous* Pacific languages are incorporated into anglophone Pacific literary texts, while the final section investigates the referencing of Indigenous mythologies in the work of various Pacific writers.

5.1 Pacific orthographies, contact languages, and the rise of English

The Pacific is one of the most linguistically complex regions in the world. Over 1,200 distinct vernaculars—around one quarter of the world's languages—are spoken in the region (Crocombe 2001: 101). Most Pacific languages belong to the Austronesian language family, deriving from a single ancestral language dating back around 5,000 years. The majority of the languages of Papua New Guinea, and some languages in the Solomon Islands, however, belong to a number of apparently unrelated non-Austronesian language families, known collectively as Papuan languages. The precise origins of these languages have not been established, but linguists estimate that the ancestors of Papuan language speakers have been in the Pacific for 50,000 years or more (Mugler and Lynch 1996: 2–3).

5.1.1 Pacific orthographies and the rise of English

None of the Indigenous Pacific languages was written prior to the arrival of Europeans in the Pacific. Orthographies (spelling systems) for a large number of Indigenous Pacific languages[1] were developed by European missionaries during the nineteenth and early twentieth centuries, in order to aid the process of converting Indigenous peoples to Christianity (Lynch 1998: 95). These orthographies were based on the letters of the Latin/Roman alphabet, and orthographers aimed to represent each phoneme (abstract unit of sound) with one letter. However, some Pacific phonemes are not found in English or French (which became the dominant metropolitan languages of the Pacific), and missionaries varied in their approach to finding suitable symbols to represent these sounds. Two examples common to many Pacific languages are the contrast between short and long vowels, and the glottal stop phoneme: the latter has commonly been represented as a quotation mark ('), while many orthographers have represented vowel reduplication with a macron (vertical bar) over the vowel (as in Māori). In this book, macrons and glottal stops are used throughout, but it is worth pointing out that many printed texts—including those by Indigenous Pacific writers—often omit these symbols.

In the early days of their missions, Christian missionaries generally used local vernaculars in their preaching and schoolteaching, but this often conflicted with the practices of European colonizers and settlers in the Pacific, who established their own mother tongues as official languages of government and communication. Although official status has been granted to Indigenous languages in some Pacific colonies (such as Vanuatu, where Bislama—a dialect of Melanesian Pidgin—is the national language), local languages were generally marginalized and stigmatized within the colonial infrastructure. English in particular became established as the primary metropolitan language in the Pacific, and it remains the official language of almost all Pacific countries and all Pacific regional organizations to this day. Other colonial languages included French, Spanish, German, and Japanese, but today only French and Spanish remain as official languages: French in the remaining French territories, and Spanish in Rapa Nui (Easter Island), a territory of Chile (Mugler and Lynch 1996: 3).

5.1.2 Pacific contact languages: pidgins, creoles, and koines

In addition to the Indigenous and introduced metropolitan languages, a number of pidgin, creole, and koine 'contact' languages also developed in the Pacific during (and beyond) the colonial period. These contact languages developed in commercial plantations where the labourers, who spoke in many different tongues, needed to develop a common language of communication. This section of the chapter will discuss three particular contact languages—Melanesian Pidgin, Hawai'ian Pidgin (also known as Hawai'i Creole English), and Fiji Hindi, a koine language—and will also explore how these languages are used or referenced in Pacific literary texts.

Melanesian Pidgin Non-specialists often assume that pidgins are simplified, 'bastardized' versions of metropolitan languages (such as English), but as linguists recognize, pidgins are discrete languages, albeit with simplified grammars and vocabularies, which develop in particular multilingual contexts. Melanesian Pidgin first developed around 200 years ago following the recruitment of Pacific Islanders to work on European-owned plantations in various locations such as

Samoa, Fiji, and Queensland (Lynch 1998: 222). The workers, having no single language in common, developed a new language with which they could communicate with each other (and with Europeans) on the plantations. As was the case with pidgins in many other parts of the British Empire, the vocabulary (lexis) of Melanesian Pidgin is based on English, the language of the colonial overseers, while its grammatical and semantic (meaning) systems are based largely on local languages (which, in this case, were the Melanesian languages spoken by the labourers). During the late nineteenth century, when the British empire was at its height, English-based pidgins were spoken throughout most of the Pacific Basin. Renditions of the trading pidgin Beach-la-Mar,[2] one of the better-known Pacific pidgins, can be found in a variety of nineteenth- and early twentieth-century European literature focused on the Pacific. In Robert Louis Stevenson's novella *The Beach of Falesá*, for example (discussed in Chapter 2), the English trader Wiltshire uses pidgin as a means by which to communicate with his Polynesian wife Uma.[3]

During the early decades of the twentieth century, many of these Pacific pidgins died out, partly due to changes in migration patterns and labour conditions, and also as a result of widespread prejudice against pidgin as a putatively 'inferior' form of 'broken English'. In Melanesia, however, Pidgin survived, largely due to the immense linguistic diversity in the region, which ensured that even after the recruitment of Melanesian labourers to overseas plantations ceased (shortly after 1900), Melanesians continued using pidgin in order to communicate with fellow plantation workers or spouses from other Melanesian linguistic communities. When a new generation of Melanesians grew up speaking Pidgin as their first language, it was thus transformed from a pidgin (used only as a second or contact language) into a creole (spoken as a first language).[4] As Melanesian Pidgin became creolized, its vocabulary expanded and its grammar became increasingly complex, and in the early decades of the twentieth century, it became the lingua franca in what were to become the independent states of Papua New Guinea, the Solomon Islands, and Vanuatu. Melanesian Pidgin has three major national dialects: Tok Pisin in Papua New Guinea, Pijin in the Solomon Islands, and Bislama in Vanuatu. Papua New Guinea also has a fourth contact language, Hiri Motu, which is a pidgin/creole spoken in the southern part of the country. Originally disseminated by the colonial police force, Hiri

Motu derives from a simplified version of the Motu language (an Oceanic language) of the Port Moresby area (Lynch 1998).

Code-switching in Melanesian literature: the case of Papua New Guinean Tok Pisin Melanesia's multilingualism makes it a productive context in which to consider the socio-cultural significance of language choice in literature. Most Melanesians are multilingual, speaking their own vernacular and often one or more neighbouring vernaculars. They also tend to speak the national variety of Melanesian Pidgin (or Hiri Motu) as a lingua franca (except in New Caledonia), and if they have been formally educated, they speak English (in Papua New Guinea, the Solomon Islands, and formerly British parts of Vanuatu), or French (in New Caledonia and former French regions of Vanuatu). A number of Melanesian creative writers have attempted to reflect this linguistic diversity in their work, by code-switching between different languages and dialects.

In its broadest sense, code-switching can be defined as the alternation between two or more languages within the same phrase, sentence, or utterance. As Ismail Talib points out, when writers code-switch between different dialects or languages in literature, they will often produce an artificial 'literary' version of the non-standard or lesser known variety in order to make it easier for non-specialist readers to understand the text. By way of example, Talib discusses Nigerian writer Amos Tutuola's first novel *The Palm-Wine Drinkard* (1952), which has achieved a wide circulation outside Nigeria due to its use of a 'literary' pidgin/creole that strikes a balance between 'raw pidgin' and standard English (Talib 2002: 124). The 'literary' or 'synthetic' Scots used by Scottish poets such as Robert Burns is a comparable example of this process of linguistic accommodation.

These kinds of strategies are clearly evident in the work of Papua New Guinean writer John Kasaipwalova. In Papua New Guinea, levels of literacy are relatively low compared to other parts of the Pacific, and much 'local' literature takes the form of dramatic works performed in Tok Pisin or local vernaculars (Beier 1980: xiii–xiv). When creative writing by Papua New Guineans first appeared in the late 1960s (see Chapter 4), the main readership for this material was located outside Papua New Guinea, in Australia and other 'Western' nations. In 1972, writer Apisai Enos noted that attempts to foster a Papua New Guinean national literature in English were foundering, as English was commonly viewed as the preserve of Papua New Guinea's educated urban élites. Enos advocated the creation of a 'Niuginian English', and of written literatures in Pidgin and Motu, in order to appeal to a wider local readership (1972: 46–9).

In the same year in which Enos's essay was published, John Kasaip-walova, a Trobriand Islander studying at the University of Papua New Guinea, published a short story which appeared to address some of Enos's concerns. The story, entitled 'Betel Nut is Bad Magic for Air-planes', is written in English, but the narrative also incorporates Tok Pisin vocabulary and grammatical patterns. The story is set during the period leading up to independence (which was formalized in 1975), and the code-switching within the narrative draws specific attention to the socio-political tensions evident during this transitional period.

The story is narrated by an unnamed university student who travels to Port Moresby's international airport with fellow UPNG students to meet some 'native people' arriving from rural Papua New Guinea. The narrator gets into an argument with a uniformed compatriot who informs the group that the chewing of betel nut (a mild stimulant customarily used by Papua New Guineans) is prohibited in the terminal area. What begins as a petty quarrel develops into a politically-charged standoff indexing the desire for self-determination among educated Papua New Guineans. The use of language in the story is crucial to this process, and becomes, as June Ellis suggests, a catalyst for the 'nascent national identity' of Papua New Guinea (Ellis 2003: 40). The airport official, for example, summons his Australian superior—referred to by the Tok Pisin word 'papa' (white man)—who attempts to put the narrator in his place by calling him 'boy', clearly invoking the insulting colonial practice of referring to local men as 'bois' (1972: 85). The narrator retaliates by first responding to the Australian in formal standard English ('on what moral grounds is it unlawful for me to chew betel nut here?') and then in 'Strine' or Australian colloquial English ('Listen mate. Why aren't you arresting those white kids inside the terminal for chewing P. K.?'[5]), demonstrating a linguistic and intellectual dexterity which confounds the Australian's attempts to belittle him. The narrator then accuses the official of intimidating the 'black people of Niugini' (85) by attempting to prevent them from exercising their civil rights in their own 'black man's country' (86). As Ellis notes, Kasaipwalova's use of the creole word 'Niugini', rather than the colonial labels 'Papua' and 'New Guinea', introduces a specifically nationalist agenda into the story (Ellis 2003: 40).

This nationalist agenda is also evident within the very style of narration: it is significant that although Standard English is used in conversational exchanges between the students and airport staff, the majority of the first-person narrative is rendered in a form of English heavily inflected by Tok Pisin vocabulary and grammar. Tok Pisin lexis (vocabulary) such as 'kalabus' for prison (86), and variant spellings such as 'polis' for police (86) are used throughout the story; similes such as 'they was standing there like bamboo, all empty' (88) and 'we wait like sleeping pigs'(90) also impart a sense of geographical specificity. At a grammatical level, the narrator's English incorporates certain features associated with Tok Pisin (and many other pidgins), such as the omission of tense markers ('The important man held his head for long time and *we wait*' (90)) and the copula ("'All right you *think you smart!*"' (84, my italics)). As is the case in Tok Pisin, pronouns are frequently used in the same form in the story whether they appear as subjects, objects or after a preposition ('*We* was standing about thirty of *we*' (83)), and prenominal articles (or determiners) are omitted ('he started . . . making his fingers round *like hard cricket ball*' (83, my italics)).

Although the narrator's 'Niuginian English' appears to be a contrived literary idiom which makes the narrative more accessible to an international readership, it is significant that the narrator uses this register to make a direct address to the reader at one point, remarking, in a description of the Australian official's enormous beer belly, that 'Maybe if you seen him too, ei, you will really laugh' (84). Such a strategy not only prioritizes the narrator's 'indigenized' English as a legitimate mode of communication, but also implicates the reader in the narrator's nationalist objectives.

Kasaipwalova's use of a Tok-Pisin-inflected English as the primary medium in his story is unusual: the use of non-standard language varieties in literature is commonly restricted to passages of dialogue or reported speech, or to individual words or phrases used sparingly throughout the text (Talib 2002: 147). The use of Melanesian Pidgin in other Pacific texts follows this conventional formula, witnessed in the use of individual Pidgin words or short phrases in texts written primarily in Standard English, such as Russell Soaba's novel *Wanpis* (1977) and Julian Maka'a's 'The Two Old Men Who Did Not Trust

Each Other' (1985).[6] At the other extreme is the use of 'pure' pidgin, as (for example) in the poem 'Brata Na Susa' ('Brothers and Sisters') by Papua New Guinean poet Rita Mamavi Pearson. Pearson's poem was published in the 1992 anthology *Te Rau Maire: Poems and Stories of the Pacific* (ed. Crocombe *et al.*), firstly in Tok Pisin and then in an English translation. Pearson uses Pidgin in a specific appeal to fellow Melanesians in the wake of various recent internal conflicts within the region, including Papua New Guinean attempts to suppress the secessionist movement in Bougainville[7] during the late 1980s and early 1990s. The English translation makes the poem accessible to non-pidgin-speaking readers outside Melanesia, but it is significant that the Pidgin version is printed first, thus signalling the existence of the Pidgin literary corpus that Apisai Enos had originally advocated in 1972.

Hawai'i Creole English   Hawai'ian Pidgin, also known as Hawai'i Creole English (HCE), is spoken by an estimated 600,000 people in Hawai'i. As is the case with Melanesian Pidgin, its vocabulary derives largely from English, and its grammatical structure from various languages spoken by labourers (including Hawai'ians, Chinese, Portuguese, Japanese, Koreans, and Filipinos) who came to work on Hawai'ian sugar plantations during the nineteenth century. When the sugar plantation era began in 1835, Hawai'ians were still in control of their islands, and Hawai'ian was privileged as the language of government and of education for all non-European children. It was also initially used as the language of administration on the plantations, but many white plantation overseers and immigrant labourers did not learn the language thoroughly, and a Pidgin Hawai'ian gradually developed. However, as the native Hawai'ian population declined and the American white settler community increased—particularly following the 1875 Reciprocity Treaty, which allowed free trade and a greater influx of Americans—English became increasingly dominant in Hawai'i. From 1878 to 1888 there was a dramatic increase in the number of English-medium schools; English gradually replaced Hawai'ian as the language of the plantations, and an English-lexified pidgin began to develop. By the beginning of the twentieth century, Hawai'ian Pidgin English was being used in a variety of contexts outside the plantation environment, and it became creolized in the 1920s as a result of intermarriage and population growth within immigrant communities. Today, Hawai'i Creole English is the mother tongue of a large proportion of Hawai'i's local population (Sakoda and Siegel 2003: viii; 2–10 *passim*).

The influence of the wide diversity of languages spoken on the plantations can be traced in the vocabulary, grammar, and semantics of HCE. Although English is the main lexifier, for example, HCE also contains around a hundred Hawai'ian words (such as 'haole', meaning white person or European); some forty Japanese words (such as 'chichi'—meaning 'breast'—from the Japanese word for milk), and a range of vocabulary from various other Pacific and Asian languages. Constituent (word) order in HCE is predominantly the same as in standard English, but the influence of Hawai'ian is evident in phrases such as 'Big, da house' ('Nui ka hale' in Hawai'ian), while the Portuguese verb 'estar' ('to be') is the source of the HCE verb 'stay' in sentences such as 'Da water stay cold' (the water is cold) (Sakoda and Siegel 2003: 11–17 *passim*).

Hawai'i Creole English, like many other pidgins and creoles, has suffered stigmatization due to prejudiced assumptions that it is a form of 'broken English' that hampers the acquisition of Standard English (which remains the privileged language of education and administration in Hawai'i). From the late 1980s, however, there have been efforts to promote HCE as a legitimate mode of expression in education, literature, and other media. A substantial body of literature in HCE has been published since the 1980s, produced by local Asian and native Hawai'ian writers such as Eric Chock, Richard Hamasaki, Lisa Kanae, Darrell Lum, Milton Murayama, Ed Sakamoto, Gary Pak, Lee Tonouchi, and Lois-Ann Yamanaka.

Literary examples of HCE: Yamanaka, Banggo, Balaz, and Apio
Lois-Ann Yamanaka's poetry anthology *Saturday Night at the Pahala Theatre* (1993) has achieved wide critical acclaim for its use of HCE. The anthology depicts the life of an Asian working class community on a Hawai'ian Big Island plantation, and many of the poems take the form of conversations in HCE between local characters. As Rob Wilson observes, Yamanaka's anthology explores the fragmentary nature of Asian (particularly Japanese) identities in Hawai'i, depicting characters who long 'to be othered into haole [white/Western] cultural styles' but also identify with 'deeper Hawaiian place values and resonance' (1999*b*: 368). In Yamanaka's poem 'Tita: Japs', for example,

two Japanese girls discuss their aspirations for 'double eyelid' operations (which will make them look more 'Western'), but also make
disparaging comments about the cultural values of schoolteachers
who have emigrated to Hawai'i from 'the mainland' US (32–3). Significantly, in a biographical footnote accompanying her short story
'Empty Heart' (published in an anthology of Asian American fiction),
Yamanaka emphasizes the sociopolitical significance of her decision
to write in pidgin: 'I write in the pidgin of the contract workers to the
sugar plantations here in Hawaii . . . Our language has been labeled
the language of ignorant people, substandard, and inappropriate in
any form of expression—written or oral . . . [but] I was encouraged
[by local mentors] to write in the voice of my place without shame or
fear' (Hagedorn (ed.) 1993: 544).

   Drawing upon precedents set by earlier native Hawai'ian poets such
as Wayne Kaumuali'i Westlake,[8] several Hawai'ian poets anthologized
in *Whetu Moana: Contemporary Polynesian Poetry in English* (Wendt
et al. (eds.) 2003) also make widespread use of HCE. Hawai'ian-
Filipino poet Kathy Banggo's 'Fly, Da Mo'o & Me', for example,
code-switches between Standard English and Hawai'i Creole English
as the speaker describes how she was raped by a male acquaintance.
The poem begins in HCE, as the speaker reveals that 'Befo time, I wuz
bright' but now 'I stay stink. / I stay ugly' (Wendt *et al.* (eds.) 2003:
13). The opening phrase 'befo time' ('earlier on') is commonly used in
HCE as a pre- or post-modifier (occurring before or after the phrase
or word(s) it modifies) in order to indicate that an event has occurred
in the past. Here, it indicates that the speaker in the poem used to be
'bright' (happy), but now feels 'stink' (bad/dirty) and 'ugly' following
the rape. The verb 'stay' here derives from the Portuguese verb 'estar'
[to be] (as discussed above), signalling the speaker's current state of
being. Banggo makes concessions for readers not familiar with HCE:
the line 'Befo time, I wuz bright', for example, is repeated in the next
stanza in Standard English ('I used to be bright'), but notably, the
description of the actual rape is rendered almost entirely in basilectal
(heavy) creole.[9] As the violation takes place, the victim focuses on a
lizard (referred to by the Hawai'ian word 'mo'o') stalking a fly on
the wall, and reports that after the lizard swallows the fly, 'Da fuckah
burp[ed]' (14). The lizard's attack on the fly thus becomes a symbolic
enactment of the rape itself: the predatory lizard, who 'burps' after
swallowing the fly, is equated with the rapist, and the fly (described

as 'my fren' [friend]) with the victim. Here, the Hawai'ian and HCE words remain 'untranslated', lending a poignancy to the moment: it appears that the experience is too painful for the woman to explain to outsiders in Standard English. A similar strategy is evident in another of Banggo's poems, 'Dey Wen Sen Me Girls' Home' ('They Sent Me to a Girls' Home'), in which the drug-addicted female speaker reveals that she stabbed her own brother after he sold her skateboard to buy himself drugs. The basilectal creole in this poem creates a vivid sense of local specificity and arguably—given the fact that HCE is frequently stigmatized as a 'lower class' mode of speech—also draws attention to the harsh social conditions which lead individuals such as the speaker into drug use and violent crime (Wendt *et al.* (eds.) 2003: 14–15).

In Joe Balaz's poem 'Da Last Squid', also included in *Whetu Moana*, HCE is used to create a sense of intimacy between the speaker of the poem, and an implied addressee (referred to as 'brah' [brother]) who is assumed to be familiar with the local people and events being described. The speaker laments the fact that commercial and residential development on O'ahu (the island on which Hawai'i's capital and tourist mecca Honolulu is located) has polluted the environment to the point where local marine species, including squid, are dying out. The speaker tells of a friend who caught a squid in an abandoned conservation area between an industrial park and a desalinization plant, and marvels that the creature could survive in that polluted environment, speculating that perhaps the mollusc 'wuz wun mutant' [was a mutant] (Wendt *et al.* 2003: 8). In retrospect, the speaker realizes that this hardy squid was the last one he ever saw in this area, as the beach subsequently became so polluted that now 'nutting [nothing] can even live' there (9). The poem implies that foreign investors (including Americans) are largely responsible for the despoliation of the island of O'ahu, which has developed 'out of control / into wun huge monstah city'. At one point, the speaker mocks the putative formality of Standard English, perhaps implying that it, too, is an unwelcome 'outsider' to Hawai'i: in describing the effluent outflow area where his friend found the squid, the speaker remarks 'You know wat "effluent" mean, eh? / Dats just wun nice word foa dodo watah'. The use of the HCE word 'dodo' for excrement here seems to suggest that Standard English euphemisms such as 'development' and 'effluent' conceal the ugly underside of (foreign) commercial enterprise, which is destroying the livelihood—fishing—upon which native Hawai'ians have relied for generations.

HCE also features in a wide range of contemporary Hawai'ian dramatic works, where the assumption of a shared linguistic paradigm among local audiences allows playwrights to use basilectal creole without the need for contextual translation. A number of dramatic works featuring HCE were brought together in the Bamboo Ridge Press anthology *He Leo Hou* (Wat and Desha (eds.) 2003), which includes plays by Alani Apio, Tammy Haili'ōpua Baker, Lee Cataluna, and Victoria Nalani Kneubuhl. Alani Apio's *Kāmau* (first performed in 1994) offers a particularly poignant commentary on the complex politics of language use among Hawai'i's ethnically diverse peoples. In one particular scene, Michael, a part-native Hawai'ian, argues with a security guard who works for a haole-owned firm that has just 'purchased' the land on which Michael's family has lived for generations. The security guard asks Michael and the rest of his family to vacate the land, using formal standard English, and Michael, assuming that the security guard is white, berates him in HCE for being 'one stupid, fagget haole who's gonna get his face bus' up real soon' [*sic*] (55). The security guard, who is in fact also part-native Hawai'ian, code-switches into HCE in an attempt to establish solidarity with Michael, arguing that 'I'm doing my job, brudda. 'Cause I get one family to feed' [*sic*] (55). Michael argues that no native Hawai'ian would evict a fellow Hawai'ian from his own family land, and he asks the security guard to prove 'what makes you Hawai'ian' (56). The security guard then code-switches into Hawai'ian as proof of his racial 'authenticity', putting a question to Michael in his native language. Ironically, Michael himself is not fluent in Hawai'ian, and he has to admit defeat at this point. This is a poignant moment in the play, as in an earlier scene, the spirit of Michael's mother had appeared to his brother Alika, lamenting the fact that her generation let much of Hawai'ian culture (including, presumably, the language) die with them due to the fact that 'They [the whites] made us so ashamed of who we are' (21). The play also investigates the economic costs of Americanization, documenting the decline of 'traditional' Hawai'ian livelihoods (such as fishing) that occurred in the wake of massive tourist development after the Second World War. Alika himself is forced to take a job with Aloha Tours, the very company that is evicting his family from their land, and the play opens and closes with Alika's tour-guide patter as he peddles a sanitized version of his culture to foreign (mainly American) tourists.

Koines in the Pacific: Fiji Hindi   Fiji, which straddles the boundary between Melanesia and Polynesia, features a unique cultural and linguistic milieu that offers an intriguing context for the study of the politics of language in literature. As discussed in Chapter 4, when Indian indentured labourers were brought to Fiji between the 1870s and 1920s, the British colonial administration discouraged close interaction between Indigenous Fijians and ethnic Indians, thereby establishing interethnic divisions that ultimately precipitated the coups of 1987 and 2000. The discrete nature of these two communities is reflected in Fiji's linguistic demography. Most Indigenous Fijians, for example, speak standard Fijian as well as their own dialect of Fijian, and many also speak English. Most Indians in Fiji, on the other hand, speak Fiji Hindi and Standard Hindi, and many speak English. Not many Fijians speak Hindi, and few Indians speak Fijian. English is the main language of interethnic communication, although in some contexts, Pidgin Fijian or Pidgin Hindi is used (Lynch 1998: 264).

Fiji Hindi, which is also known as Fiji Baat ('baat' is Hindi for 'language'), is a contact language which developed as a result of Fiji's plantation history. In linguistic terminology it is known as a koine (dialect mix) deriving from a variety of North Indian dialects spoken by the original indentured labourers who came to Fiji in the late nineteenth century. Over time, Fiji Hindi also incorporated words from English and Fijian, and today it is the first language of nearly all Indo-Fijians and is spoken by over 300,000 people (Mugler and Lynch 1996: 4; Lynch 1998: 220). Fiji Hindi is only used in informal contexts, however, while Standard (Indian) Hindi is used in schools, in print, on the radio, and in other formal contexts. Linguists describe this as diglossia, a situation where one variety (in this case, Standard Hindi) is privileged in formal situations and the other variety (Fiji Hindi) is used in informal situations (Lynch 1998: 236).

Fiji Hindi in Indo-Fijian literature: Subramani and Sudesh Mishra
In a direct protest against the marginalization of Fiji Hindi as a written language, in 2001 Indo-Fijian writer Subramani published *Dauka Puraan*, a novel written in the Fiji Hindi that he spoke while growing up in rural Labasa (on Vanua Levu). The novel is

the first major literary work to be published in Fiji Hindi, and has created controversy not only due to its linguistic medium, but also because of its subject matter. The narrative begins with the arrival of an overseas academic, Vidyadhar Shrivastow, in a rural Indo-Fijian village, where he convinces a local man, Fijilal, to tell him the history of the local people. Fijilal jokingly introduces himself as 'Fijilal Girmit Ram Dauka', thereby using a symbolic name that draws attention to the history of indenture within the community, and to the 'subaltern' status of the local people (who are the 'dauka' referenced in the novel's title). The title of the novel also indexes the puraanas—the Hindu religious scriptures—but Subramani's 'epic' documents the adventures not of gods and mythical heroes, but rather of the 'dauka', the lower-caste ethnic Indians who belong to Fijilal's community. As Subramani puts it, the novel therefore becomes 'a scoundrel's tale' or 'comic Puraan' (Ali 2001: n.p.). The novel's intermingling of the sacred and the profane has been viewed as 'offensive' by some critics: reviewer Rameshwar Prasad, for example, criticizes Subramani for substituting 'vulgar tongues for standard language', arguing that Fiji Hindi is mere 'slang', and suggesting that the novel's title is an insult to those who 'take the *Puraanas* as sacred' (2003: n.p.). Subramani has responded to such criticisms by arguing that Fiji Hindi is 'the language of the subalterns I wanted to write about', and that there are 'histories, secrets, silences, omissions, nuances, intuitions, ironies in the language that no amount of what Rushdie calls "chutnification of English" (1991: 414) will be able to draw out of the memories of subalterns who dream and imagine in a different idiom' (2003: 11). Subramani's assertions here bear some resemblance to Gayatri Spivak's arguments that the Indian historians who belonged to the 'Subaltern Studies' research group (which flourished in India in the 1980s) were frustrated in their attempts to document the experiences of Indian peasants, due to the fact that the testimonies of these illiterate 'subalterns' remained unrecorded and therefore inaccessible (Spivak 1999: 270–3).

In an autobiographical short story entitled 'Lila' (1994), Indo-Fijian writer Sudesh Mishra, like Subramani, celebrates Fiji Hindi as a diasporic language that indexes the history of indenture. The story describes the narrator's experience of taking part in a lila Rama, a week-long dramatization of the poet Tulasidasa's Hindi translation of Valmiki's Sanskrit epic the *Rāmāyana*. In Mishra's story, the narrator

plays the role of Shatrugun, youngest brother of the hero Rama, whose
adventures form the focus of the epic. According to the *Rāmāyana*,
Rama—an incarnation of the god Vishnu—was sent into exile for
fourteen years before returning to the Kingdom of Ayodhya to take
up his father King Das(h)haratha's crown, which had wrongfully been
awarded to Rama's brother Bharata upon the old king's death. Rama
has been adopted as a symbol of the girmitiya experience in a wide
range of Indo-Fijian literature and theory: as Vijay Mishra points
out, the story of Rama's banishment and eventual return has been
interpreted as an allegory for the experience of the girmitiyas in Fiji,
many of whom anticipated a return to their homelands after their
period of indenture ended. In actuality, few girmitiyas could afford the
costs of transportation back to India, and as future generations have
remained in Fiji, Rama's mythical return to Ayodhya has endured as
a 'millennial' dream for Indo-Fijians anticipating an eventual reward
for their patience, labour, and suffering (1992: 3–4).

In 'Lila', the narrator recalls struggling with his lines in the lila Rama,
due to the differences between shudh Hindi (in which Tulasidasa's
version of the epic is written), and the Fiji Hindi with which he
has grown up. In retrospect, the narrator revels in this difference,
describing Fiji Hindi as growing 'out of the girmit experience, at
once vital, ribald, earthy, poetic, ironic, impure, maligned, a hybrid
monster of a Hindi that drew sustenance from Fijian and English,
among other languages, a Hindi that made the proper names of other
languages improper, the better to enlist them for its own unfolding'
(1994: 651). The narrator notes that Tulasidasa's shudh Hindi has been
altered by the 'carnival of voices' in Fiji, so that his lines become
those of 'a diasporic self, releasing the perfume of cowpats, wet
mongoose pelts and gecko droppings' (655). Mishra's choice of the
word 'carnival' here is significant, not only echoing the work of Russian
theorist Mikhail Bakhtin,[10] but also drawing attention to the politics
of language in a postcolonial setting. As Mishra puts it, his polyphonic
narrative (which switches between Standard English, Standard and
Fiji Hindi, Urdu, and Fijian) is designed 'to alter from within the
architecture of the great colonial bungalow' (655), disrupting the
authority of the colonial English language he was forced to learn as a
schoolchild.

5.2 Oceanic oral and textual culture

5.2.1 *Linguistic deterritorialization: code-switching between Indigenous and colonial languages*

Another major category of code-switching within Pacific literatures involves the alternation between (former) colonial and Indigenous languages. The degree to which Indigenous language is used in Indigenous anglophone literatures is, of course, contingent upon the relative status of Indigenous and colonial languages within each particular national context. In settler colonies such as Hawai'i, Aotearoa/New Zealand, and New Caledonia/Kanaky, for example, Indigenous languages are in a far more precarious position than in many other former colonies in the Pacific. Most Pacific Islanders are at least bilingual and many are multilingual, but in Aotearoa/New Zealand and Hawai'i, where the descendants of Euro-American settlers are in the majority, only a small proportion of Māori and native Hawai'ians speak their own languages fluently, and although Māori and Hawai'ian are recognized as official languages, English remains the main language of communication. In both countries, however, the establishment of language revival programmes from the 1970s onwards has ensured that these Indigenous languages have featured prominently in Māori and Hawai'ian literature, both at a metalinguistic level, and as a medium of expression through strategic code-switching.

Included below are two case studies from different poles of the linguistic continuum described above. First discussed is the Māori language, which is under threat due to the dominance of English within Aotearoa/New Zealand. The second language to be discussed is Samoan, which has retained its vernacular status within Samoa, and is still spoken by a large proportion of diasporic Samoans living in Australia, Aotearoa/New Zealand, and the United States. Examples are taken from the work of Māori writer Patricia Grace, and Samoan writer Sia Figiel, in order to compare code-switching strategies and language politics in their prose fiction.

The status of Māori   The Māori language was spoken universally in the nineteenth century and by most Māori in the early decades of the twentieth century, but during the post-war period, the large-scale migration of Māori to urban centres, where they were compelled to 'assimilate' into the dominant Pākehā culture, had a dramatic impact on the use of Māori as a first language. As discussed in Chapter 4, an important language survey undertaken in the 1970s revealed that most native speakers of Māori were over thirty years of age, and only around two per cent of children were growing up speaking Māori as a first language (McRae 1991: 2; Waite 1992). This had come about partly as a result of Māori parents and grandparents becoming convinced that learning English was the key to success in the Pākehā world, and partly due to government education policy. In 1905, for example, the Inspector of Native Schools instructed teachers to encourage Māori children to speak English in school grounds. As Ranginui Walker notes, this injunction was rapidly translated into 'a general prohibition of the Māori language within school precincts' which lasted for the next five decades and 'was in some cases enforced by corporal punishment' (Walker 2004: 147). In response to growing concerns about the Māori language, and galvanized by the political and social activism which developed out of the Māori Renaissance, various Māori community groups established language programmes for Māori children from the late 1970s. These include Kōhanga Reo (Māori language 'nests' for those below school age) and Kura Kaupapa Māori (Māori-medium primary and secondary schools), and more recently, Māori-administered universities (whare wānanga) and adult literacy programmes. These measures have effected an increase in the number and fluency of Māori speakers, but it is not clear at this stage whether or not Māori will regain its vernacular status among the majority of the Māori population (Harlow 2005). At the very least the grammar of the language is changing significantly due to the influence or transference of English grammatical structures across to Māori.

Māori language in literature: Patricia Grace   As a result of the social conditions described above, prominent 'first-generation' Māori writers such as Witi Ihimaera and Patricia Grace have grown up speaking very little Māori and have only achieved greater fluency in the language in adult life. Patricia Grace, in particular, has been preoccupied with the status of the Māori language throughout her literary career, and her writing offers a rich range of examples of the way in which code-switching between English and Māori can be used as a means by which to advocate Māori cultural revival and self-determination. The linguistic theories of Gilles Deleuze and Félix Guattari offer a useful framework within which to consider the subversive potential of

Grace's code-switching strategies. In *Kafka: Toward a Minor Literature* (1986), Deleuze and Guattari argue that the 'minor' writer, writing in a 'major' or dominant language, can 'deterritorialize' the dominant language by allowing the grammatical and conceptual categories from the 'minor' language to infiltrate the syntax of the 'major language'. According to this argument, the 'minority' language therefore 'inhabits' or 'occupies' the dominant language, undermining any sense of univocal authority and shifting the parameters of meaning towards the 'minor' writer's own cultural milieu (Deleuze and Guattari 1986: 26; Keown 2003: 421–2 and 2005: 162–3). While the terms 'major' and 'minor' are problematic due to their homological relationship to strategies of domination and subjection in colonial discourse, Deleuze and Guattari's arguments are nevertheless relevant to a reading of the linguistic strategies used in Grace's fiction.

Like many of her peers, Grace grew up speaking English as her first language: during her childhood, her Māori relatives—particularly the older ones—tended not to speak Māori in front of the children because it was generally believed at the time that it was more advantageous to speak English (Tausky 1991: 90). In spite of this, Grace recalls a certain degree of exposure to Māori, and she reveals that she has incorporated Māori words and phrases into her 'English sentences' ever since her childhood (1999: 72). This practice of code-switching between English and Māori is apparent throughout Grace's fiction, and is used as a marker of cultural identity particularly among middle-aged or older characters, in keeping with the demographic profile of Māori speakers in the post-war period. While Grace's early publications included glossaries and contextual translations of Māori words and phrases, from the publication of *Potiki* (1986), Grace has made far fewer concessions for non-Māori-speaking readers, and has recently argued that writers from 'small population cultures' should not have to 'other' their languages and cultures by providing glossaries and other explanatory information for readers (Grace 1999: 71–2). A sense of the range and depth of Grace's explorations of the politics of language can be gained by examining a few examples from different stages of her literary career.

In Grace's first novel *Mutuwhenua* (1978), and in her first three short-story collections (1975, 1980, 1987), for example, glossaries of Māori words are provided at the end of each text, but code-switching between English and Māori is also frequently elucidated within the texts themselves. Translations are often provided in the sentence or phrase immediately preceding or following the Māori word or phrase, as in the following example from the story 'A Way of Talking' (1975), when the narrator observes the antics of her friend's children:

> They kept jumping up and down on the sofa to get Rose's attention and I kept thinking what a waste of a good sofa it was, what a waste of a good house for those two nuisance things. I hope when I have kids they won't be so *hoha*.
>
> (1994: 12; my italics)

Here, the reader is able to work out from the context that 'hoha' means 'tiresome' or 'irritating', the equivalent to the 'nuisance things' described in the previous sentence. A similar example appears in the short story 'The Dream' (1975), where a character utters a phrase in Māori and then gives an English translation:

> 'E ta, ka haunga to tuna,' said Ritimana, slicing the air with his hand. 'Your eel stinks.'
>
> (1994: 31)

Here, the translation is not exact—the Māori version of the sentence is prefaced with 'e ta', a mode of address to a young man which roughly translates here as 'hey, mate . . . '—but the English translation is close enough to give a clear sense of the meaning of the original Māori version.

As mentioned above, by the time Grace published *Potiki* (1986), she had decided not to provide glossaries of Māori words any longer, and her use of Māori within the novel itself is less accommodating of non-Māori-speaking readers. In the following example, an elderly woman named Granny Tamihana switches from Māori to English during a conversation with her grand-daughter Mary, and Granny Tamihana's English utterances serve only as a partial translation of the original Māori:

> 'Haere mai te awhina o te iwi. Haere mai ki te kai, haere mai ki te inu ti.'
> 'See, Gran?'
> 'Very beautiful my Mary.'
> 'Beautiful and nice.'
> 'Very beautiful and nice . . . You come and have a cup of tea now.'
> 'Cup of tea.'
> 'Come and have a cup of tea and a bread.'
> 'Come back after and do my work.'
> 'When you had your cup of tea and a kai.'
>
> (20)

Here, non-Māori-speaking readers will have more difficulty interpreting Granny Tamihana's initial address to Mary. Her first utterance could be translated as follows: 'Come here, helper of the people. Come and eat, come and drink tea.' Granny Tamihana's subsequent English sentence 'come and have a cup of tea and a bread' goes some way towards translating the Māori utterance, but it is not a simple matter of matching phrase to phrase, as in some of Grace's earlier fiction. The final sentences of the novel take this process even further; they are rendered entirely in Māori with no translation whatsoever:

No reira, e kui ma, e koro ma, e hoa ma. Tamariki ma, mokopuna ma—Tena koutou. Tena koutou, tena koutou katoa. Ka huri.

(185)

The passage can be translated thus: 'Therefore, (elder) women, (elder) men, friends. Children, grandchildren—greetings. Greetings, greetings to you all. It's your turn.' The last sentence, 'ka huri', literally meaning 'it turns', is used in Māori oratory to indicate that one speaker has finished and another is to begin. By using this phrase, Grace offers the ending of her novel as a challenge to the reader who understands Māori. Coming at the end of a narrative which has focused specifically on Māori self-determination in the face of Pākehā institutional and discursive hegemony, it suggests that the (Māori) reader should take up where Grace left off, continuing the battle for Māori self-expression and sociopolitical autonomy. Grace's use of Māori language is central to this political agenda, and it is significant that in 1987, the year after *Potiki* was published, Māori finally achieved status as an official language (alongside English) in Aotearoa/New Zealand following a claim (filed in 1985) for protection of the language under the terms of the Treaty of Waitangi (Benton 1996: 214). In her later novel *Cousins* (1992), Grace incorporates specific references to these and other developments in the status of the Māori language: one of the narrators (Makareta) tells of her involvement in petitioning for the Māori language to be accorded official status, and also describes her subsequent role in establishing kōhanga reo in the hope that 'our language, through our own initiatives and via the little children, would revive and survive after having been suppressed for so long' (1992: 211).

Grace's commitment to the revitalization of the Māori language is also encoded at a more complex stylistic level in her writing: in some cases, Māori grammatical patterns are transferred across to the English language used by her Māori characters. A particularly common example of grammatical 'interference' evident throughout Grace's fiction is in the rendering of mass and count nouns, which are not differentiated in Māori. For example, 'a book' and 'some food' would be expressed using the same indefinite article 'he' (as in 'he pukapuka' and 'he kai'), although in English 'book' is a count noun and 'food' is a mass noun (Keown 2003: 425). In Grace's fiction, elderly characters whose first language is Māori often make 'errors' in their use of English mass and count nouns, appearing to revert to Māori grammatical patterns. In Grace's story 'Waimarie' (1987), for example, an elderly woman asks her niece to 'get me *a* leaves from my little tree' (Grace 1994: 193, my italics), while Granny Tamihana in *Potiki* tells her grandchildren to 'Butter you *a* bread.... And I'll pour us *a* tea' (20, my italics).

Another form of grammatical transference found in Grace's early fiction in particular is the process of agent deletion, which commonly occurs in Māori narratives in which the identity of the subject has already been established earlier in the text. An awareness of this grammatical process may account for the absence of subject pronouns in the following example from Grace's story 'Toki' (1975): 'To the hills next morning, and from there saw the little boat head straight for the deep' (1994: 19). In Standard English, this sentence would normally read something like this: '*I* went to the hills the next morning, and from there (*I*) saw the little boat head straight for the deep'. In 'Toki', however, agent or subject deletion is used throughout the story, effectively establishing the fact that the elderly speaker's first language is Māori.

A third common form of 'interference' evident in Grace's fiction centres upon Māori methods of expressing tense and mood, which are realized not through modification to the verb itself (as in English) but rather through the choice of a preceding verbal particle. Within the context of Māori oral narrative, verbal particles marking particular tenses are often replaced by the non-specific verbal particle 'ka', which precedes the verb but has no specific tense value in itself, merely marking the phrase in which it occurs as verbal (Harlow 1989: 202). Tense is judged from context, therefore if a speaker begins a story in the past tense (i + verb), s/he can mark all subsequent verbs with 'ka' with the tacit understanding that the past tense is being expressed. This may account for the fact that in the following utterance from an elderly Māori man in Grace's novel *Baby No-Eyes*, all verbs except the first 'was' are in the present tense, even though the old man is clearly talking about past events:

There *was* this old man Hori who *talk* to me about Anapuke. Well that hill, that Anapuke, you *don't* hardly talk about. *It's* from the far, old times, where *there's* only the Maori . . . You go there *it's* trouble.

(1998: 151, my italics)

A similar example appears in Grace's *Potiki*, where Granny Tamihana tells of an event in the past but consistently uses the present tense, even code-switching into Māori and using the 'ka' construction as she speaks of the occasion when her brother was killed after his horse was 'spooked' by a kehua (ghost):

The horse *get* a very big fright. My brother *fly* out in the air you see, because of the big kehua *make* his horse very wild. And down, down, and splash in the small water. And bang. His head *break* on that rock there with a big kehua on it. My poor brother, *ka pakaru te upoko.*

(1986: 56; my italics)

Here, Grace draws specific attention to the function of the 'ka' construction in Māori, as Granny Tamihana's final phrase 'ka pakaru te upoko'—which corresponds with the English phrase 'his head break'—makes explicit the grammatical rule that she has transferred to the English sections of her utterance. The use of 'ka' here therefore signals the need to retrieve temporal information from a preceding utterance.

While these examples of grammatical transference clearly imbue Grace's writing with a sense of socio-linguistic realism, in some cases her language strategies are also put to more explicitly political purposes. In her story 'Letters from Whetu' (1980), for example, the disjunction between Māori and English grammatical patterns is explored in order to challenge the adherence to grammatical ortho-doxy within the English-medium education system in Aotearoa/New Zealand. The story is epistolary, comprising a series of letters written by a Māori high school student named Whetu-o-te-moana (whose name translates as 'Star of the sea') to allay his boredom during class time. Whetu addresses his letters to various Māori friends who have now left school, and expresses frustration at the fact that his teacher (Ms Fisher) has taken him under her wing as 'her honourable statis-tic, her minority person MAKING IT' in an education system where

Māori students frequently drop out as soon as they reach school-leaving age (1994: 122). In order subtly to undermine the well-meaning but condescending behaviour of his teacher, Whetu sometimes uses putatively 'incorrect' grammar in order to elicit a reaction:

> I sometimes do a bit of a stir with Fisher, like I say 'yous' instead of 'you' (pl.). It always sends her PURPLE. The other day I wrote it in my essay and she had a BLUE fit. She scratched it out in RED and wrote me a double underlined note—'I have told you many times before that there is no such word as 'yous' (I wonder if it hurt her to write it). Please do not use (yous heh heh) it again.' So I wrote a triple underlined note underneath—'How can I yous it if it does not exist?'

(122)

Here, Whetu's playful sally makes a serious ideological point. The word 'yous' as a second person plural pronoun is often associated with non-standard dialects of English within the United Kingdom, for example, but in Aotearoa/New Zealand it is also strongly associated with Māori ethnicity. This possibly stems from the fact that unlike modern English, Māori has distinct singular, dual and plural second-person pronominal forms, so that the modern English pronoun 'you', which is used to express all three number categories (singular, dual and plural), has three separate counterparts in Māori: 'koe' ('you', singular); 'kōrua' ('you two') and 'koutou' ('you' plural). In this context, Whetu's 'yous' is equivalent to 'koutou' ('you' plural), and is therefore not only a legitimate plural form in non-standard varieties of English, but also arguably reflects an existing (and more complex) number distinction in Māori. Whetu's behaviour therefore draws attention to the way in which non-standard usages featured in Māori English are proscribed by the Pākehā-dominated education system, exacerbating the sense of exclusion that makes Māori students (such as Whetu's friends) desperate to leave school as soon as they are able.

Samoan language in literature: the case of Sia Figiel   In contrast to Māori (and Hawai'ian), the Samoan language enjoys a much more secure status as the vernacular language of Samoa. Although Western Samoa was a European colony, first under Germany and subsequently under New Zealand, relatively few Europeans settled there, and although European missionaries were extremely successful in Christianizing Samoans, many other aspects of the fa'a Sāmoa

(Samoan way of life), including the status of the Samoan language as the mother tongue, have endured throughout and beyond the colonial period. Today, Samoan is used as the sole medium of instruction during early schooling, with English language introduced as a subject later in a child's education, thus preserving Samoan's vernacular status at an institutional level. Many contemporary Samoan writers, however, write primarily in English in order to make their work accessible to a wider international audience. When Samoan language is used in Samoan literature, it frequently appears in the service of socio-linguistic realism, although it is notable in examining the work of Albert Wendt (Samoa's most prolific contemporary writer) that his early publications are relatively sparing in their use of Samoan language and contain glossaries, whereas in later works such as his 1991 novel *Ola* and his short story 'Robocop in Long Bay' (2002), untranslated (and unglossed) Samoan is much more widespread (Wendt 1991: 260; see also Sharrad 2003: 191). This points towards a more general tendency, among contemporary 'postcolonial' Pacific writers, to make far fewer concessions for monolingual English-speaking readers.

Wendt's compatriot Sia Figiel, who published her debut novel *Where We Once Belonged* in 1996, is notable for her widespread use of untranslated Samoan in her work. She is highly critical of Western discursive representations of Samoans in her writing, and the use of untranslated Samoan is at times used in order to satirize particular individuals responsible for these representations. In *Where We Once Belonged*, for example, the anthropologist Ernest Beaglehole is dubbed 'Fa'ipula [ripe banana] Beaglehole' (69), while the name of the anthropologist Derek Freeman is conferred upon two Samoan brothers who eventually become trans-sexuals:

Freeman (Pagoka-ua-faasolokoiga) and Derek (Keleki) both turned out to be fa'afafige. Keleki returned from Hawai'i with breast implants, and Pagoka-ua-faasaolokoinga leads a life of sin in Apia with sailors and unhappily or happily married men.

(1996*a*: 68)

Here, Freeman's name is comically (and subversively) indigenized and transformed, translated into Samoan firstly through direct parallel translation ('Pagoka-ua-faasolokoiga' means 'man/prisoner who has been freed'), and secondly through phonetic adaptation ('Keleki' being a close approximation to 'Derek' in Samoan phonology) (Keown 2005:

46). The joke here, of course, is the fact that these two trans-sexuals have been named after an anthropologist who focused specifically upon Samoan *hetero*sexuality and the putatively assertive masculinity of Samoan men (see Chapter 2). The fact that these linguistic puns remain untranslated lends them a subversive quality, particularly given that the quips are made about anglophone Western academics.

There are other linguistic strategies in Figiel's work that are significant for a local readership but not readily apparent to non-Samoan-speaking readers. Figiel, an experienced performance poet, has pointed out that the rhythms of vernacular speech are central to her work, and in passages of Samoan dialogue in *Where We Once Belonged* (1996a) and her novella *The Girl in the Moon Circle* (1996b), she uses a form of Samoan commonly reserved for informal social contexts. Samoan has two distinct registers, one formal and respectful, and the other informal and more intimate. Traditionally the two registers were reserved for talking to or about matai (chiefs or titled persons) and commoners respectively, but as John Lynch points out, '[f]ormality and politeness can be signaled by the use of the respect register even when those involved do not merit this by virtue of their status', while 'intimacy or common purpose can be conveyed by using the ordinary register even if one or more of the participants is *matai*' (1998: 258). Each register has variations in pronunciation: the formal Samoan 't' and 'n' become 'k' and 'g' (pronounced 'ng') in the informal register, for example. In her writing, Figiel makes widespread use of the 'speakerly' k dialect,[11] and of Samoan (and English) expletives. In a society that maintains strict protocol regarding appropriate forms of speech and writing in Samoan, these are bold strategies that have made her work particularly appealing to young Samoan readers (Marsh 1997: 5). Figiel herself has pointed out that there is a political dimension to her use of the informal register: she is motivated not only by a personal desire to 'capture people speaking in the vernacular—in their own language which is often very grassroots level' [*sic*], but also by a belief that 'it is important for Samoans and other Pacific people to realize that their language is being prioritized *in an English context*' (1998: 101; Keown 2005: 41).

In addition to using Samoan language in her work, Figiel, like Grace, also transfers Samoan grammatical patterns across into her English: a notable example is her use of reduplicated verbs (such as 'zoom-zoom' and 'swimming-swimming') to indicate continuous or repetitive movement (1996a: 88; 85). This replicates a common practice in Samoan and other Polynesian languages (such as Māori), where a verb such as pati (which means 'to clap hands together' in Samoan) is reduplicated as 'patipati' to indicate a repetitive or frequentative action such as clapping or applause (Pratt 1984: 14). Full reduplication is also applied to loanwords such as, for example, 'afa'afa ('to take equal shares' or 'go halves'), and it therefore seems appropriate that Figiel should apply this rule to the English verbs she reduplicates in her narratives (Mosel and Hovdhaugen 1992: 219).

5.2.2 Orality in the printed text: Figiel and Grace

Both Figiel and Grace use their Indigenous languages not only at a lexical or grammatical level in their work, but also at a deeper structural level, basing their narratives on the rhythms and patterns of their respective oral traditions. Grace, for example, makes frequent use of multiple narrators in her novels, approximating the Māori tradition of whaikōrero or speechmaking, in which different orators take turns to offer individual perspectives on a topic of discussion. This practice is particularly important in *Potiki*, where various members of a Māori coastal community, finding that the Pākehā-dominated world of the media and print culture tends to exclude Māori, choose to produce their own narratives in order to empower themselves and reinforce a sense of shared cultural identity. These narratives are intimately linked with the whare whakairo or carved meeting house in which the people gather for various community events, and in which there are carved ancestral figures (poupou) that each record the place of particular ancestors within the history of the iwi (tribe). In this sense, the whare whakairo, like other Māori figurative art forms, becomes a 'book' which can be 'read' by the people of the community. Further, the figure of the spiral, a central motif in Māori carving and other art forms, is used in the novel as a symbol of the storytelling process and of social history, which (in Māori cosmogony) is viewed not as a linear process but rather as a spiralling phenomenon:

[A]lthough the stories all had different voices, and came from different times and places and understandings ... each one was like a puzzle piece which tongued or grooved neatly to another. And this train of stories defined our lives, curving out from points on the spiral in ever-widening circles from which neither beginnings nor endings could be defined.

(Grace 1986: 41)

Significantly, this spiralling pattern is integral to the narrative structure of the novel. While the conflict and confrontations between the Pākehā land developers and the Māori community emerge as a linear sequence of events, the actual 'stories' of the various narrators in the novel make continual temporal shifts, doubling back on each other and, as Miriam Fuchs notes, slipping 'between the various stages' of the unfolding conflict between the developers and the Māori community (1993: 574). The process of narration continues even after death, when Tokowaru-i-te-Marama—a young boy, gifted with foresight, who is killed in a booby-trap set by the developers—delivers a final spoken chapter from within the whare whakairo where he now appears as a carving. Toko's post-death utterance thus enfolds and encircles his narrative back into the collective history of the iwi as recorded in the ancestral meeting house. Within this context, it is entirely appropriate that the novel should finish with a final address in Māori (as discussed earlier) that signals the end of one orator's speech and the beginning of another's: Grace, having delivered her 'speech' advocating self-determination for the Māori people, now invites other Māori to continue this process of cultural regeneration.

Like Grace, Sia Figiel also locates her own Indigenous oral tradition as an organizing principle behind the narrative frameworks in her writing. Where Grace focuses on the spiral as a central symbol of the Māori oral tradition, Figiel draws attention to the circle as a powerful 'metaphor' and 'philosophical concept' that is central to Samoan ontology, and to her own creative writing:

[The circle] is in our architecture, our social structure, our traditional calendar, our poetic and musical compositions . . . I was interested . . . in experimenting with the idea of the ula or lei or flower necklace as a working metaphor for the composition [of my narratives]. In Samoan poetry (solo) or specifically in singing (pesepesega), we call it suifefiloi [sic]—the weaving or the threading of many different songs/tunes to make one long long song. Stylistically that was my intention. In The Girl, the book begins with a song and ends with a song—thus closing the circle. One might say that there are big bright flowers blooming all over the composition, interspersed by small ones.

(Subramani 1996: 126)

The suʻifefiloi pattern Figiel describes here is clearly evident in the narrative structure of *Where We Once Belonged* and *The Girl in the Moon Circle*, both of which comprise a series of interwoven short narrative fragments and poems. Both narratives feature central adolescent narrators whose perspectives alternative with those of a more knowing, unnamed third-person narrator, and this strategy gives texture to Figiel's narrative garland, as the stories of various young women within each main narrator's community are interwoven to create a multilayered whole. Figiel's 1999 novel *They Who Do Not Grieve* develops this technique even further by featuring two young female narrators who thread together the life stories of three generations of Samoan women (Keown 2005: 39–42).

At a syntactical level, the influence of oral storytelling techniques is also evident in the frequent repetition of particular words and phrases throughout Figiel's writing. A particularly vivid example of this technique is found in her short story, 'The Poet as a Girl':

She had the same dream over and over. Over and over she dreamt of the tribe fighting in her liver. Sticking poisonous fish into their enemy in her liver. Smashing their heads with stones and clubs in her liver. Swimming too in the pool of their blood in her liver . . . Into the mouths of sharks. IN HER LIVER.

(1995: 17)

Here, the repetition of particular phrases ('over and over' and 'in her liver'), and the use of alliteration and parallel grammatical constructions (with verbs such as 'sticking', 'smashing' and 'swimming' placed at the beginning of consecutive sentences), is redolent of the sound patterning found in oral narratives. Such constructions are clear evidence of Figiel's efforts to capture orality in print: she has pointed out that during the process of composition, she reads everything she writes aloud to ensure that it captures the rhythms of oral performance (Subramani 1996: 121).

Figiel's and Grace's techniques of incorporating oral literary patterns into their printed narratives can be situated within a more general resurgence of oral literary forms in Pacific literature produced since the decolonization period. As discussed in Chapter 4, since the emergence of the Hawaiʻian nationalist movement in the 1970s, for example, there has been a revitalization of 'traditional' Hawaiʻian oral performance genres (such as speechmaking, poetry, chant, and song), and literacy in Hawaiʻian has increased dramatically as a result. In Tonga, which has a long tradition of courtly poetry, the literary journal *Faikava* (issued during the late 1970s and early 1980s) reproduced a range of verse by Queen Salote (1900–65), the most famous of Tonga's poet-monarchs. In Fiji, the traditional genre of meke—dances accompanied by sung poetry—has been revived in the work of dramatist Jo Nacola and poet Pio Manoa, both of whom have translated ancient meke into English. More recently, musicians and dancers at the Oceania Centre (established at the University of the South Pacific in 1997) have experimented with composing new meke which combine traditional and modern instruments and gestures. Epeli Hau'ofa, Director of the Oceania Centre, has pointed out that these modern meke, like other artistic forms and genres produced at the Centre, have been composed not in order simply to replicate past traditions, but to combine these traditions with contemporary motifs and energies in order to 'free' ancestral spirits and 'invite' them into the modern world (Keown 2001: 77).

5.2.3 Polynesian 'Tall Tales': Epeli Hau'ofa's Tales of the Tikongs

Many oral traditions within the Pacific also include the genre of the 'tall tale': these are stories, featuring exaggerated and sometimes risqué plot scenarios, which are often rendered in colloquial language. As Subramani notes, 'tall-tale' elements have been incorporated into a wide range of post-1970s Pacific literature, evident (for example) in the drama of Jo Nacola, the novels of Albert Wendt, and the short stories of Epeli Hau'ofa. Hau'ofa's writing, particularly his short story collection *Tales of the Tikongs* (1983), has been described as 'serious comic writing' (Edmond 1990: 143), as it blends humour with social critique in order to pinpoint particular post-independence socio-economic problems in the Pacific. Hau'ofa draws specifically upon Tongan storytelling practices, which use the 'tall tale' as a medium through which to critique particular individuals and institutions. Because it is considered extremely rude to offer such criticisms directly, the satire is instead conveyed through comic allegorical tales that are shared in storytelling circles. Each individual in the group attempts to outdo the previous orator by infusing his or her narrative with increasingly exaggerated and ribald plot embellishments (Keown 2001: 73).

In *Tales of the Tikongs*, Tongan 'tall tale' conventions inflect both the structure and narrative style of the text. The allusive nature of 'tall-tale' satire, for example, is evident in the fact that Hau'ofa's tales are set on a fictional Pacific island (Tiko): this plot device allows Hau'ofa a certain freedom of movement in critiquing socio-economic problems throughout the post-independence Pacific. Further, as Rod Edmond notes, the tales are recounted by 'a deadpan narrator with an alter ego, Manu', who appears as a kind of ventriloquist's dummy, making direct criticisms and bald statements which contrast with the studied neutrality of the narrator (1990: 143). Several of the tales in the collection satirize hypocrisy and worldliness among Tiko's clergy, and where the narrator treads delicately around the subject, more direct criticisms are attributed to Manu, who is described as 'the only teller of big truths in the realm' (7). In 'The Winding Road to Heaven', for example, the boldest attack upon ecclesiastical corruption in the story is attributed to Manu ('as Manu says, not even the clergy are safe from Temptation' (10)), and it is Manu who offers the most trenchant criticisms of the various economic development initiatives described throughout the collection.

Although the comic strategies in Hau'ofa's fiction have been likened to Mikhail Bakhtin's notion of the carnivalesque (Edmond 1990; Griffen 1997*b*; Keown 2005), the relationship between Manu and the unnamed narrator is also redolent of Polynesian comic theatre traditions. In Polynesian societies, authority figures are accorded great respect and deference, and in Samoa for example, songs and comedy sketches known as fale aitu (which translates as 'house of spirits'), performed at community gatherings, are often the only outlet for public criticism of 'figures and institutions of authority' (Sinavaiana-Gabbard 1999: 184). As Caroline Sinavaiana-Gabbard explains, in fale aitu comic sketches, the lead comedian is customarily 'considered by the audience to be a ghost (aitu) while in character during the sketch, and it is the ghost who delivers the social or political criticism, relieving the actor of responsibility for these criticisms' (1999: 186). An analogous role is assumed by Manu in Hau'ofa's collection: he suddenly materializes at key moments in order to deliver blistering criticisms of various sociopolitical problems discussed in these narratives, thereby protecting the narrator (and the author, by association) from censure.

Many of the tales in the collection also blend elements of the tall tale formula with biblical parody: 'The Wages of Sin', for example, relays the misadventures of Ti Pilo Siminī, a chain smoker who tears a page from the Bible by mistake in order to roll a cigarette. Afterwards, Ti has a terrifying dream in which he is berated by Moses and Joshua, who explode a stick of dynamite in his mouth in punishment for his act of sacrilege. Ti then embarks on a series of disastrous attempts to atone for his sin, each attempt bringing him more terrifying dreams and more sticks of exploding dynamite, until Manu solves the problem by advising him to tear another leaf from the other side of his bible and smoke it in an 'equal and opposite sin' that will cancel out the first (41). With its series of escalating catastrophes and farcical events, the story follows a recognizable 'tall tale' formula, but like other stories in the collection, it is daringly irreverent in its representation of Christian doctrine, with Moses and Joshua represented as sadistic heavies who join forces with 'the entire Israeli Armed Forces' in their eagerness to punish Ti for his misdemeanours (39). Christianity is a firmly established and strictly observed institution in many nations of the Pacific, and Hauʻofa's subversive parodying of biblical discourse in this and other stories in the collection also, therefore, challenges one of the central institutions regulating Pacific social behaviour.

This irreverent approach to Christianity is also a feature of the writing of Albert Wendt, who has targeted elitism and hypocrisy among the Samoan clergy in his early fiction in particular. In early stories such as 'Pint Size Devil on a Thoroughbred' (1974), Wendt also draws upon the tall tale formula, recounting the story of a diminutive confidence trickster named Pili whose exploits have entered into folk legend within his local Samoan community. Significantly, Wendt dedicates *Flying Fox in a Freedom Tree* (the collection in which the story appears) to his grandmother Mele Tuaopepe, whom he describes as 'the greatest storyteller I have ever known'. The influence of Wendt's grandmother is evident in Wendt's incorporation of Samoan fagogo or 'yarning' narrative techniques into a wide range of his writing, while other Samoan performative traditions such as fale aitu and pese (popular song-making) are also referenced throughout his work (see Sharrad 2003: 21–2).

5.3 **Mythology and cultural memory**

5.3.1 *Gods and tricksters: Polynesian mythological figures in Pacific literature*

Pacific mythopoeic traditions are another important source of inspiration for Wendt and other Pacific writers. In establishing Pili's character in 'Pint Size Devil on a Thoroughbred', for example, Wendt draws specifically upon Polynesian mythology, basing his central character upon aspects of the pan-Polynesian trickster and demi-god Māui-Tikitiki-a-Taranga, and his Samoan counterpart, Pili. According to Māori legend, Māui was born deformed and was abandoned (presumed stillborn) by his mother Taranga, but he later went on to perform various heroic and subversive feats, including forcing the sun to slow its passage across the sky; fishing up the North Island of Aotearoa/New Zealand with his grandmother's magic jawbone; and bringing fire to humankind by persuading the fire-goddess Mahuika to relinquish her flaming fingernails. Māui is eventually killed when, in an attempt to achieve immortality, he crawls into the vagina of the sleeping death-goddess Hine-Nui-Te-Pō with the intention of emerging through her mouth. A bird (fantail) watching Māui's attempt bursts out laughing, waking the death goddess who crushes Māui with the teeth of obsidian within her vagina.

Like Māui, the Samoan demigod Pili is also a trickster and adventurer: according to one version of the myth, Pili, sired by the Supreme Creator Tagaloaalagi upon a mortal woman, Sina, was ejected from Tagaloaalagi's domain (the ninth heaven) due to his mischievous exploits, and he fell to earth in the form of a lizard. Pili convinced Tagaloaalagi to restore his human form on the satisfactory completion of three herculean tasks in which—unbeknown to Tagaloaalagi—he was assisted by three spirit companions, thereby achieving his objectives. Wendt became fascinated with the Māui and Pili myths during his early career, and in early novels such as *Sons for the Return Home* (1973) and *Leaves of the Banyan Tree* (1979), he fuses elements of Māui and Pili together to create an 'existential mythical Everyman', as Paul Sharrad puts it (2003: 63). Pili in 'Pint-Sized Devil on a Thoroughbred' bears a clear resemblance to the mythical Māui and Pili: he is '[b]orn a small bundle of barely live flesh' (1974: 42) and barely reaches five feet when he is fully grown, but he becomes an expert thief and confidence

trickster. Like his mythical counterparts, Pili is also a cunning oppor-
tunist, supplying the 'American G.I. hordes' with home-brew and
prostitutes during the Second World War (1974: 52). Other notable
Māui/Pili figures in Wendt's fiction include Tagata (literally, 'man'),
a dwarf who appears in the novella 'Flying Fox in a Freedom Tree'
(1974) and again in *Leaves of the Banyan Tree*, and Lemigao, a club-
footed (and light-fingered) illegitimate who appears in *Pouliuli* (1977),
a novel that also offers Wendt's most extended exploration of the Pili
myth. Notably, Wendt's early writing also blends aspects of the Māui
myth with elements of the absurdist philosophies of Albert Camus as
outlined in his existentialist manifesto *The Myth of Sisyphus* (1942),
which Wendt read as a student. Wendt identified connections between
Māui's ignominious death and the fate suffered by Sisyphus (eternally
condemned to push a rock up a mountain only to have it roll down
again), and a number of disaffected young male characters in Wendt's
early fiction are modelled upon the absurdist anti-heroes described in
Camus's philosophical tract (Keown 2002).

The Māui myth-cycle is also referenced by a range of Māori writers as
a means by which to reconcile Māori oral traditions with contemporary
literary narrative techniques. In *Potiki* (1986), for example, Patricia
Grace blends aspects of the Māui myth with elements of the life of Jesus
Christ in creating the character of Tokowaru-i-te-Marama, a young
disabled boy gifted with foresight. Several of Toko's experiences follow
Māui's, including his birth (he is deformed, like Māui); the episode
where he catches a 'big fish' (just as Māui 'fished up' the North Island);
and the circumstances of his death (the booby-trapped doorway in
which he perishes is described as 'the toothed aperture through which
all must pass' (183), a clear reference to Hine-Nui-Te-Pō's *vagina
dentata*). On the other hand, Toko's mother's name is Mary, and a
man called Joseph is named as his father, thereby linking him with
Christ. His ability to predict the future links him both with Christ
the prophet, and with Māui, who had the gift of matakite (foresight).
Like Wendt, Grace therefore blends Polynesian mythology with non-
Polynesian mythopoeic discourses, thus exploring the relevance of
Pacific oral traditions to contemporary sociopolitical realities.

In addition to referencing the Māui myth-cycle, *Potiki* also draws
upon the Māori creation myths, in particular the story of the separation
of Ranginui, the sky father, and Papatūānuku, the earth mother.
According to Māori mythology, Rangi and Papa were once locked

in a tight embrace that allowed their progeny no space in which to move or breathe. Rangi and Papa's children eventually succeeded in forcing them apart, however, and when rain falls, it is said to be the tears of Rangi, grieving over his separation from his beloved Papa. In Grace's narrative, husband and wife Roimata and Hemi are linked with Rangi and Papa: Roimata (whose name translates as 'tears') is described as a 'patient watcher of the skies' (Rangi's domain), while Hemi dedicates himself to working the land (the body of Papa) (Grace 1986: 159). Roimata and Hemi's links with their mythical counterparts appear to bring a balance to their community, aiding the journey towards self-sufficiency and strengthening the people's bonds with the mythical and ancestral past. A similar process takes place in Grace's 1998 novel *Baby No-Eyes*, which returns to the very beginning of Māori mythological time, positing te kore—the 'void' which existed before life began—as a metaphor for the process of artistic (including literary) creation (Keown 2005: 156).

Māori poet Hone Tuwhare also makes widespread use of Māori mythology in his work: his poem 'We, who live in darkness' (1982) describes the separation of Rangi and Papa from the perspective of one of their children (frustrated with perpetual 'wriggling and squirming in the swamp of night'), who urges his brothers, 'let us kill him—push him off' (1994: 158). Tuwhare's 1978 poem 'Papa-tu-a-nuku (Earth Mother)' interweaves Māori myth and contemporary politics, describing the Māori Land March of 1975 (discussed in Chapter 4) as a journey down the spine of Papatūānuku, who shivers with pleasure as the land march participants 'massage' her 'ricked back' with their tramping feet (1994: 126). In this short poem, Tuwhare succinctly conveys the spiritual significance of the land—the body of the earth mother—to the Māori people, grounding the political activism of the march participants in Māori cosmogony and thereby legitimizing their protests.

5.3.2 Female goddessess as feminist icons

In a variety of contemporary Pacific women's writing, female goddesses are invoked as legitimizing or galvanizing forces for female activism and independence. Sia Figiel, for example, frequently cites the powerful Samoan war goddess Nafanuā as a role model for young Samoan women battling against various forms of oppression and discrimination. American Samoan poet Caroline Sinavaiana-Gabbard, who spent much of her childhood in California, describes her first encounter with the legends of Nafanuā as a formative moment in which she discovered a meaningful alternative to familiar 'American' female role models such as Miss America, Marilyn Monroe, and 'the disneyesque Snow White' (2001: 22–3). She cites as a particular source of inspiration the myth in which Nafanuā defeats an army of invaders and restores stolen land to her people, assisted by an invisible horde of ancestors 'in the guise of dragonflies and cicadas' (2001: 23). Sinavaiana-Gabbard's mythopoeic poem 'Sā Nafanuā [the canoe-riding kin group of Nafanuā]', which has been republished in *Whetu Moana*, describes modern Samoan women as a 'band of warriors', Nafanuā's 'frisky daughters'. These contemporary warrior-women, like Nafanuā, are armed, but their arsenal takes the form of 'paintbrush & camera / laptop & lawbook', weapons that equip them for survival in the contemporary technocratic metropolitan world (Wendt *et al.* (eds.) 2003: 185).

In Hawai'ian mythology, Nafanuā has a comparable counterpart in the volcano-goddess Pele, renowned for her explosive temper and capacity for visiting terrible vengeance upon those who offend her. Hawai'ian poet Haunani-Kay Trask has referenced Pele in a range of her work, invoking her destructive power as a method by which to purge Hawai'i of 'the foreigner[s]' who have damaged the landscape and disenfranchised native Hawai'ians (2002: 8). Trask's invocation of Pele (and various other Hawai'ian gods and goddesses associated with the natural world) in this and many other of her poems suggests that although Hawai'ians are outnumbered by 'foreigners' and have lost much of their land, it is still possible to connect with and symbolically 'reclaim' those places through an awakened knowledge of the mythical past. In this respect, Trask's poetry shares much in common with the work of other Polynesian writers such as Henri Hiro (Tahiti), Sia Figiel (Samoa), and Hone Tuwhare (Aotearoa/New Zealand), all of whom celebrate the dominion of various Polynesian 'departmental' gods over the natural world. While these representations are generally respectful, occasionally one finds a more irreverent literary treatment of these deities. In John Kneubuhl's drama *A Play: A Play* (1997), for example, the goddess Pele appears as a liquor-guzzling, mischievous shape-shifter who manipulates helpless humans into committing various sexual indiscretions. Similarly, Richard Hamasaki's poem

'Kamapua'a had balls . . .' offers a playful exploration of the love-hate relationship between Pele and Kamapua'a, the Hawai'ian demigod and shape-shifter who often took the form of a pig (his name translates as 'pig-man'). The poem offers an ironic commentary on Kamapua'a's libidinous masculinity ('your balls contain your power'), making reference to the moment when he subdued and seduced Pele after extinguishing almost all of her volcanic fires with mud (2000: 38).

Within Aotearoa/New Zealand, a number of Māori women writers and poets have invoked Māori goddesses as a source of inspiration and empowerment for modern Māori women. Patricia Grace's referencing of various female mythical figures (such as Papatūānuku, Hine-Nui-Te-Pō, and Mahuika) in her novel *Potiki*, for example, was stimulated by her involvement (with the artist Robyn Kahukiwa) in producing *Wahine Toa* (1984), an illustrated guide to women in Māori mythology. In her poem 'Me aro koe ki te hā of Hineahuone' (anthologized in *Whetu Moana*), feminist poet Jacq Carter traces the 'strength' of contemporary Māori women back to powerful Māori mythical figures such as Hine-Nui-Te-Pō and Hineahuone (the first woman) (Wendt *et al.* (eds.) 2003: 41). In 2003, Māori feminist Ngahuia Te Awekotuku published *Ruahine*, a short story collection which presents new versions of traditional myths centred upon strong Māori mythic women. As Te Awekotuku explains, these stories were passed down to her by various close female relatives, and the collection celebrates 'the dignity and passion of Ruahine, the energy of being female' (2003: 141).

5.3.3 Revision and syncretism: the confluence of Indigenous and European mythologies in contemporary Pacific literature

The incorporation of Indigenous Pacific mythology into contemporary Pacific literature is clearly an important aspect of the dialogue between oral and written traditions in Pacific discourse, and as was the case with other traditional oral genres (as discussed above), it was a central feature of the developing corpus of Indigenous Pacific (written) literature which began to accumulate from the early 1970s. As Subramani points out, early issues of *Mana* and other literary magazines produced in the 1970s feature a 'proliferation' of myths and oral literature, both in the original vernaculars, and in English translation (1992: 34). Some recorders and translators have tried to remain 'faithful' to the original oral narratives, but many Pacific writers (such as Grace and Wendt) have experimented with synthesizing aspects of Pacific and Western mythologies and ontologies, exploring the syncretic nature of postcolonial subjectivities. Such techniques date back long before the 1970s, of course: as discussed in Chapter 2, Robert Louis Stevenson had experimented with blending Pacific and European myths and fictions in his 'South Seas' stories of the 1890s, and Albert Wendt has revealed that the stories his own grandmother told him during childhood blended Samoan mythology with aspects of Aesop's fables and the brothers Grimm's fairytales (Subramani 1992: 33). Syncretism is also evident in Pacific religious discourse: in parts of Vanuatu, for example, Tamakaia (the grandson of Māui) is identified with Jehovah (Subramani 1992: 33), and the Melanesian and Māori syncretic religions discussed in Chapters 2 and 3 blend aspects of Christian and Indigenous sacred doctrine. As Witi Ihimaera points out, while 'Westerners' often make a distinction between 'fictitious' myth and 'factual' history, in Māori culture myth *is* history, and in Māori and other Indigenous Pacific texts, myth is invoked as a means by which to assert land and other cultural rights through descent from the deities who created and still protect the natural world (Ihimaera 1991: 53–4). Yet Ihimaera, like other Pacific writers, also acknowledges that the flexibility of the oral mode means that myth as 'history' will change over time and vary between different individuals and social groups (Ihimaera 1991: 53–4). A further layer of complexity is added when one acknowledges that many Pacific 'traditional myths' were first recorded in print by Europeans, who themselves censored and manipulated oral literary material. Solomon Islander Rexford T. Orotaloa explores these dynamics in his story 'Raraifilu' (reprinted in Wendt's *Nuanua*), where the narrator tells of a ne'er-do-well uncle who attempts to lay sole claim to a plot of family land in order to collect royalties from a mining company. In court, the uncle recites a complex genealogy that apparently proves his claim through descent from ancestral spirits, but ironically, his claims are dismissed as they don't match with the 'official' family genealogy recorded by a European missionary in collaboration with a local man. While this story demonstrates the uncertain status of oral narratives in a textual age, other Pacific writers such as Dan Taulapapa McMullin and Sia Figiel have celebrated the transcendental qualities of Polynesian mythologies, creating new 'magic realist' narratives which adapt the mythical exploits of the ancestors to a postmodern present. Postmodernism, magic realism and other literary devices used in contemporary Pacific literature are discussed in further detail in Chapter 6, which focuses upon a range of developments in Pacific literature since the 1990s.

6

Conclusion: Pacific Diasporas

In ancient days navigators sent waka between.
Now, our speakers send us on waka. Their memories,
memory of people in us, invite, spirit,
compel us aboard, to home government, to centre:
Savai'i, Avaiki, Havaiki, Hawaiiki, from where we peopled
Kiwa's Great Sea.

(Robert Sullivan, *Star Waka*)

So, distance and travel are in my blood, in the genes. Polynesian
navigator DNA, plus a few strays from the European side . . . All
that sailing in the blood, all that moving in the family. Migratory
birds, circling the great water, looking for the other shore, a place
to land.

(Caroline Sinavaiana-Gabbard, *Alchemies of Distance*)

This chapter concludes our journey through the literatures of the contemporary Pacific. Resuming the chronological focus followed in Chapters 2, 3, and 4, the chapter outlines some of the most significant developments in Pacific writing since the 1990s and into the new millennium. The first section of the chapter (6.1) investigates the preoccupation with globalization and diaspora culture within contemporary Pacific literature and theory, selecting two major diasporic centres—Aotearoa/New Zealand and the United States—as case studies. The second part of the chapter (6.2) discusses a range of other theoretical and thematic developments in Pacific literature since the 1990s, while the final part of the chapter (6.3) explores key developments in Pacific theatre and film since the 1990s, closing with a short discussion of potential future developments in Pacific literary studies.

6.1 Globalization and Pacific diaspora culture

6.1.1 Globalization and diaspora culture: the theoretical context

Since the 1980s, diaspora has become a key focus issue in international postcolonial studies, reflecting an expanding interest in globalization, trans-national travel, and patterns of migration among (formerly) colonized peoples in the contemporary world. Postcolonial writers and theorists such as Homi Bhabha (1994), Abdul R. JanMohamed (1992), and Salman Rushdie (1988, 1991), for example, have explored the positive, intellectually liberating aspects of migration and the diasporic experience. Conversely, figures such as V. S. Naipaul (1969), Avtar Brah (1996), and Robin Cohen (1997) have drawn attention to the disorienting and disempowering aspects of migration for members of 'minority' or non-hegemonic cultures. Brah and Cohen—like other theorists such as Revathi Krishnaswamy (1995)—have also advocated an attentiveness to the particular socio-historical circumstances affecting different diasporic communities, rather than simply celebrating migrancy as an abstracted theoretical category. In exploring diasporic formations within Pacific literature, this section of the chapter aims to strike a balance between these various theoretical positions, remaining attentive to the distinctive patterns of migration and settlement within the Pacific region, while also exploring a range of issues that are putatively common to diasporic communities across the globe. As David Pearson points out, theorists generally agree that diasporic communities emerge though a process of 'multidirectional migration' and are characterized as follows:

> The diaspora's population must be dispersed from a homeland to two or more other territories; its presence abroad must be reasonably enduring, although permanent exile is not a necessity; and there must be some kind of (continuing) exchange—economic, political or cultural—between homeland and hosts. In short, if diasporic, journeys are multiple, transnational and recurrent.
>
> (2001: 69)

These features are common to a range of diasporic communities within the Pacific. Prior to the arrival of Europeans, the Pacific was already a vibrantly diasporic space, with successive waves of migration and island-hopping taking place across several centuries. Some of these journeys were short, but others involved travel over thousands of miles. It is now widely held that these journeys, rather than involving chance discoveries, were often carefully planned expeditions involving complex systems of navigation by stars, wind, and waves (Spickard 2002: 3). As we have seen, European colonial incursion into the Pacific gave rise to further forms and phases of migration among Pacific Islanders. Commercial trading networks prompted many islanders to leave their countries of birth throughout the nineteenth century: some were transported as far as North America in order to work in the whaling, fur, and timber industries, while others worked on colonial plantations throughout and beyond the Pacific. As discussed in Chapter 4, large numbers of Indians and other South Asians were also brought into the Pacific to work on European plantations, and many of their descendants remain in the region today.

The twentieth century saw several waves of Pacific Islander migration to three industrialized anglophone neighbouring countries: Aotearoa/New Zealand, Australia, and the United States. This process of out-migration accelerated after the Second World War, when there was a demand for manual labour during a time of industrial expansion. By this time, Western economic imperialism in the Pacific had made many island nations dependent upon their powerful neighbours for imports and financial aid, and many islanders went abroad for employment and education opportunities, sending money back to their home countries in order to keep their fragile economies afloat. The acronym MIRAB—conflating 'migration, remittances, aid, and bureaucracy'—was coined as a label for Pacific Island cultures characterized by these conditions, which continue today (Watters 1987; Goss and Lindquist 2000). Even by the mid-1980s, over 37 per cent of ethnic Polynesians were living outside their home countries, and in countries such as Niue, the Cook Islands, and Tokelau, the number of expatriates currently far exceeds those remaining at home (Hayes 1991: 3; Subramani 2003: 7).

Patterns of migration vary significantly between the three geo-cultural regions of the Pacific. The majority of Polynesian migrants originate from the Samoan archipelago, with Aotearoa/New Zealand and the US the main destinations. Large numbers of Polynesians have also emigrated to Australia, though exact numbers are difficult to determine as Australia does not particularize ethnicity on its census forms. Thousands of Micronesians emigrated to the US during the 1990s, when free entry was granted to citizens of the Federated States of Micronesia, Palau, the Republic of the Marshall Islands, and the Commonwealth of the Northern Mariana Islands. (The Chamorro of Guam already had free entry to the US by this time.) Melanesian migration has been largely internal (as Melanesians are generally denied free access to 'Western' nations), with increasing numbers of rural peoples settling in urban centres such as Port Moresby in Papua New Guinea (Fischer 2005a: 263–5).

6.1.2 Diaspora culture in Pacific literature, theory, and art

Inspired by these diasporic developments, and in response to the recent revival of traditional canoe-building and travel across the Pacific, imagery of Pacific voyaging has featured prominently in Pacific literature produced since the 1990s. Much of this activity has been concentrated within Polynesia: Cook Islander Tom Davis's novel *Vaka* [*Canoe*] (1992), for example, describes the history of the Polynesian voyaging canoe Takitumu over a period of three hundred years, while Māori poet Robert Sullivan's poetry collection *Star Waka* (1999) meditates upon various forms of travel by land and sea within Māori culture across the centuries. A selection of poems from Sullivan's collection is published in the anthology *Whetu Moana* (2003), the title of which translates as 'ocean of stars',[1] and in their editorial introduction, Wendt, Sullivan and Reina Whaitiri celebrate the Polynesian seafaring heritage after which the collection is named (2003: 1). As we have seen, a range of Pacific theory and literary criticism focused upon Pacific diaspora culture has also appeared in the last few decades, with Vijay Mishra's work on the Indo-Fijian diaspora, and Epeli Hau'ofa's theories on the 'Oceanic' heritage of Pacific Islanders, being two notable examples.

References to navigation and sea travel also appear frequently in the work of contemporary Pacific artists. A notable example is a work by Samoan artist Fatu Feu'u, who was commissioned to paint a large mural for the Aotea Centre in Auckland in 1990. Entitled 'Tautai Matagofie' ('The Wonderful Navigator'), the mural takes the form of a tableau celebrating the journeys of Pacific Island peoples to Aotearoa/New Zealand (see Figure 6.1). It draws upon iconography found in Polynesian art forms such as tapa (decorated barkcloth) and tatau (tattooing), featuring stylized motifs of the frigate bird and migratory schools of tuna fish, both of which were used as navigational aids by early Pacific voyagers (Vercoe 2002: 192). The inclusion of Rangitoto and the Manukau Heads in the background of the painting locates the end-point of the 'journey' within the coastal city of Auckland—the largest Polynesian city in the world—while the central panel, which features repeated motifs redolent of siapo or Samoan barkcloth patterns, draws attention to the successful transposition of Polynesian 'traditions' to the new land.

The importance accorded to seafaring and migration in Pacific literature, theory, and visual arts would suggest that, rather like the trans-Atlantic slave ship described in Paul Gilroy's *The Black Atlantic* (1993), the Polynesian waka/vaka, or the various sea-going vessels used throughout the Pacific over the centuries, could serve as key chronotopes of Pacific diaspora culture. Without careful contextualization, however, such formulations run the risk of reproducing abstract, 'celebratory' models of diaspora culture (as discussed above), rather than recognizing that some Pacific migration has taken place under imperialist coercion. Hau'ofa's influential 'oceanic' theories, for example, have been charged with bearing a 'superficial resemblance' to utopian models of postcolonial diaspora culture (Edmond and Smith 2003: 10), but it is also worth noting that Hau'ofa modulates his more abstract theoretical claims by acknowledging that some Pacific diasporic communities have been formed as a result of involuntary exile. In 'The Ocean in Us' (1998), for example, Hau'ofa discusses the forced evacuation of the Banaba and Bikini Islanders, the former to make way for phosphate mining operations in the early twentieth century, and the latter to expedite atomic tests by the US during the Cold War (397). Hau'ofa's essay also draws attention to the ways in which climate change threatens Pacific ecosystems, identifying the problems that rising sea levels pose to the inhabitants of low-lying Pacific island nations such as Tuvalu (400).

In addition to Hau'ofa, many other Pacific creative writers have also offered nuanced responses to the complexities of the diasporic experience, exploring the social pressures bearing upon migrant Pacific Islanders in 'Western' metropolitan centres. Below is an analysis of

Fig. 6.1 'Tautai Matagofie' ('The Wonderful Navigator'), by Fatu Feu'u (1990)

literary representations of diaspora in two major diasporic centres in the Pacific: Aotearoa/New Zealand, and the United States.

6.1.3 Pasifika diaspora culture in Aotearoa/New Zealand

As outlined above, large numbers of Pacific Islanders came to Aotearoa/New Zealand following the Second World War, and are now well-established as substantial 'minority' populations in metropolitan centres such as Auckland and Wellington. At the time of the 2001 Census, one in sixteen (or 231,801) people in Aotearoa/New Zealand were of Pacific Island ethnicity, with Polynesians making up the vast majority of those numbers (**www.stats.gov.nz**, accessed 14 March 2006). Half (115,017) of those registered as Pacific Islanders by ethnicity were Samoan, while the next largest groups (in descending order) were Cook Island Māori (52,569), Tongans (40,716), Niueans (20,148), Fijians (7,041), Tokelauans (6,204), and Tuvalu Islanders (1,965). The composition of these immigrant communities reflects New Zealand's status as a former colonial power in the Pacific: Western Samoa, the Cook Islands, Niue, and Tokelau were all New Zealand territories, while Tonga (like Fiji and Tuvalu) has had close administrative links with Aotearoa/New Zealand, particularly in the education sector.

Since the 1990s in particular, Samoans and other Pacific Island immigrant communities have made significant contributions to the creative arts within Aotearoa/New Zealand. While the 1970s and early 1980s were characterized by the politics of biculturalism which emerged in the wake of the Māori Renaissance, from the 1990s

Aotearoa/New Zealand has become increasingly multicultural, with increasing recognition and representation of Pacific Island and Asian immigrant communities in politics, media, and the arts. As mentioned above, Samoans represent the largest of Aotearoa/New Zealand's Pacific Island immigrant communities, and it is therefore not surprising that Samoans are the most prolific among the Pacific Island artistic communities in Aotearoa/New Zealand.

The work of Samoan writer Albert Wendt, who spent a considerable proportion of his childhood and adult life in Aotearoa/New Zealand, offers one of the most extended literary explorations of Samoan diaspora culture in Aotearoa/New Zealand. Born in Western Samoa in 1939, Wendt completed his secondary and tertiary education in Aotearoa/New Zealand, and while he spent his early career in Samoa and Fiji, he returned to New Zealand in 1988 to take up a professorship at Auckland University. In early novels such as *Sons for the Return Home* (1973) and *Leaves of the Banyan Tree* (1979), and in later works such as *Ola* (1991), 'Robocop in Long Bay' (2002), and *The Songmaker's Chair* (2004), Wendt has explored what sociologist Cluny Macpherson terms 'moral communities': networks of diasporic Samoans characterized by strong social integration and shared beliefs about morality and social behaviour. As Macpherson points out, these social formations have created intergenerational conflict within Samoan communities, where the children of Samoan migrants are often less committed to maintaining Samoan values and cultural practices than their parents and grandparents (1992; 1999). Wendt's narratives probe these tensions, exploring the ways in which young Samoans break free of the social restrictions imposed by their elders. *Sons for the*

Return Home, for example, features a Samoan university student who begins a relationship with a Pākehā girl against the wishes of his parents, who expect him to return 'home' and marry a Samoan woman after his graduation. Similar issues are taken up in 'Robocop in Long Bay', where an Auckland university student resorts to deceit in order to evade the constraints of his close-knit Samoan diasporic community.

Indo-Fijian scholar Subramani has described *Sons for the Return Home* as a 'classic text within the definitions of diaspora worked out by scholars' such as James Clifford: it addresses key themes such as 'expatriation, collective memory, dreams of ancestral home, visions of return, and self-definition in terms of a lost home' (Clifford 1994: 310; Subramani 2003: 7). In these respects, Wendt's novel is a forerunner of later New Zealand-based 'diasporic' novels such as Sia Figiel's *They Who Do Not Grieve* (1999), which explores the pressures faced by Samoan immigrants in New Zealand and the US, and John Pule's novels *The Shark that Ate the Sun* (1992) and *Burn My Head in Heaven* (1998), which centre upon the Niuean diasporic community in Auckland. Pule's novels share with Alan Duff's *Once Were Warriors* (1990) a focus on the social problems (such as poverty, domestic violence, and alcoholism) faced by working-class Polynesians in Aotearoa/New Zealand. In spite of—and partly because of—these hardships, Pule's characters maintain strong links with their ancestral homeland through exchanges of letters, family histories and legends, and financial remittances.

A significant epoch in the post-war history of Pacific Island immigration to Aotearoa/New Zealand were the 'dawn raids' of the late 1970s. High levels of immigration between 1971 and 1974 had prompted the New Zealand government to impose stricter immigration controls, and in 1976, a series of early-morning raids on Pacific Island residences took place in Auckland for the purposes of locating and subsequently deporting 'overstayers'. These included individuals whose work permits and visas had expired, as well as those who had arrived without permission to take up employment. Anxieties surrounding the pursuit of 'overstayers' by New Zealand immigration authorities have been explored in a wide range of creative work by Pacific Islanders, from the lyrics of hip hop artists such as King Kapisi, and dramatic texts by playwrights such as Oscar Kightley, to poems such as Vinepa Aiono's 'Adapting', included in Wendt's poetry anthology *Whetu Moana*. Kightley's plays 'Dawn Raids' (1997) and *Fresh off the Boat*

(1993/2005) engage with the racial discrimination suffered by Samoan and other Pacific Island immigrant communities during the raids of 1976, while Aiono's 'Adapting' takes the form of an impatient address by a New-Zealand based Samoan to a maladjusted uncle who has 'overstayed' after arriving from Samoa (Wendt *et al.* (eds.) 2003: 5).

While these texts explore the negative aspects of the immigrant experience in Aotearoa/New Zealand, other Pacific Island artistic production in New Zealand, particularly from the 1990s, records a qualified shift from alienation to a new sense of belonging. Albert Wendt's own writing has followed this trajectory: while his novels *Ola* (1991) and *Black Rainbow* (1992), and his short story 'Robocop in Long Bay' (2002), acknowledge the continuing social pressures faced by the Samoan diasporic community in Aotearoa/New Zealand, his play *The Songmaker's Chair* (2004) explores the way in which Samoans and other Polynesians, particularly those born in New Zealand, have increasingly laid claim to Aotearoa as 'home' through strengthening interrelationships with other ethnic groups. As Wendt argues in his introduction to *The Songmaker's Chair*:

Since I came to Aotearoa in 1952, I have observed and written poetry and fiction about the Samoan and Pacific migrant experience. This play is my latest attempt to encapsulate that, and celebrate the lives of those courageous migrant families who have made Auckland and Aotearoa their home . . .

> Why is it we've stayed this far?
> We think we've found a firm fit to this land.
> To our children and mokopuna [grandchildren] it's home.
>
> (2004: 2)

It is significant that Wendt uses a Māori word (mokopuna) here, acknowledging the ways in which Samoan culture has entered into meaningful dialogue with other Polynesian communities within Aotearoa/New Zealand. Māori writer Patricia Grace has also celebrated pan-Polynesian cultural affiliations, remarking in particular upon shared historical and mythological narratives:

Our stories all say that we came from Hawaiki.[2] So we have this history that links us. We call [other Polynesians] our older brothers and sisters to honour the fact that we came from them. Languages are similar. The stories are all similar.

(DeLoughrey and Hall 1999: 14)

The sense of pan-Polynesian solidarity Grace expresses here is central to *Whetu Moana* (2003), the anthology of Polynesian poetry edited by Albert Wendt, Robert Sullivan, and Reina Whaitiri. The collection includes the work of poets from Aotearoa/New Zealand, Hawai'i, Tonga, Samoa, the Cook Islands, Niue, and Rotuma, but the editors have deliberately arranged the poets by alphabetical order of surname rather than by country of origin. The editors argue that this structure 'juxtapose[s] the poetries of the Pacific' in order to generate multiple readings and thematic cross-currents (2003: 3), but it also signals the fact that the bloodlines of a number of these poets cross multiple national and cultural boundaries: many are of mixed Polynesian, Asian, and European descent.

In keeping with this genetic profile, several poets in the anthology engage directly with socio-cultural affiliations between different Polynesian communities within Aotearoa/New Zealand. In his poem 'Disgrace', Tim Pa'u, born in Aotearoa/New Zealand of Samoan and German descent, expresses a sense of political kinship with Māori (who, like Samoans, have experienced colonization by Pākehā New Zealanders). Pa'u advocates Samoan support for Māori 'rights' to self-determination, condemning the Pākehā betrayal of the terms of the Treaty of Waitangi, and paying tribute to Māori warrior-chief Hone Heke (who repeatedly felled the British flagpole at Waitangi during the 1840s in protest against treaty violations) and prophet Tahupotiki Wiremu Ratana (faith healer and founder of the Ratana religious and nationalist movement in the 1920s) (Wendt *et al.* (eds.) 2003: 155). 'Two-in-one', by Samoan poet Lemalu Tate Simi, expresses similar sentiments: the poem is dedicated to John Rangihau (a Tūhoe leader who advanced Māori welfare and cultural revival initiatives), and declares that Māori and Samoans are 'still one in Polynesia', united in their quest for self-determination (Wendt *et al.* (eds.) 2003: 179).

6.1.4 *Pacific diaspora culture in the US*

While much of the poetry in *Whetu Moana* is written by New Zealand-based Polynesians, also included is work by Polynesian poets living in the United States. As Paul Spickard notes, within the US mainland, Pacific Islanders, like other immigrants to the United States, have generally been absorbed within an 'assimilation model' whereby immigrants are expected to shed their 'ancestral identities' and assume an 'undifferentiated American identity' (2002: 9–11). Although certain pan-ethnic labels such as 'Latin American' and 'African American' are long-established in the US, Pacific Island writers and artists in the US have often been subsumed within other pan-ethnic categories. Work by Dan Taulapapa McMullin (of American Samoan descent) and Kiana Davenport (of Hawai'ian descent), for example, has appeared in anthologies of Asian American writing (McMullin 2000; Davenport 1993), while 'The Story of Susana' by Hawai'ian playwright Victoria Nalani Kneubuhl has been published in *An Anthology of Native American Plays* (D'Aponte (ed.) 1999).

There is evidence, however, that a new category of 'Pacific Islander American' is emerging in the mainland US. Further, there is now an established community of Pacific Island writers, artists, and musicians in California in particular, though Hawai'i remains the primary 'American' publishing centre for Pacific Islander Americans (Spickard 2002: 18; see Chapter 4). One of the most notable 'diasporic' writers to have published within Hawai'i is Caroline Sinavaiana-Gabbard, whose poetry and prose collection *Alchemies of Distance* (2001) reflects extensively upon her experiences as a diasporic American Samoan. In a series of autobiographical prose pieces, she describes her life as a succession of journeys: born in American Samoa, she grew up on a military base in Florida (where her father was stationed), later travelling back to American Samoa as a teacher and finally securing an academic position at the University of Hawai'i at Mānoa. She describes her life as characterized by 'distances, leave-takings and arrivals somewhere else', arguing that travelling is part of her genetic makeup, carried in her 'Polynesian navigator DNA' (13). While these statements imply a rather celebratory model of migration, Sinavaiana-Gabbard also acknowledges the social problems faced by members of the Samoan diaspora: in her prose piece 'Journey', she laments the fact that young Samoans in Honolulu, Los Angeles, Auckland, and Sydney are becoming increasingly involved in drugs, crime, and consumerism, 'washing down the colonial poison of self-hatred with Mountain Dew and Budweiser, self-medicating with stock options and Jerry Springer' (24). Exploring the negative potentialities of voyaging and exile, she argues that like many of the African slaves transported across the Middle Passage (between Africa and America), many 'modern day'

Samoans are being 'lost at sea' as they become increasingly distanced from their cultural heritage (24).

Other writers and poets such as Dan Taulapapa McMullin and Sia Figiel have explored a different form of ethnic alienation, referencing the way in which the American tourist industry conflates the various cultures of the Pacific into the archetypal image of the exoticized, hula-dancing Hawai'ian. In Figiel's novel *They Who Do Not Grieve* (1999), for example, a Samoan woman studying and working within the US is dubbed 'hula-girl' by her Dominican housemate (115), while McMullin's poem 'Untitled, to J. K. Kauanui' (2001*b*) describes various peoples of the Pacific who have been mistaken for, or have pretended to be, Hawai'ian. The speaker, who is Samoan, recalls being identified as Hawai'ian in Waikīkī, and reveals that his own brother 'used to tell women / he's Hawai'ian' as a pick-up line. Drawing upon the work of James Clifford, Teresia Teaiwa describes this process as 'a metonymic condensing of identities' whereby the Polynesian body—specifically the Hawai'ian body, in this case—becomes a sign which 'may be imposed on' (or appropriated by) various ethnic groups (1999: 255).

6.2 Pacific literary culture since 1990

While diaspora culture has formed a major focus in Pacific literature produced since the 1990s in particular, there are also many other important trends and developments evident in contemporary Pacific writing. It is not possible to discuss the full range of these developments here, so what follows is an overview of three significant trends in particular: the shift in focus from anticolonialism to post-independence corruption; from realism to postmodernism; and from phallocentrism to gender inclusiveness.

6.2.1 Anticolonialism and post-independence corruption in Pacific literature

Lali (1980), *Nuanua* (1995), and *Whetu Moana* (2003), the three anthologies of Pacific writing edited by Albert Wendt, offer a useful index of the ideological shifts that have taken place from the independence era to the new millennium. *Lali*, for example, emerged at a time when many Pacific Islands had already gained or were fast approaching independence, and much of the writing in this anthology is therefore overtly anticolonial and nationalistic. The essence of this dynamic is captured in 'Kros', a poem in the collection written by ni-Vanuatu writer Albert Leomala. Printed first in Bislama and then in English translation (under the title 'Cross'), the poem targets the crucifix as a synecdoche for the entire European colonial apparatus, and eagerly anticipates the eventual expulsion of the foreigner (120–1). The poem contains many of the features that Albert Wendt has located as central to the literature of the decolonizing period: it places the colonial and the Indigenous 'in irreconcilable opposition'; it sees 'no benefits' in colonialism or in 'fusions of the Indigenous and the foreign'; it offers a 'tragic, pessimistic vision' of the times; and it evinces a modernist 'search for originality and uniqueness' (Wendt (ed.) 1995a: 4). As Wendt points out, in its reliance upon realist and modernist modes and techniques, a large proportion of early Pacific literature shows the influence of the predominantly Eurocentric university education received by many first-generation Indigenous writers. As he also points out, however, some of this writing is equally inflected by the work of established 'postcolonial' writers such as V. S. Naipaul, George Lamming, Derek Walcott, Chinua Achebe, Wole Soyinka, Bessie Head, Ngugi, and Ayi Kwei Armah, who were beginning to appear on literature courses at Pacific universities during the 1970s (Wendt (ed.) 1995a: 4). Wendt's own early writing offers a good example of these processes at work: his novel *Leaves of the Banyan Tree* (1979), for example, describes a Samoan village in a state of cultural transition and crisis reminiscent of Chinua Achebe's *Things Fall Apart*, but it also draws upon the nihilist and existentialist philosophies found in the work of V. S. Naipaul, Fyodor Dostoevsky, and Albert Camus (Keown 2002).

By the time *Nuanua* was published in 1995, some fundamental shifts had taken place in the parameters of Pacific literature. In particular, the anticolonial stance taken in much earlier literature had transmuted into a closer focus on the internal sociopolitical problems that followed independence in many Pacific countries. As is the case in a variety of postcolonial literature from Africa and the Caribbean, the corruption of post-independence political and social élites has formed a particular satirical target in Pacific writing. Epeli Hau'ofa and Albert Wendt are two of the best-known exemplars of this phenomenon. As discussed in Chapter 5, Hauʻofa's *Tales of the Tikongs* (1983) and his novel *Kisses in the Nederends* (1987), for example, satirize worldliness, nepotism and fraud among the clergy and bureaucracy. Hauʻofa's texts are set on fictional Pacific Islands, allowing him to critique social problems which are shared by many post-independence Pacific nations. However, both texts also contain more specific allusions to Fiji and Tonga, where Hauʻofa has worked closely with political and academic élites over the years. Both narratives contain characters with Fijian names, and much of the satire in *Kisses*, as Hauʻofa himself points out, is directed at certain academics and ideologues—many based at USP—who supported the 'Pacific Way' ideology (discussed in Chapter 4) in the pre-coup years (Keown 2001: 74).

Much of Wendt's fiction and poetry also satirizes corruption among political and religious figures, particularly within Samoan society. In a manner reminiscent of the work of West African writers of the 1960s and 1970s (such as Ayi Kwei Armah, Chinua Achebe, Ama Ata Aidoo, Wole Soyinka, and Kofi Awoonor), much of Wendt's writing represents obesity or bodily dysfunction as metaphors for political corruption and the excesses of conspicuous consumption (Innes 1995: 1; Keown 2005: 28–34). Images of corpulent and corrupt politicians appear in his poetry collection *Inside Us the Dead* (1976*b*) and his novel *Leaves of the Banyan Tree* (1979), while in his novel *Pouliuli* (1977), a powerful elderly matai (titled leader) delegates his authority after becoming disgusted with the corrupt scheming of Samoan political and religious leaders. In Wendt's 1992 novel *Black Rainbow*, conspicuous consumption and obesity are linked with the colonial exploitation of Aotearoa/New Zealand's Indigenous Māori people (Keown 2005: 31–6).

Wendt's attitude towards post-independence Pacific élites is shared by other Pacific writers represented in the *Nuanua* anthology. 'Neo-Colonialism', by ni-Vanuatu poet Grace Molisa, attacks 'civil servants/and weak politicians' who allow foreign economic powers to continue dominating Vanuatu's economy (Wendt (ed.) 1995*a*: 391–2), and Molisa's compatriot Sampson Ngwele similarly condemns the self-indulgence of ni-Vanuatu bureaucrats in his poem 'Peripheral Politicians' (395). In his poem 'Freedom Day', Wendt's compatriot Ruperake Petaia satirizes the Samoan 'Big Men' and 'so-called liberators' who boast of heralding in a 'Freedom' which remains, in reality, 'Unreachable' (277–9).

6.2.2 Realism and postmodernism in Pacific literature

Wendt's fiction, in particular, also exemplifies a central fin-de-siècle development in Pacific literature: the increasing experimentation with postmodernist literary modes such as magic realism, pastiche, parody, and metafiction. Wendt has used these techniques throughout his literary career: his 1974 novella 'Flying Fox in a Freedom Tree' (later incorporated into the middle section of *Leaves of the Banyan Tree*) contains metafictional elements, and his own Masters thesis on the Samoan Mau movement (see Chapter 3) ends with a dialogue between Wendt and an imaginary alter ego (who claims to be his 'conscience') about the legitimacy of claims to truth and objectivity in the interpretation of history. While these kinds of postmodernist literary conceits are evident throughout Wendt's oeuvre, they become increasingly dominant in works produced from the 1990s. Notable examples include *Black Rainbow* (1992), a futuristic dystopian novel in which New Zealand citizens are programmed with state-simulated identities, and *Ola* (1991), a flagrantly metafictional novel in which the male narrator 'writes' a biography of a Samoan woman based largely on an assemblage of her personal documents left on his doorstep. The narrative takes the form of a series of 'biographical' fragments interspersed with snippets of conversation, aphorisms, poems, and rhetorical questions. This 'discontinuous narrative' technique is also favoured by Wendt's compatriot Sia Figiel, who frequently mixes poetry and prose, and switches between realist and 'magic realist' modes, in her fiction.

Wendt has suggested that the emergence of postmodernist literary techniques in Pacific literature can be attributed in part to the influence of 'international' writers such as Jorge Luis Borges, Gabriel Garcia Márquez, Italo Calvino, and Umberto Eco, but he also argues that many so-called 'postmodernist' techniques can be traced back to pre-colonial Pacific oral, artistic, and philosophical traditions (1995a: 4–5; Ellis 1994). He claims, for example, that narrative features such as digression, metafiction, and pastiche as deployed in novels such as *Ola* and *Black Rainbow* are not borrowed from Western postmodernist fiction, but are instead characteristic of Samoan fagogo and other Pacific storytelling traditions, which contain a 'rich mix of fantasy, parody, pastiche, poetry' (Ellis 1997: 84; 89). Again, Sia Figiel's writing also contains a variety of these modes and techniques: her narratives intersperse realist scenes of domestic violence with fantasy sequences in which her young female characters interact with spirits, forest creatures, and deities (such as Taema and Tilafaiga, the mythical Siamese girl-twins who putatively introduced the art of tattooing to Samoa) (Figiel 1999: 43). Critics of postcolonial literature often describe this blending of 'mythical' and 'realist' elements as 'magic realism'—a term first applied to Latin American literature in the 1950s—but as Wendt has observed, this technique is also central to Indigenous Pacific oral traditions.

As we have seen, the blurring of the boundaries between 'realism' and 'fantasy' has also been a common feature of Māori literature in English. In terms comparable to Wendt's analysis of oral storytelling in the Pacific, Witi Ihimaera has argued that Māori historiography and storytelling have been influenced by the 'frameworks of the unreal as well as the real' since precolonial times (1991: 53–4). Such an analysis is in keeping with a major strand of Ihimaera's own writing, from early stories such as 'The Greenstone Patu' (1977), where a hand-held weapon comes to life in order to resolve a family dispute, and 'The Makutu on Mrs Jones' (1972), where an elderly tohunga gains control over the mind of a feisty postmistress by casting a spell over her handkerchief, to later works such as The Dream Swimmer (1997), where the protagonist's mother is able to travel in time and space while sleeping. Patricia Grace's writing also includes 'magic realist' elements: novels such as Potiki and Cousins contain post-death narration, and in Baby No-Eyes (1998)—which resonates with Toni Morrison's gothic novel Beloved (1987)—the spirit of a deceased child returns to trouble a living relative.

While the events described in these narratives are consistent with beliefs in animism and the existence of kēhua (ghosts) in Māori culture, their presence has caused some disquiet among non-Māori critics, who have questioned the extent to which Polynesian representations of 'the supernatural' are appropriate to textual forms derived from a 'western literary tradition' (Arvidson 1991: 121; Pearson 1982). In response to such reservations, Wendt has always argued that notions of cultural 'purity' are spurious, and that writers and critics should celebrate cultural syncreticity rather than becoming preoccupied with notions of cultural 'origins' and 'authenticity' (1976a; 1983). Wendt's arguments may seem particularly apposite in a postmodern critical context where fundamentalist notions of 'truth', 'value', and 'tradition' are frequently destabilized. However, other Pacific theorists such as Subramani have expressed concerns about the viability of postmodernism in a postcolonial context:

> Postmodernism, as the expression of late capitalism, in which the movement is away from meaning, a style that is inclined toward the pleasures of form, the playful, and the pastiche, that talks endlessly about the 'death of man' and the 'end of history' has little utility in postcolonial societies, where the real problem is the threat by transnational capital and its capacity to destroy all previously accepted values.
>
> (2003: 8)

In spite of his scepticism about the relevance of postmodernist poetics to postcolonial literature, Subramani nevertheless acknowledges that Pacific writers such as Sia Figiel, John Pule, Sudesh Mishra, and Teresia Teaiwa are able to engage with postmodernism while remaining 'aware of its reactionary politics and its indifference to local struggles' (2003: 8). Such a caveat could also be applied to Wendt's work, particularly *Black Rainbow*, where many of the 'postmodernist' aspects of the novel also function as colonial allegory, interweaving artifice and postmodern 'play' with 'serious' politico-cultural critique. For example, the process of 'reordinarinisation' (citizen identity programming) described in the novel is conceptualized as a latter-day colonial assimilation policy which serves to disavow cultural difference and to obscure the historical and continuing dispossession of the Indigenous Māori people (see Keown 2005: 32). Several of the poets included in *Whetu Moana* similarly blend postmodernist experimentation with political commentary. Poems by Audrey Brown (of Cook Island Māori and Samoan descent) offer disjointed sentence fragments, abbreviations, and font shifts redolent of postmodern cyber-culture, but they also index cross-cultural tensions in contemporary New Zealand society. Her poem 'o'er dose on the self-indulgence of self-importance', for example, questions the viability of government policy requiring Māori employees to speak the Māori language, criticizing the way in which important government decisions are often made on the basis of recommendations by self-important 'aka-dem-ick[s]' who produce narrow(-minded) definitions of ethnicity (Wendt *et al.* (eds.) 2003: 22–3). In her poem 'Tropical Fantasia', Samoan writer Emma Kruse Va'ai presents a playful pastiche of European children's tales such as Cinderella and Rapunzel situated within a Samoan landscape, but the poem also contains more pointed observations on the damaging effects of Western consumer capitalism and popular culture within the Pacific Islands.

While these and many other poets in *Whetu Moana* combine an exploration of contemporary cultural issues with postmodern play, others adhere to the realist mode in their engagement with social problems such as unemployment and domestic violence. Many of the women poets in the anthology (including Kathy Banggo, Jacq Carter, Hinewirangi Kohu, Roma Potiki, and Caroline Sinavaiana-Gabbard) explore male violence against women and celebrate female solidarity, reflecting a significant increase in the number of Pacific women writers documenting women's's issues since the 1990s. Gender and sexuality are the final issues to be discussed in this section of the chapter.

6.2.3 The politics of gender and sexuality in Pacific literature

In structural terms, international postcolonial debates have drawn upon and intersected closely with debates on gender, and particularly feminist theory, which typically investigates and contests the marginalized position of women under patriarchy. As Ashcroft *et al.* point out, 'both patriarchy and imperialism can be seen to exert analogous forms of domination over those they render subordinate. Hence the experiences of women in patriarchy and those of colonized subjects can be paralleled in a number of respects, and both feminist and post-colonial politics oppose such dominance' (1998: 101). These homologies have informed various theorizations of the position of both 'third world' and 'first world' women in colonial contexts. Analyses of so-called 'third world' women have often focused on their 'double marginalization' both under colonialism and under patriarchy within their own societies, while studies of 'first world' settler women have investigated the degree to which their own complicity in the colonial endeavour is complicated (or even compromised) by their own marginalization under patriarchy (Petersen and Rutherford 1986; H. Tiffin 1997; McLeod 2000). During the 1980s, however, a number of 'third world' feminist critics (such as Hazel Carby, Chandra Talpade Mohanty, and Gayatri Spivak) began to question the foundations of Western feminism and its relevance to the experiences of 'third world' women. These critics argued that Western feminism was operating from a Eurocentric bias, in some cases ignoring the experiences of 'third world' women altogether, and in others constructing 'third world' women as an undifferentiated mass victimized by putatively 'backward' social practices. Gayatri Chakravorty Spivak, perhaps the most influential postcolonial feminist, has raised important questions about the ideological positioning of the feminist critic, who must be aware of the potential disparities between his or her own cultural, institutional, and class background, and those of the women under discussion. Spivak argues that the feminist theorist must learn to speak 'to' rather than 'for' these women in order to circumvent the homogenizing imperatives of what she calls a 'UN-style universalist feminism' that represents 'third world' women as a victimized 'collectivity' (1999: 361).

These international debates on gender and ethnicity have had a clear impact on analyses of the position of Indigenous women in Pacific literature and scholarship. The rise of feminist political movements in the 1960s and 1970s coincided with the process of decolonization in several Pacific nations, and many 'first-generation' Pacific women writers—such as ni-Vanuatu poet Grace Mera Molisa—became closely involved with initiatives designed to increase the involvement of Pacific women in post-independence political and public life. Molisa's poetry collections *Black Stone* (1983) and *Black Stone II* (1989) contain a number of critical reflections on the disempowerment of ni-Vanuatu women after marriage, while her poem 'Ni-Vanuatu Women in Development' (1987), reprinted in *Nuanua*, takes the form of a statistical table revealing the disparity in the numbers of men and women involved in politics and other professions (Wendt (ed.) 1995a: 394). Other 'first-generation' Pacific women writers include Konai Helu Thaman of Tonga, Jully Makini (née Sipolo) of the Solomon Islands, and Momoe Von Reiche of Samoa. In poems such as 'You, the Choice of My Parents' (1974) and 'Pacific Woman' (1987), Thaman is critical of the way in which some Pacific Island women lose agency after marriage (Wendt (ed.) 1980: 238; Jones *et al.* (eds.) 2000: 122), while her poem 'Women's Lib' (1974) offers an ambivalent response to the feminist movement, appearing to resist the notion that formerly colonized women can 'liberate' themselves simply by rejecting Western or 'modern' values and commodities and returning to 'traditional' ways of life (1999: 131). Makini and Von Reiche have critiqued the way in which Western ideals of female beauty have adversely affected the sexual aspirations of Pacific Islanders: Makini's well-known poem 'Civilised Girl' (1981) targets the observance of Western beauty trends as a product of a misplaced aspiration to so-called 'Civilization', while Von Reiche's poem 'My Guest' (1979) is written from the point of view of an overworked housewife observing a 'bottle beauty' beguiling her husband (Wendt (ed.) 1995a: 341; 299).

Although the women poets discussed above—along with writers such as Vanessa Griffen and Prem Banfal of Fiji—have made important and ongoing contributions to debates on gender in the Pacific, as late as 1999, feminist scholars Selina Tusitala Marsh (of Samoan descent) and Teresia Teaiwa (of Banaban, I-Kiribati, and African-American descent) were arguing that contemporary Indigenous Pacific literature and academic scholarship remained 'male-dominated' (Marsh 1999: 343; Teaiwa 1999: 257). In their respective essays on this subject, Teaiwa and Marsh both attempt to address the shortfall in feminist Pacific literary scholarship, Teaiwa by undertaking a feminist reading of Paul Gauguin's *Noa Noa* and Epeli Hau'ofa's *Kisses in the Nederends*, and Marsh by advocating a Pacific feminism based on local concepts rather than international theoretical models. Marsh's essay thus identifies some of the universalizing tendencies of 'Western' feminisms as critiqued by 'international' feminist scholars such as Mohanty, Spivak, and Sara Suleri, but she also argues that Pacific women's experiences have been overlooked by *Indigenous* Pacific writers and theorists such as Albert Wendt (Marsh 1999: 343).

Marsh's views are shared by Samoan writer Sia Figiel, who produced a series of publications focused upon Samoan girls and women in the late 1990s in order to address what she viewed as a lack of attention to female experience in Pacific writing (Subramani 1996: 130). Her novels *Where We Once Belonged* (1996a) and *They Who Do Not Grieve* (1999), and her novella *The Girl in the Moon Circle* (1996b), contain adolescent and teenage narrators whose naive perspectives alternate with those of a more mature, unnamed narrative voice, allowing Figiel to explore the 'coming of age' of Samoan women from various points of view (Keown 2005: 38–60). As Samoan scholar Annemarie Tupuola points out, fa'a Samoa values forbid young women from rebelling against established codes of conduct and from speaking or writing publicly on 'topics relating to the human body and sexuality' (2000: 64), and Figiel's bold engagement with controversial social issues such as domestic violence, extra-marital sex, and suicide have earned her criticism from a number of compatriots, including women (Holt 1997: 48). Figiel's interest in female histories and genealogies links her with other Pacific feminists such as Hawai'ian playwright Victoria Nalani Kneubuhl, whose 1988 play *The Conversion of Ka'ahumanu* (2002) explores the role of Ka'ahumanu (c. 1768–1832), wife of Hawai'i's first monarch King Kamehameha I, in the pivotal historical context of the 1820s (when Christian missionaries first gained a foothold in Hawai'i).

Māori feminism and Māori women's literature in Aotearoa/New Zealand has also developed in new directions during the 1990s. Māori feminists such as Donna Awatere—author of the controversial nationalist text *Maori Sovereignty* (1984)—have published a range of polemical writing in the wake of the feminist and Māori Renaissance movements of the 1970s, but the 1990s witnessed a more intense focus on lesbian identity politics. In 1989, writer and feminist scholar Ngahuia Te Awekotuku published her début short story collection *Tahuri*, the first fictional text to engage in detail with lesbian Māori sexuality. Many of the stories in the collection—which draw upon Te Awekotuku's own childhood experiences—are written from the point of view of Tahuri, an adolescent Māori girl who becomes gradually aware of her lesbian identity. As critics Aorewa McLeod and Nina Nola point out, Te Awekotuku's collection is notable for its representation of lesbianism as an established and 'accepted' sexual orientation in Māori culture (1998: 16). Although the final story in the collection (entitled 'Red Jersey') describes the homophobic beating of a lesbian teenager (Whero), many of the other stories witness Tahuri's affirming encounters with other (Māori) lesbians. In her own discussion of *Tahuri*, Te Awekotuku points out that Māori lesbians and gay men belong to an established 'Polynesian tradition' of same-sex relationships: 'We are the inheritors...of the *māhu* of Hawaii, Tahiti, the Cook Islands, the Marquesas, of the *fa'afafine* of Samoa, of the *fakaleiti* of Tonga' (1992: 288). Te Awekotuku is here referring to a widespread Polynesian custom whereby male children (especially in families without female children) are dressed as females, undertake female domestic tasks, and often continue living as women in adulthood. Te Awekotuku argues that while there are no Māori equivalents of terms such as māhu and fa'afafine (though some Māori now use the term 'takatāpui' in this context), Māori culture has its own model of cross-gendering in the famous legend of Hinemoa and Tutanekai, one version of which contends that Hinemoa (a high-born woman from the Te Arawa tribe of Rotorua) masqueraded as a man in order to seduce the male warrior Tutanekai, who favoured a male 'intimate friend' named Tiki (1992: 288). In *Ruahine* (2003), her collection of short-story 'retellings' of mythological narratives focused on powerful Māori women, Te Awekotuku includes a new version of the Hinemoa-Tutanekai story which endorses this version of events: when Hinemoa and Tutanekai first meet, Tiki tries to head off Hinemoa's advances towards Tutanekai by placing a proprietorial hand upon his lover's thigh (109).

Te Awekotuku's exploration of same-sex attraction as a well-established (though often misunderstood) aspect of Māori society stands in stark contrast to Witi Ihimaera's fictional representations of Māori gay and lesbian relationships in his 2000 novel *The Uncle's Story*. The novel explores in detail the prejudice against homosexuality (and lesbianism) as a perceived threat to the continuation of family whakapapa (genealogies) in Māori society. In a similar vein, Samoan-American writer and artist Dan Taulapapa McMullin has written of the difficulties he has faced as a gay man in Samoan culture, which has a long-established fa'afafine tradition, but appears less accommodating of homosexuals who choose not to assume a feminine persona (1999: 120–1). McMullin's poetry collection *A Drag Queen Named Pipi* (2004) contains a number of poems exploring gay and fa'afafine sexual relationships, including his renowned performance poem 'The Bat', which is also published in *Whetu Moana*. His short story 'Sunday' (2001*a*) playfully satirizes Western fantasies about sexually uninhibited Polynesians, focusing on a Samoan seminary student in Minnesota who piously resists homosexual advances from a predatory white Reverend, but then succumbs to the charms of a well-built assistant pastor. McMullin's engagement with fa'afafine and gay sexualities resonates with the work of a range of dancers, fashion designers, and playwrights within Aotearoa/New Zealand, which has a vibrant urban fa'afafine community (Taouma 2002: 144).[3] A more detailed discussion of cross-gendering and sexuality in Pasifika theatre is included in the final section of this chapter, which engages with post-1990 developments in Indigenous Pacific drama and film.

6.3 Contemporary developments: drama and film

Drama and film are two of the most significant areas of expansion in the Pacific creative arts since the 1990s. Indigenous peoples have been involved in theatrical and media production since the emergence (and resurgence) of Pacific literature and other creative arts in the 1970s, but due to the relative lack of funding and other resources for Indigenous film-makers, activity in this area has been fairly limited, with only a small number of feature films produced since the 1980s. In comparison to film, drama has flourished, with major theatrical movements developing in various parts of the Pacific. Drama is discussed immediately below, while film is discussed at the end of the chapter.

6.3.1 Drama in the Pacific

Drama has formed a major strand in Indigenous Pacific literature produced since the 1970s, and as discussed in Chapter 4, countries such as Papua New Guinea and Fiji have well-established theatrical traditions, although many Papua New Guinean plays, for example—which are often improvised and performed in local languages—remain unpublished. This section of the chapter discusses three major focal points in Pacific theatre that have not been discussed elsewhere in this book: Māori theatre; 'Pasifika' theatre within Aotearoa/New Zealand; and representations of gender, sexuality, and the body in a range of contemporary Pacific drama.

Māori theatre Māori drama, like other genres of Māori 'literature' in English, began to gather momentum in the wake of the Māori Renaissance of the 1970s. Māori plays of the 1970s—such as Harry Dansey's *Te Raukura* (1974) and Rowley Habib's *Death of the Land*[4] (inspired by the Māori land march of 1975)—frequently engaged directly with colonial injustices against Māori, particularly the expropriation of land, and as Māori playwright Hone Kouka points out, these plays were 'easily pigeonholed as the political, the worthy or the spiritual' (1999: 9). As was the case with Māori fiction in English, however, Māori theatre of the late 1980s began to focus more specifically on contemporary urban Māori life: Riwia Brown's 1988 play *Roimata*, which centred on a young Māori woman's move to the city, marked this transition. Brown was the scriptwriter for the film version of Duff's *Once Were Warriors*, and there are clear points of intersection between the two works, particularly in their exploration of the psychological and physical abuse of Māori women.

The main locus of Māori theatrical activity has been the city of Wellington, and in particular the Depot theatre (established in 1983), now known as Taki Rua.[5] In the 1980s, Taki Rua theatre practitioners Jim Moriarty and Rangimoana Taylor developed the highly influential concept of 'marae theatre' (also known as 'theatre marae'). Pre-European Māori culture had its own performance traditions centred upon the whare tapere (house of entertainment),[6] but the 'marae theatre' concept is based specifically on the premise that various aspects of Māori marae ritual *per se* are highly theatrical and can therefore be incorporated into contemporary dramatic performances. The word 'marae' is often used to refer to the entire complex of buildings (meeting/sleeping house, kitchen/dining hall, ablution block, and other outbuildings) that forms the core of a 'traditional' Māori community, but it is also used more specifically to refer to the marae atea, the sacred ground in front of the wharenui (meeting house) upon which particular rituals are performed. 'Marae theatre' therefore conceptualizes theatrical space as comparable to the marae atea.

Some of the key elements of a hui (ceremonial gathering) on the marae include an exchange of calls (karanga) between women who represent the tangata whenua (hosts) and the manuhiri (visitors coming onto the marae); a pōwhiri (welcome); a sequence of formal greetings (mihi), speeches (whaikōrero), songs (waiata), and prayers (karakia) given by selected members of the respective parties; tūtakitanga (a physical welcome in which hosts and visitors shake hands (hariru) and press noses (hongi)); and the taking of refreshments (kai), after which further discussions may take place within the meeting house (wharenui) (Tauroa and Tauroa 1986). The wharenui (literally, 'big house'), also known in many cases as the whare whakairo (carved house) or whare tupuna (ancestral house), is commonly conceptualized as the body of an important ancestor of the tribe, and poupou (carved images of various other ancestors) frequently line the internal walls of the building. On entering the meeting house, the individual therefore enters the body of the ancestor: the carved figure (kōruru) on the roof top at the front of the building represents the head; the bargeboards (maihi) which curve from the head towards the ground represent the arms, the central post (tāhū) running along the roof from front to back is the spine, and the rafters (heke) which connect to the carved ancestors (poupou) are conceptualized as the ribs (see Figure 6.2). Māori writers such as Witi Ihimaera, Patricia Grace, and Alan Duff have acknowledged the importance of the whare whakairo as a storehouse of tribal history and artistic expression,[7] and Grace in particular has used the construction of the whare whakairo as a metaphor for the role of the Māori writer, who represents his or her culture through literary narrative 'construction' (see Melbourne 1991; Keown 1998; Arvidson 1992).

Many 'marae theatre' performances since the late 1980s have also acknowledged the symbolic importance of the whare whakairo by incorporating marae ritual and spatial dynamics into the dramatic process. During the 1990 International Festival of the Arts in Wellington, for example, the Depot foyer and theatre was consecrated as a marae (with the theatre as wharenui), and members of the audience were welcomed with a pōwhiri and a karanga, and were then asked to remove their shoes (as they would upon visiting the whare whakairo) before entering the performance space. Karakia and whaikōrero were central aspects of each performance, with the audience invited to respond to the actors and the play, again reproducing marae protocol (Kouka 1999: 16). As Helen Gilbert observes, marae theatre 'thereby alters the status of the audience from the Western theatrical norm of unacknowledged and silent observers who judge the performance, to that of participants in a ritual, collective experience' (2001: 348; see also Balme 1999).

In addition to using marae ceremonies to 'frame' Māori theatrical productions, a number of playwrights have also incorporated aspects of marae ritual into the dramatic substance of their works. Dunedin-based Māori dramatist John Broughton, for example, has written two plays—*Te Hokinga Mai/The Return Home* (1988) and *Marae* (1992)—which centre specifically upon the marae and its rituals. *Te Hokinga Mai* was performed in front of Mataatua, the wharenui housed within the Otago Museum (Dunedin), and the wharenui and marae atea are central both to the stage 'set' and to the play's action, which involves the performance of various marae rituals. Similarly, Broughton's *Marae*, first performed during the 1992 Wellington International Festival of the Arts, took the form of a hui, and included a formal Māori welcome to both cast and audience as they arrived

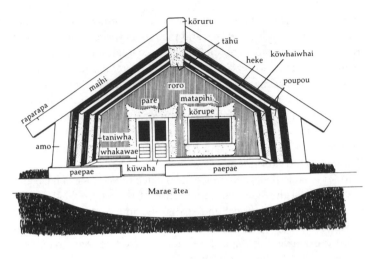

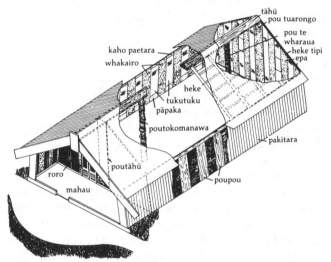

Fig. 6.2 The whare whakairo (carved meeting house): Tānenuiarangi

at Waiwhetu, the temporary marae at which the play was performed (McNaughton 1998: 381). Hone Kouka has also adopted marae theatre conventions in his 1994 play *Ngā Tāngata Toa* (discussed in Chapter 3), which includes a pōwhiri scene and whaikōrero.

Kouka is one of the most prominent of a new generation of Māori playwrights who emerged in the 1990s. *Ngā Tāngata Toa* was followed two years later by his highly successful play *Waiora* (1996), which returns to the mid-1960s when many Māori were leaving their ancestral land in search of opportunities within the urban centres. As Kouka himself points out, the play is an 'immigrant's story' which has relevance both to Māori and non-Māori New Zealanders, thus connecting narratives of Māori migration (from Hawaiki to Aotearoa/New Zealand, and then from the rural lands to the cities) with the wider preoccupation with diaspora culture within Pacific literature of the 1990s (1997: 8). Kouka's *Waiora*, along with a number of other Māori plays of the 1990s, has been published by Huia, a Wellington-based organization (founded in 1991) which is specifically dedicated to fostering and disseminating Māori and Pacific Island literature. Among Huia's dramatic titles is Briar Grace-Smith's *Ngā Pou Wāhine* (1995/1997), which has been reprinted in Helen Gilbert's anthology *Postcolonial Plays* (2001). Grace-Smith's play, which enacts the cultural awakening of a young Māori woman, incorporates aspects of marae theatre, beginning with a karanga and including poupou (carved ancestral panels) as a central element of the set. Where *Ngā Pou Wāhine* indexes the Māori art of wood carving, *Purapurawhetū* (1997/1999), another of Grace-Smith's plays, uses the weaving of tukutuku panels—another artistic form traditionally displayed within the wharenui—as a central conceit.

Another landmark publication in the Huia series is Witi Ihimaera's *Woman Far Walking* (2000b), a play in which 160 years of colonial history are embodied in the figure of Te Tiriti o Waitangi Mahana, a woman born in the year of the Treaty signing (after which she is named). Like Ihimaera's historiographical novels *The Matriarch* (1986) and *The Dream Swimmer* (1997), the play explores key phases in Māori history such as Te Kooti's guerilla campaign against the Pākehā in the 1890s, the 1918 'Spanish' influenza pandemic (which killed disproportionate numbers of Māori), and the 1981 Springbok rugby tour of New Zealand (which many Māori opposed due to South Africa's apartheid policy). As Ihimaera himself points out, the drama records 'the survival, struggles and resilience of the Māori people' since the colonization of Aotearoa/New Zealand (2000b: 3), while also exploring established themes such as the expropriation of Māori land,

and incorporating aspects of marae ritual including karanga, waiata, and whaikōrero.

Pasifika theatre in Aotearoa/New Zealand   The rapid expansion of Māori dramatic activity since the 1990s has been accompanied by an equivalent movement among diasporic Pacific Islanders in Aotearoa/New Zealand. This transcultural, diasporic phase of creative production is often referred to by the adjective 'Pasifika', an indigenized version of 'Pacific' that references orthographic conventions shared across a range of Pacific (particularly Polynesian) languages.

As around half of Aotearoa/New Zealand's immigrant Pacific Islanders are Samoan, much of the new Pasifika drama based within New Zealand has focused upon, and been produced by, Samoans. The first full-length Samoan play to be performed in Aotearoa/New Zealand was *Le Matau*, a play by Stephen Sinclair and Samson Samasoni that premiered at the Depot Theatre (Wellington) in 1984. This play set a trend for ensuing Pacific theatre and other creative art forms in its focus on a Samoan immigrant (Ioane) who suffers cultural alienation after coming to New Zealand in search of employment opportunities. The establishment of two theatrical organizations—Pacific Theatre in Auckland in 1987, and Pacific Underground in Christchurch in 1991—created a wider support base for Pacific drama, which gathered momentum in the 1990s. 1993 saw the debut production of American Samoan playwright John Kneubuhl's *Think of a Garden* (discussed in Chapter 3) at Auckland's Watershed theatre, and later that year *Fresh Off the Boat*, a play about Samoan immigrant culture written by Oscar Kightley and Simon Small, was performed for Pacific Underground in Christchurch. Kightley, who was born in Samoa in 1969 and emigrated to Aotearoa/New Zealand as a child, has become a key figure in Pasifika theatre and media production. He was co-founder of Pacific Underground, and in addition to writing several plays, he has also toured as a member of the renowned comedy theatre troupe 'The Naked Samoans', and has participated (both as scriptwriter and performer) in television comedy series such as 'Skitz' (which included comic sketches centring on the Semisis, a 'dysfunctional' Pacific Island family) and 'Bro' Town' (a comedy cartoon television series, set in Auckland, which features Pacific Islander and Māori characters). Kightley also acted in (and co-wrote the script for) the acclaimed Samoan comedy feature-film *Sione's Wedding* (directed by Chris Graham), which premiered in New Zealand and Samoa in March 2006.

A particular feature of the work of Kightley, the Naked Samoans, and other Pacific Island writers (and film-makers) in Aotearoa/New Zealand is their use of humour to explore the position of Pacific Island immigrant communities. Sensitive issues such as racism and socio-economic deprivation are handled in a manner that differs considerably from much contemporary Māori literature and film, which often explores similar topics through a politicized and uncompromising social realism (O'Donnell and Tweddle 2003). While comi-satirical strategies are common in 'postcolonial' or 'ethnic minority' comedy in other national contexts—such as Britain, where the South Asian comedy series 'Goodness Gracious Me' and 'The Kumars at No. 42' became popular BBC shows—comic theatre also has a specific and established history within Samoan culture. As outlined in Chapter 5, Samoan *fale aitu* (which translates as 'house of spirits') is a theatrical tradition in which actors perform a series of sketches under various comic personas. These sketches often involve satirical attacks upon community values and authority figures, but actors are protected from censure by the customary belief that performers are temporarily 'possessed' by spirits of the dead who have returned to offer criticism of the living (Sinavaiana-Gabbard 1999).

The influence of the *fale aitu* tradition is clearly evident in Samoan television comedy such as 'Bro' Town' and 'The Semisis', where the values and prejudices of the dominant palagi/Pākehā community, as well as those of Pacific Islanders, are satirized under the veil of humour. Oscar Kightley and Simon Small's play *Fresh off the Boat* (2005) offers another example of these strategies in practice. On the one hand, the play explores some of the 'serious' issues contingent upon the Pacific Island diasporic experience, depicting the cultural dislocation of a Samoan man (Charles) who has recently arrived in Aotearoa/New Zealand. Another character in the play, a young man named Samoa, also explores the sociocultural problems facing Polynesians in Aotearoa/New Zealand, but his pronouncements are often replete with the verbal punning and sexual innuendo characteristic of *fale aitu* performances. In scene ten of the play, for example, Samoa prefaces a persuasive discussion of the stereotyping of black and Pacific Island characters in the media with a claim that in a packet of M & M's sugar-coated chocolates there are only three brown ones 'because white people are afraid of the sexual potency of eating brown M & M's [which] are proven aphrodisiacs' (27). Samoa's playful invocation of sexual stereotypes thus leavens his discussion of racial prejudice, and he uses a similar strategy in scene twelve, where Charles is teaching his New Zealand-born niece Evotia how to perform the Samoan siva dance. Watching the lesson approvingly, Samoa fantasizes about creating a movie centring on the diasporic experience: 'I'll start it with a shot of you guys doing that in the Islands and then cut to a Samoan gangster in South Central L.A., telling us how he's lost count of the people he's shot. . . . [It's] going to be called "Where the Fobs Have No Names" ' (34). Here, Samoa incorporates the pejorative nickname 'fob' (short for 'fresh off the boat', an epithet conferred upon recently-arrived Pacific Island immigrants) into an adaptation of a line from Irish band U2's song 'Where the Streets Have No Names', comically undermining his more 'serious' political assertions with a flash of postmodern intertextuality. Samoa's 'over-the-top' political activism (as Kightley and Small put it) therefore adds a humorous aspect to the play's exploration of more weighty inter-racial issues, thereby referencing the comi-satirical strategies of the fale aitu tradition (2005: iii).

Gender, sexuality, and the body in Pacific theatre Fale aitu and other Pacific comic theatrical conventions have also been adopted by dramatists elsewhere in the Pacific. Playwright Vilsoni Hereniko, who has published a monograph (*Woven Gods*, 1995) on the subversive aspects of clowning on his home island of Rotuma, has incorporated comic theatrical conventions into *Last Virgin in Paradise* (1993), a play co-written with Teresia Teaiwa (of Banaban and African-American descent). The play is subtitled 'a serious comedy', underscoring the dialectic between humour and social criticism which is also a feature of fale aitu and other Pacific comic theatre. While the play offers a sobering social critique of enduring Western conceptions of the Pacific as a sexual and environmental paradise, the cast includes a male clown figure whose behaviour references ritual clowning traditions in various parts of the Pacific (including Fiji and Rotuma, Samoa, Tahiti, Tokelau, Vanuatu, and Papua New Guinea). In a wedding reception scene towards the end of the play, the clown performs a series of sexually suggestive songs and sketches for the entertainment of the guests, thus engaging in the improvised 'secular' clowning often performed at Pacific social gatherings. There is also a political edge to the clown's antics: during the wedding scene he dances with the bride Hina's aunt Mere, who dons a wig resembling the toupee worn by Hina's lecherous European husband, Helmut. Helmut had come to Marawa, the fictional Pacific Island on which the play is set, in order to find a mythical virginal Polynesian bride, and Mere satirizes Helmut's sexual imperialism by informing the male clown (who is playing Hina) that 'I come all the way from Jamani [Germany] to find virgin' (16). Mere and the clown also undermine Helmut's self-important attitude by implying that Hina is only marrying him for his money, and by mistranslating his wedding speech to make it appear that instead of 'gaining a son', Hina's parents are 'gaining a useless old thing, like chewed bubble gum' (21). In addition to deploying the sexual innuendo and role reversals characteristic of fale aitu, therefore, the scene also incorporates the satirization of 'authority figures or foreign persons and their behaviour' that Hereniko locates at the heart of Pacific clowning traditions (1993: 66). A more direct reference to the Rotuman clowning tradition appears in Hereniko's dramatic feature film *The Land Has Eyes* (2004), in which an elderly woman performs the ritual clown role at a wedding, 'subjugating' various male guests in a carnivalesque inversion of mainstream gender dialectics.

John Kneubuhl's drama *A Play: A Play* (1997) is also heavily influenced by Pacific comic theatre, and in particular the fale aitu tradition of his ancestral homeland (American Samoa). The play ostensibly dramatizes the experiences of some local actors in Hawai'i rehearsing a comedy about the volcano goddess Pele, but the work—in keeping with the fale aitu tradition—is flamboyantly metatheatrical, with the actors frequently stepping out of character to question the motives of the playwright (who is himself a character in the play). Like the wedding scenes in *Last Virgin in Paradise* and *The Land Has Eyes*, Kneubuhl's play also draws upon the cross-gendering and sexual innuendo that characterizes fale aitu and other Polynesian comic theatre. Further, Kneubuhl blends the fale aitu tradition with aspects of Hawai'ian culture, including in the cast a māhū (transvestite) playing the role of Pele, who is herself able to switch gender at will. In Act Two of the play, Pele makes love to various characters after taking alternate male and female physical forms. In this respect, Kneubuhl's play also intersects with the work of Indigenous Hawai'ian playwrights such as Tammy Haili'ōpua Baker, whose play *Kupua [Shapeshifter]* (2001) adapts two traditional mo'olelo (legends) involving shape-shifting and seduction (see Wat and Desha (eds.) 2003). By referencing Pacific narrative and performance traditions, playwrights such as Hereniko, Kneubuhl, and Baker therefore challenge strategies of exoticization and eroticization in European representations of the Polynesian 'body', repositioning Polynesian debates on gender and sexuality within specific socio-historical contexts.

The 1990s also witnessed the emergence of a number of Pacific women playwrights who have focused more specifically upon the female body in performance space. Many contemporary Pacific theatre practitioners and dancers have reacted against the trope of the 'exotic' (and passive) 'dusky maiden' swaying to languorous melodies by adopting 'hard-core' or androgynous stances for female dancers, and by blending traditional Pacific musical traditions with contemporary, urban international musical styles such as hip-hop and gangsta rap (Taouma 2002: 133–4). Samoan playwright Makerita Urale engages with the stereotype of the sensuous Polynesian female dancer in her play *Frangipani Perfume* (1997/2004), the first Pasifika play in Aotearoa/New Zealand to be written and performed entirely by women. The play opens with 'Three Dusky Maidens' performing a dance 'of sleepy sensual beauty', but as the lights come up, these 'maidens' are revealed to be three Samoan cleaners (all sisters) scrubbing a dirty floor. The scene thus effectively juxtaposes the myth of the exotic Polynesian 'dancing girl' with the hardships suffered by many working-class Pacific Island women in Aotearoa/New Zealand (O'Donnell 2004: iii). Similar strategies of demystification are evident in Hawai'ian playwright Victoria Nalani Kneubuhl's *Emmalehua* (1996/2002), which contrasts crass appropriations of Hawai'ian hula dancing in the post-war Hawai'ian tourist industry with the specific spiritual and cultural significance of the hula within Indigenous Hawai'ian culture.

Dianna Fuemana, whose parents migrated to Aotearoa/New Zealand from Niue and American Samoa, is another prominent female playwright within Aotearoa/New Zealand's Pasifika community. Her play *Mapaki* (1999)—published jointly with Urale's *Frangipani Perfume* in 2004—bears resemblance to the prose narratives of Sia Figiel both thematically (in its focus on domestic violence) and stylistically (it was originally performed as a solo performance poem, and incorporates alternating sections of song and narrative poetry in Niuean and English). The play includes harrowing scenes in which Fisi (a New Zealand-born Niuean) suffers verbal and physical abuse from her boyfriend Jason; however, the influence of Polynesian comic theatre is discernible in other scenes in the play where Gina—a fa'afafine and Fisi's best friend—indulges in outrageous sexual banter.

6.3.2 Indigenous film in the Pacific

In addition to their achievements in the field of drama, Māori and other Indigenous Pacific creative artists have also made significant contributions to film and television production in the last few decades. This final section of the chapter discusses a range of developments in Indigenous Pacific film since the late 1980s, focusing in particular upon dramatic feature films and literary adaptations made by Māori film-makers, who have been the most prominent Indigenous Pacific film-makers to date.

From the origins of New Zealand film in the early twentieth century, and until the 1970s, images of Māori in New Zealand film were produced almost exclusively by Pākehā or European film-makers (Blythe 1994: 34). The Māori Renaissance of the 1970s, however, created a cultural dynamic in which Māori film-makers began to emerge alongside Māori creative writers such as Witi Ihimaera and Patricia Grace. The first full-length Māori feature film, *Ngāti* (1987), was made by Barry Barclay, a Māori film-maker whose career began in 1974 with the filming of *Tangata Whenua*, a documentary television series focused primarily upon rural Māori life. Barclay was one of the founding members of Te Manu Aute, a national organization of Māori 'communicators' formed in 1986, and from the beginning of his career, he has been committed to Māori self-determination in the media as well as other sectors of political and social life (Barclay 1990: 7). In his own film-making efforts, he has always aimed to respect Māori communalist ethics, often featuring pairs or groups of people rather than individual 'talking heads' in his various documentaries, and giving participants a sense of 'ownership' of the filmed material by organizing special screenings and depositing unedited footage with the community (Barclay 1990: 10–11; 1999: 410–11). He has compared his role as film-maker to that of a traditional itinerant Māori carver, who travels to various communities, carving images of local ancestors according to the local style of carving, but nevertheless also leaves his own individual creative 'signature' on the final product (personal communication, 24 October 2005).

These philosophies were put into practice during the filming of Barclay's *Ngāti*, most of which was shot in Waipiro Bay near Tokomaru (on the east coast of the North Island), where the film's scriptwriter Tama Poata spent his childhood. Barclay aimed 'to have Māori attitudes control the film', employing as many Māori as he could on the film crew as well as in the cast, and he describes the film as a 'determined attempt to say what it's like being Maori [*sic*]' (Lomas 1987: 4). Set in a late 1940s rural Māori community struggling to preserve its local economy and population in a period of rapid industrialization and urbanization, the film clearly intersects with the work of Māori writers such as Witi Ihimaera and Patricia Grace, both of whom have explored the consequences of post-war urban migration upon Māori communities (see Chapter 4). Similar issues are explored in Merata Mita's *Mauri* (1988), the first fiction feature film to be made solely by a Māori woman. The film dramatizes the effects of post-war urbanization and cultural 'assimilation' upon members of a small Māori community on the East Coast of the North Island, and Mita has described it as a 'parable about the schizophrenic existence of so many Maori in Pakeha society'.[8] The film can be interpreted as tino rangatiratanga (self-determination) in action: ninety per cent of those involved in the film's production were Māori, and the film dramatizes key aspects of Māori culture (such as marae hui and rituals surrounding birth, death, and marriage) and uses a high proportion of untranslated Māori, making very few concessions for a Pākehā or international audience.

Barclay and Mita have also made other important feature-length films: Mita's documentary *Patu!* (1983) explored Māori involvement in the anti-apartheid protests during the 1981 South African rugby tour of New Zealand, and Barclay's fiction feature *Te Rua* (1991) depicts the recovery of Māori taonga (treasured objects) from a Berlin museum, exploring issues of self-determination also featured in many of his documentaries. However, the relative lack of funding and support for Indigenous film-makers in Aotearoa/New Zealand has ensured that many established and emerging Māori and Pacific directors (such as Lisa Reihana and Sima Urale) have channelled their energies into video and short film-making rather than feature-length film projects. There are notable exceptions to this general rule: a range of 'Māori-focused' feature-length films have been produced during and beyond the 1990s, including Don Selwyn's *The Maori Merchant of Venice* (2001), based on Pei Te Hurinui Jones's 1945 Māori translation of Shakespeare's original play; Lee Tamahori's 1994 adaptation of Alan Duff's *Once Were Warriors*; Ian Mune's *What Becomes of the Broken Hearted* (1999), an adaptation of Duff's 1996 sequel to *Once Were Warriors*; and Niki Caro's *Whale Rider* (2002), adapted from Ihimaera's 1987 novel *The Whale Rider*. In 2004, a Māori television channel was launched, and in addition to providing news, documentaries, and children's programmes in both Māori and English (Aotearoa/New Zealand's two official spoken languages), the channel has screened a variety of short and feature-length films made by Māori.[9]

The considerable international success enjoyed by *Once Were Warriors* and *Whale Rider* in particular has prompted lively debates about the degree to which cultural 'integrity' or 'authenticity' in Indigenous film is compromised by the commercial demands of the international film industry. In his article 'Colonialism Continued' (2000), Stephen Turner argues that antipodean media production has entered a post-nationalist phase of 'export consciousness' in which films are commonly tailored to a 'globalizing market'. He argues that this process of globalization has eroded the once productive dichotomy between 'metropolis' and 'margin': the 'margin' is no longer a potential site of resistance but is instead incorporated into a homogenizing 'virtual space' (Turner 2000: 218–19). Turner's analysis focuses primarily upon work produced by members of Australian and New Zealand 'settler' cultures, but his arguments are also relevant to a consideration of Māori-focused films such as *Once Were Warriors* and *Whale Rider*. Lee Tamahori (of Ngāti Porou descent) has argued that he set out to emphasize the status of *Once Were Warriors* as a 'Māori film' both at home and abroad. Filters were used during filming in order to 'enrich' the brown skin tones of the Māori actors, and Tamahori made a conscious decision to downplay the influence of American popular culture on New Zealand urban Māori (youth) culture (McKenzie 1995: 65). Māori hip-hop and reggae songs, and fashions inspired by Māori motifs, featured prominently in the film in order to foreground its 'New Zealand' context (McKenzie 1995: 65; Staff 1993: 9). In spite of these culturally specific references, however, the film nevertheless has a recognizably 'Hollywood' or 'international' veneer which has arisen from Tamahori's professed desire to make *Once Were Warriors* appealing to a wide audience 'beyond the film festivals' (Martin 1995: 3). Further, some Māori have expressed disquiet over the fact that traditional Māori moko (tattoo) patterns worn by gang members in the film have entered international popular culture, thereby 'compromising' the function of moko as a culturally specific graphic code recording the lineage and achievements of the bearer (see Sumner 1999; Keown 2005: 184).

Niki Caro's 2003 film version of Witi Ihimaera's novel *The Whale Rider* (1987), another movie that has enjoyed wide international circulation, has also sparked debates about the cultural particularism of 'Māori' film in an international context. Barry Barclay, for example, has discussed the film within the context of his own theories on 'Fourth Cinema'—that is, films that feature and are directed by Indigenous peoples, particularly those within white 'settler colonies'—and has argued that because Caro is not ethnically Māori, *Whale Rider* cannot be classified as an 'Indigenous' film (2003: n.p). According to Barclay's definition of Fourth Cinema, there are to date only seven 'Indigenous' Pacific Island dramatic feature films. These include the Māori films *Ngati, Mauri, Te Rua, Once Were Warriors*, and *The Maori Merchant of Venice*; *The Land Has Eyes* (2004), Vilsoni Hereniko's dramatic feature-film set in Rotuma; and *No. 2* (2006), a film adaptation of a 1999 play by Toa Fraser.[10] If Australia is included in the equation, Tracey Moffatt's *BeDevil* (1993), the first aboriginal dramatic feature film, and *Beneath Clouds* (2002), a dramatic feature by aboriginal director Ivan Sen, also qualify as 'Indigenous' Oceanic films.

Film critic Claire Murdoch has contested Barclay's rejection of *Whale Rider* as a 'Māori' film, pointing out that Caro drew extensively upon the expertise of Māori cultural advisers and worked in consultation with Witi Ihimaera (appointed deputy director) and the Ngāti Kanohi people of Whangara (where the filming took place), thereby preserving the consultative and community-centred values associated with independent and small-budget Māori film-making (Murdoch 2003: 98). Barry Barclay, however, has pointed out that the film was crewed by white technicians, excluding and thereby offending many experienced Māori technicians who wished to participate in the project (personal communication, 2 March 2006). Further, Murdoch herself points out that the circumstances of the film's funding problematize claims for its status as an autonomous local 'Māori' production. It was the first film produced under the New Zealand Labour government's Film Production Fund, which resulted from Prime Minister Helen Clark's belief that film is a powerful medium through which to create positive representations of New Zealand 'national identity' both at home and abroad (Murdoch 2003: 102). Clark's aspirations for *Whale Rider* are in keeping with Stephen Turner's arguments on the 'export consciousness' of antipodean cinema. Further, the film's vision of an 'unspoilt' rural New Zealand resonates with other twenty-first-century antipodean film successes such as Peter Jackson's *Lord of the Rings* trilogy,[11] which has (re)generated tourist-industry constructions of New Zealand as a prelapsarian paradise far removed from global terrorism and the worst excesses of late capitalism.

The success of Caro's *Whale Rider* has also had a marked effect upon sales of Ihimaera's books: new 'international' editions of a variety of Ihimaera's novels (including *The Whale Rider*) have been published since 2003. While these new editions are closely based on the originals, certain adjustments (such as the removal or translation of Māori words and concepts) have been made in order to accommodate a global market unfamiliar with Māori or wider New Zealand culture. The increased international availability of Ihimaera's *The Whale Rider* in the wake of the film's successes might go some way towards addressing Murdoch's concerns that international audiences are deprived of some of the cultural particularities of Ihimaera's original text: while the new edition does make some concessions for a global readership, the stylistic and ideological integrity of the original largely remains.

However it is interpreted, this increasing 'internationalization' of Māori film and literature resonates with a variety of developments in Indigenous Pacific creative arts since the 1990s. In the wake of expanding international travel networks and the global dissemination of information through the internet and other media sources, much contemporary Pacific cultural production has moved towards the transcultural, the postnational, and the global. The prevalence of global/local rhetoric in twenty-first-century Pacific literary conferences, art exhibitions, and publishing initiatives suggests that transnationalism will feature prominently in Indigenous Pacific cultural production for some years to come, resonating with contemporary debates on the nexus between the 'global' and the 'local' in international postcolonial studies (Hall 1997; Dirlik 1998; Wilson 2000; Hardt and Negri 2001, 2004; Boehmer 2004). The emergence of various English-language translations of francophone literature from New Caledonia and Tahiti (see Chapter 4) also points towards a growing interest in non-anglophone literatures of the Pacific, again corresponding with an increasingly polylingual orientation within 'international' postcolonial studies (see Forsdick and Murphy (2003); Murdoch and Donadey (2005); and McMullin (2005)). This movement towards transculturalism and globalization in Pacific studies does not mean, however, that indigeneity and cultural specificity have become marginalized within contemporary Pacific cultural production. Texts such as Albert Wendt's *Black Rainbow* (1992) suggest that the global and the local, postmodern pastiche and indigeneity, can exist alongside each other, while Epeli Hau'ofa, in advocating a regional 'oceanic' identity shared by the peoples of the Pacific, has also emphasized the importance of local creative traditions for Indigenous Pacific artists and writers. As noted in Chapter 1, Hau'ofa has put these theories into practice as Director of the Oceania Centre for Arts and Culture, which was established at the University of the South Pacific in 1997. The Centre brings together a range of visual and performing artists from throughout the Pacific region, and the complex is designed so that these various individuals can work alongside each other, building creative links while maintaining a sense of the uniqueness of their own cultural traditions. The Red Wave Collective, a group of artists based at the Oceania Centre, exemplify this ethos: they have toured Australia (in 2000) and the UK (in 2006), and their work responds both to the unique visual artistic traditions from the artists' home nations (including Fiji, the Solomon Islands, Tonga, and Samoa), as well as drawing upon artistic movements from beyond the Pacific. The dawning of the new millennium has witnessed an increasing Pacific presence in the international creative arts scene: exhibitions featuring the work of contemporary 'Pasifika' artists (including Māori and other Pacific Islanders) have toured the US (in 2006)[12] and the UK (in 2006–8),[13] and a growing number of Indigenous Pacific writers are attending literary events both within and beyond the Pacific. The fact that these writers and artists are now commonly identified through pan-ethnic and regional labels such as 'Pasifika' and 'Oceania' draws attention to the importance of the interconnected local, regional, and global spatial formations that Hau'ofa has identified as a central aspect of contemporary Pacific cultural production. The following statement, from Hau'ofa's opening address for the Red Wave exhibition at the James Harvey Gallery (Sydney) in 2000, encapsulates this creative interchange:

The development of new art forms that are truly Oceanic, transcendant [sic] of our national and cultural diversity, is very important in that it allows our creative minds to draw on far larger pools of cultural traits than those of our individual national lagoons. It makes us less insular without being buried in the amorphousness of the globalised cultural melting pot . . . We learn from the great and wonderful products of human imagination and ingenuity the world over, but the cultural achievements of our own histories will be our most important models, points of reference, and sources of inspiration.

(Hau'ofa 2000: n.p.)

Hau'ofa's use of aquatic metaphors here resonates with his arguments for a shared Oceanic identity based on a relationship with the Pacific ocean as a source of subsistence as well as inspiration. Hau'ofa's rhetoric exemplifies the 'place-consciousness' that theorist Arif Dirlik has identified in a range of contemporary discourses and social movements reacting against the forces of globalization in today's world. As Dirlik notes, conceptualizations of the 'local' often focus on the attachment of people—particularly Indigenous peoples and 'peasants'—to the physical environment and to the traditions associated with a particular 'place'. The 'global', on the other hand, is commonly associated with more abstract economic and political formations that are seen as a threat to the survival of the 'local' (1998: 8). It is certainly true that a large proportion of the literature and Indigenous social movements discussed in this book engages with the relationship between the 'global' and the 'local' in these terms. The Māori Land March and the Kaho'olawe demilitarization campaign, for example, both emphasized Indigenous claims to the 'local' physical environment against the incursions of 'foreign' colonizers and military forces (see Chapter 4), and Hawai'ian writers such as Haunani-Kay Trask and Alani Apio have critiqued the devastating effects of multinational commercial development upon the environment and livelihoods of Hawai'i's Indigenous peoples (see Chapter 5).

However, this opposition between the 'local' and the 'global', or the 'Indigenous' and the 'foreign', has become less absolute with the increasingly diasporic orientation of Pacific creative production since the 1990s, as witnessed in poems from *Whetu Moana* such as Samuel Cruickshank's 'Urban Iwi' and Caroline Sinavaiana-Gabbard's 'Sā Nafanuā' (discussed in Chapters 4 and 5). Such transitions point towards a reconfiguration of the global/local binary in which the 'local' is no longer seen as threatened by, or subsumed within, the 'global'. Dirlik has developed the term 'glocal' to describe formations in which the global and the local are seen as mutually dependent and interwoven rather than in hostile opposition: as he observes, multinational companies are, after all, dependent on 'local' producers and consumers for their continued survival and expansion. As Dirlik suggests, the politics of place articulated in 'local' social movements can therefore mediate—and potentially obviate—systemic problems posed by the forces of 'globalization':

In their simultaneous attachment to places and local cultures, on the one hand, and their critical engagement with the global, on the other, social movements offer the most hopeful arena for a defence of place and a more balanced perspective between the global and the local. They suggest ways for relearning and seeing communities as anchoring points for reconceiving and reconstructing the world from the perspective of place-based cultural, ecological, and economic practices.

(1998: 12)

As Dirlik argues, when considered in these terms, 'glocalism' can be viewed not as an abstract and utopian ideology, but rather as a new form of place-centred politics that can challenge the discourse of developmentalism, which seeks to render 'local' places across the globe increasingly homogenous through the processes of commercialization and 'modernization'. Place-centred politics are crucial to Hauʻofa's arguments for a regional identity for Pacific Island peoples, who, as individual small-population nation-states, are vulnerable to the depredations of multinational corporations, and are becoming increasingly marginalized within externally-imposed politico-economic formations such as APEC (the Asia-Pacific Economic Cooperation) (Hauʻofa 1998: 397). Viewed in these terms, the notion of a shared regional identity for Indigenous Pacific peoples becomes more than just a creative paradigm: it also becomes a means of material and ideological survival. As this book has demonstrated, the contemporary Indigenous literatures of the Pacific, and the social movements with which they are inextricably connected, are a testament to the continued survival of the manifold and diverse cultures within Te Moana Nui ā Kiwa: the great Pacific Ocean.

NOTES

CHAPTER 1

1. Hauʻofa was born in Papua New Guinea to Tongan missionary parents.

2. As an example of the former see Priscilla Rasmussen's 'Polynesian Poetry', in which she pays homage to a variety of first-generation Pacific writers (Wendt *et al.* (eds.) 2003: 168). Conversely, Samoan writer Sia Figiel (for example) has indicated that she began writing about girls and young women partly in response to a masculinist bias in earlier Pacific writing (Subramani 1996: 129–30).

3. With its mix of Polynesians and Melanesians, Fiji, for example, is often included as part of Polynesia, but as Viktor Krupa points out, linguistic evidence suggests that the 'Polynesian-Fijian' linguistic unity terminated during the second millennium BC (approx.), when Tonga was first settled (Krupa 1982: 2).

4. Cythera is the legendary Greek 'isle of dreams' near which the goddess Aphrodite (Venus to the Romans) is said to have risen from the sea.

5. There are a variety of Pacific countries that remain under colonial jurisdiction. French Polynesia, Wallis and Futuna, and New Caledonia all remain French territories. Hawaiʻi (annexed by the US in 1898) became the fiftieth US state in 1959, and as is the case in Aotearoa/New Zealand and New Caledonia, its Indigenous population in many ways remains sociopolitically marginalized by the dominant white settler culture. American Samoa and Guam are still US territories, while the Northern Mariana Islands became a Commonwealth of the US in 1986. Easter Island remains a province of Chile, and West Papua remains under Indonesian jurisdiction.

6. The British monarch is still the head of state in both Australia and New Zealand, but both countries gained political autonomy in the first decade of the twentieth century.

CHAPTER 2

1. Taʻunga wrote in the Cook Island Māori language, but a selection of his writings were published in English translation (under the title *The Works of Taʻunga*) by Ron and Marjorie Crocombe in 1968.

2. In Wendt's 2003 novel *The Mango's Kiss*, Stevenson is reincarnated under the pseudonym Leonard Roland Stenson, and generously distributes copies of his books among Indigenous Samoans.

3. Lady Barker's epistolary memoir *Station Life in New Zealand* (1870), like Mander's novel, contains vivid details of the practical hardships faced by settler women, but its emphasis on the putatively *déclassé* nature of colonial life, and its often playful reworkings of misfortunes Barker suffered while living on a Canterbury sheep station in the 1860s, brings it closer to a 'comedy of manners' than the more sober reflections of other women settler-writers such as Sarah Amelia Courage (see Gibbons 1998: 50).

CHAPTER 3

1. Tonga's constitutional monarchy (which remains to this day) was established in 1875, and the Hawai'ian monarchy in 1810.

2. Wendt's thesis is now available online at www.nzetc.org/tm/scholarly/tei-WenGua.html.

3. Samoan society contains variations on the pyramidal descent-group structure found in most other parts of Polynesia, featuring an assemblage of honorific titles for which high-born men compete on the basis of their personal and martial prowess, and with the support of their tulafale or talking chiefs.

4. The taiaha is also used as an important symbol of Māori 'warriorhood' in films such as Lee Tamahori's *Once Were Warriors* and Niki Caro's *Whale Rider* (discussed in Chapter 6).

CHAPTER 4

1. In addition to writers from the USP nations, Papua New Guinean writers are also included in both anthologies.

2. The characters' names mean 'first' and 'second' in Rotuman.

3. A wide range of this material has been published in the journal *'ōiwi*, established in 1998, which is specifically dedicated to native Hawai'ian literature, criticism, politics, language, and art.

4. These include, for example, the communal ownership of land, and the matai system, under which leaders from extended family groups (*'aiga*) are elected to sit on the village council (*fono*). Social structures are strictly hierarchical, with juniors deferring to seniors, children to parents, and commoners to chiefs (Sharrad 2003: 25).

5. This book follows the current convention of rendering Easter Island's Polynesian name (as a geographical term) in Chilean fashion as Rapa Nui, while labelling its people and language in pan-Polynesian fashion as Rapanui (see Fischer 2005*b*: 11).

CHAPTER 5

1. There are still a number of Pacific languages (particularly in Melanesia) for which orthographies have yet to be developed.

2. This trading pidgin is also known as Bêche-de-Mer, named after the sea slugs harvested from various Pacific Islands during the early nineteenth century (Fischer 2005*a*: 101).

3. Wiltshire makes frequent use of common pidgin terms such as 'all-e-same' (meaning 'same as' or 'similar to') and 'savvy' (meaning 'know'), for example.

4. Some linguists view pidgins and creoles (such as Melanesian pidgin) as two aspects of (or stages in) the same linguistic process, rather than two separate entities (Crowley 1990: 385).

5. A brand of chewing gum, here used as a generic label.

6. In Soaba's text, a few well-known pidgin words such as 'dimdim' ('white man') and 'misinare' (missionary) are presented in italics (7, 8), and occasionally, a Tok Pisin phrase is included and then translated directly or contextually. In Maka'a's story, Solomon Islands Pijin is used in sections of dialogue between characters ('"Iumi tufala go klaem kokonat fren," suggested Gina' (36)), but the majority of the story is in Standard English.

7. Bougainville, a large island to the east of Papua New Guinea, was incorporated into the German province of New Guinea, which was taken over by Australia during the First World War. When Papua New Guinea became independent it retained Bougainville, but Bougainvilleans view themselves as ethnically distinct from New Guineans, and continuing resentment over the continued exploitation of Bougainville's rich copper reserves helped trigger a civil war which raged between 1988 and 1997 (Denoon *et al.* (eds.) 2000: 455–6).

8. Westlake's 'Native-Hawaiian', published in *Mālama: Hawaiian Land and Water* (Hall (ed.) 1985) is an oft-quoted lyric poem in HCE that draws attention to the cultural schizophrenia experienced by native Hawai'ians living in an Americanized and commercialized modern Hawai'i.

9. In linguistic parlance, 'strong' Pidgin is termed the basilect, 'light' pidgin (closer to Standard English) is the acrolect, and varieties in between are known as mesolects.

10. In *Rabelais and His World* (1965), Bakhtin discusses European carnival traditions as temporary inversions of social (including linguistic) hierarchies.

11. See, for example, 'keigeiki' [little girl] (Figiel 1996*b*: 10), which would be 'teineiti' in the formal dialect.

CHAPTER 6

1. Traditionally, stars were used as navigation aids by Pacific voyagers.

2. According to Māori cosmogony, Hawaiki is the ancestral/spiritual homeland of the Māori (and other Polynesian) people, to which they return after death.

3. Oscar Kightley and David Fane's 1996 play 'A Frigate Bird Sings', for example, dramatizes a young fa'afafine's attempts to reconcile family commitments with his involvement in the New Zealand urban gay scene.

4. Printed in Garrett (ed.) 1991: 16–50.

5. As playwright Hone Kouka explains, the name 'Taki Rua' describes a Māori weaving pattern incorporating dual strands, encapsulating the bicultural ethos of the theatre (1999: 17).

6. As Charles Royal (1997, 2004) explains, while the concept of mimetic 'acting' did not exist in pre-European Māori culture, whare tapere featured other forms of entertainment including dance, storytelling, songs, instrumental performances, and various games and amusements.

7. See in particular Ihimaera's 'The Whale' from *Pounamu, Pounamu* (1972), Grace's *Potiki* (1986), and Duff's *Once Were Warriors* (1990).

8. Mita 1992: 49.

9. Te Māngai Paho, a Crown organization established under the 1993 Broadcasting Amendment Act, also provides funding for Māori-language television programmes and music, as well as supporting the national network of Māori radio stations. The government also contributed funding for the inaugural Wairoa Māori Film Festival, held in 2005.

10. Fraser was born in New Zealand of Fijian ancestry. He was both scriptwriter and director for the film, which focuses on Aotearoa's diasporic Fijian community.

11. The trilogy is not 'set' in New Zealand but was filmed on location there.

12. The exhibition 'Turning Tides: Gender in Oceania Art' was held at the University of California San Diego Graduate Gallery, February 2006.

13. The exhibition 'Pasifika Styles 2006', featuring the work of Māori and Pacific Island artists from Aotearoa/New Zealand, opened at the Cambridge University Museum of Archaeology and Anthropology in April 2006, and the Red Wave Collective exhibited at the October Gallery (London) in May–July 2006.

GLOSSARY AND LIST OF ACRONYMS

A number of the words listed here are shared across various Pacific languages and in some cases meanings vary. Translations given here are selective and specific to the contexts in which these terms have been used in this book.

GLOSSARY

Aotearoa	Māori name for New Zealand, with various translations including 'Land of the Long White Cloud'
dauka	lower-caste Indian(s)
fa'afafine	trans-sexual or transvestite (Samoan)
fa'a Sāmoa	Samoan way of life
fagogo	stories; storytelling (Samoan)
fale aitu	'house of spirits': Samoan comic theatre
girmit	indenture agreement (Fiji Hindi)
haka	rhythmical dance (Māori)
haole	person of European descent (Hawai'ian)
Hawaiki	mythical ancestral homeland of the Māori people
Hine-Nui-Te-Pō	'Great woman of the night': Māori death goddess
hui	gathering of people (Māori)
iwi	tribe; bone (Māori)
kanaka	meaning 'person' or 'man' in a variety of Pacific languages, this term was used by Europeans as a derogatory term for Pacific Islanders but has more recently been reclaimed by Indigenous New Caledonians as a positive term
kava	non-alcoholic but intoxicating drink, made from the roots of the kava plant, and consumed within various Pacific nations. Also known as yaqona (Fiji) and 'ava (Hawai'i)

Kiwa	legendary Polynesian navigator and guardian of the sea
māhu/māhū	homosexual; transvestite (Tahitian/Hawai'ian)
mana	a word, shared across many Pacific languages, that carries connotations of power, psychic force and socio-political influence
Mā'ohi	Indigenous person/people of Tahiti/French Polynesia
Māori	Indigenous person/people of Aotearoa/New Zealand
marae	sacred meeting area (Māori). The term is often used to refer to the ceremonial meeting house and surrounding buildings within a Māori community.
Māui	Polynesian demigod and trickster
Mau	name attached to the Samoan independence movement. Its various meanings in Samoan include 'hold' and 'keep'
meke	dance accompanied by sung poetry (Fijian)
moana	Polynesian word for sea/ocean
moko	tattoo (Māori)
mo'olelo	legend (Hawai'ian)
Nafanuā	Samoan war goddess
Pākehā	New Zealander of European descent
Pālagi/papalagi	European/white person (Samoan)
Papatūānuku	mythical earth-mother (Māori)
Pele	Hawai'ian volcano goddess
pēpeha	proverb (Māori)
Pili	Samoan demigod and trickster
pōtiki	youngest child (Māori)
Pouliuli	primeval darkness; void (Samoan)
pounamu	greenstone (Māori)
Ranginui	mythical sky-father (Māori)
su'ifefiloi	Samoan oral literary form in which songs are linked together to form one continuous song
Tagaloaalagi	Supreme creator (Samoan)
tagata/tangata	man, person (Samoan/Māori)
takatāpui	intimate friend of the same sex (Māori)
talanoa	Polynesian word referring to storytelling or 'yarning'

tangata whenua	'people of the land'; hosts (Māori)
tangi	funeral; to weep (Māori)
taonga	treasured item(s) (Māori)
tapa	barkcloth
tapu/kapu	Polynesian religious system that places certain people, places, and objects off-limits
tatau	tattoo (Samoan)
Te Kore	Māori mythical void preceding life
Te Moana Nui ā Kiwa	'The great ocean of Kiwa' (Polynesian name for the Pacific ocean)
tino rangatiratanga	full sovereignty/chiefly authority (Māori)
toa	champion; warrior (Māori)
tupuna	ancestor(s) (Māori)
tusitala	writer of tales (Samoan)
Waitangi	weeping water(s) (Māori). Site of 1840 Treaty signing
waka/vaka/vaʻa	Polynesian term for a canoe or other means of conveyance
whaikōrero	speechmaking (Māori)
whakapapa	genealogy (Māori)
whānau	family; to be born (Māori)
whare	house; building (Māori)
whare whakairo	carved meeting house (Māori)
whenua	land; afterbirth (Māori)
whetu	star (Māori)

LIST OF ACRONYMS

CMS	Church Missionary Society
HCE	Hawaiʻi Creole English
LMS	London Missionary Society
SPCAS	South Pacific Creative Arts Society
UH	University of Hawaiʻi
UHP	University of Hawaiʻi Press
UPNG	University of Papua New Guinea
USP	University of the South Pacific

REFERENCES

Ali, Noora (2001) 'A Scoundrel's Tale has Fiji Hindi Literary World Talking', *Wansolwara Online*, 7 November. www.sidsnet.org/pacific/usp/journ/docs/news/wansolnews/wansol0711011

Arvidson, Ken (1991) 'Aspects of Contemporary Māori Writing in English', in G. McGregor and M. Williams (eds.), *Dirty Silence: Aspects of Language and Literature in New Zealand* (Auckland: Oxford University Press), pp. 117–28.

—— (1992) 'Some Maori Versions of Pastoral', in B. Bennett and D. Haskell (eds.), *Myths, Heroes and Anti-Heroes: Essays on the Literature and Culture of the Asia-Pacific Region* (Nedlands: CSAL), pp. 1–10.

—— (1993) 'The Emergence of a Polynesian Literature', in Paul Sharrad (ed.), *Readings in Pacific Literature* (Wollongong: New Literatures Research Centre), pp. 20–38.

—— (2001) 'Editor's Introduction', in J. E. Gorst, *The Maori King* (Auckland: Reed), pp. vii–xix.

—— (2003) 'Widening the Tasman: 1940s New Zealand Literary Nationalism Writes Out Oz', in N. Bierbaum, S. Harrex, and S. Hosking (eds.), *The Regenerative Spirit Volume 1: Polarities of Home and Away, Encounters and Diasporas, in Post-colonial Literatures* (Adelaide: Lythrum Press), pp. 68–76.

Ashcroft, Bill, Griffiths, Gareth, and Tiffin, Helen (eds.) (1998) *Key Concepts in Post-Colonial Studies* (London: Routledge).

Awatere, Donna (1984) *Maori Sovereignty* (Auckland: Broadsheet).

Baker, Heretaunga Pat (1975) *Behind the Tattooed Face* (Whatamongo Bay: Cape Catley).

Ballantyne, R. M. (1995 [1858]) *The Coral Island* (London: Penguin).

Balme, Christopher (1999) *Decolonizing the Stage: Theatrical Syncretism and Post-Colonial Drama* (Oxford: Clarendon).

Barclay, Barry (1990) *Our Own Image* (Auckland: Longman Paul).

—— (Fall 1999) 'The Vibrant Shimmer', *The Contemporary Pacific*: 390–413.

—— (February 2003) 'An Open Letter to John Barnett from Barry Barclay', *Onfilm*: www.archivesearch.co.nz/ViewEditorial.asp?EditorialID=9301&pubcode=ONF

Beavis, Bill (1971) 'Brown is Beautiful: Witi Ihimaera', *Listener*, 11 January: 53.

Beer, Gillian (1990) 'The Island and the Aeroplane: The Case of Virginia Woolf', in H. Bhabha (ed.), *Nation and Narration* (London: Routledge), pp. 265–90.

Behdad, Ali (1996) *Belated Travelers: Orientalism in the Age of Colonial Dissolution* (Durham, NC: Duke University Press).

Beier, Ulli (1980) 'Papua New Guinea: Voices of Independence', in U. Beier (ed.), *Voices of Independence: New Black Writing from Papua New Guinea* (St Lucia: University of Queensland Press), pp. xi–xvi.

——— (2005) *Decolonising the Mind: The Impact of the University on Culture and Identity in Papua New Guinea, 1971–1974* (Canberra: Pandanus).

Belich, James (1986) *The New Zealand Wars and the Victorian Interpretation of Racial Conflict* (Auckland: Penguin).

Benton, Richard (1996) 'The Māori Language in New Zealand Education and Society', in Mugler and Lynch (eds.), *Pacific Languages in Education* (Suva: Institute of Pacific Studies), pp. 209–27.

Bertram, James (1953) 'Robin Hyde: A Reassessment', *Landfall* 7.2: 181–91.

Bhabha, Homi (1994) *The Location of Culture* (London and New York: Routledge).

Binney, Judith (1996) 'Ancestral Voices: Maori Prophet Leaders', in K. Sinclair (ed.), *The Oxford Illustrated History of New Zealand*, 2nd edn (Auckland: Oxford University Press), pp. 153–84.

——— Chaplin, G., and Wallace, C. (1979) *Mihaia: The Prophet Rua Kenana and His Community at Maungapohatu* (Wellington: Oxford University Press).

Blythe, Martin (1994) *Naming the Other: Images of the Maori in New Zealand Film and Television* (Metuchen, NJ and London: Scarecrow).

Boehmer, Elleke (2004) 'Global Nets: Or What's New about Empire?', *Postcolonial Studies* 7.1: 11–26.

——— (2005) *Colonial and Postcolonial Literature*, 2nd edn (Oxford: Oxford University Press).

Bornholdt, J., O'Brien, G., and Williams, M. (eds.) (1997) *An Anthology of New Zealand Poetry in English* (Auckland: Oxford University Press).

Brah, Avtar (1996) *Cartographies of Diaspora: Contesting Identities* (London: Routledge).

Broughton, John (1994) *Michael James Manaia* (Dunedin: Department of Preventative and Social Medicine, University of Otago).

——— (2000 [1998]) *Te Hokinga Mai (The Return Home)* (Dunedin: Aoraki).

Brown, Peter (2004) 'Introduction', in *Sharing as Custom Provides: Selected Poems of Déwé Gorodé*, ed. and trans. Raylene Ramsay and Deborah Walker (Canberra: Pandanus), pp. ix–xliv.

Brown, Ruth (1989) 'Maori Spirituality as Pakeha Construct', *Meanjin* 48.2: 252–8.

_____ (2003) 'Beyond the Myth: Janet Frame Unframed', *Journal of New Zealand Literature* 21: 122–39.

Campbell, I. C. (1989) *A History of the Pacific Islands* (Christchurch: Canterbury University Press).

Campbell, Alistair (2001) *Maori Battalion: A Poetic Sequence* (Wellington: Wai-Te-Ata Press).

Clifford, James (1994) 'Diaspora', *Cultural Anthropology* 9.3: 302–38.

Cody, J. F. (1956) *28th (Maori) Battalion* (Wellington: War History Branch).

Cohen, Robin (1997) *Global Diasporas: An Introduction* (London: Routledge).

Conrad, Joseph (1973 [1899]) *Heart of Darkness* (London: Penguin).

Crocombe, Marjorie (1974) 'Introducing *Mana* 1974', *Mana Annual of Creative Writing*, 1.

_____ (1977) '*Mana* and Creative Regional Co-operation', in *Third Mana Annual of Creative Writing*: 5–6.

_____ (ed.) (1982) *Te Mau Aamu Maohi/Poesie Tahitienne/Tahitian Poetry*, spec. issue of *Mana* 7.1.

Crocombe, Marjorie Tuainekore, Crocombe, Ron, Kauraka, Kauraka, and Tongia, Makiuti (eds.) (1992) *Te Rau Maire: Poems and Stories of the Pacific* (Rarotonga, Suva, Wellington, and Auckland: Tauranga Vananga, the Institute of Pacific Studies, SPCAS, the University of Victoria and the University of Auckland).

Crocombe, Ron (1995) *The Pacific Islands and the USA* (Suva: Institute of Pacific Studies).

_____ (2001) *The South Pacific* (Suva: Institute of Pacific Studies).

Crowley, Terry (1990) *Beach-La-Mar to Bislama: The Emergence of a National Language in Vanuatu* (Oxford: Clarendon).

Curnow, Allen (1945) 'Introduction', in A. Curnow (ed.), *A Book of New Zealand Verse 1923–45* (Christchurch: Caxton), pp. 13–55.

_____ (1960) 'Introduction', in A. Curnow (ed.), *The Penguin Book of New Zealand Verse* (Harmondsworth: Penguin), pp. 17–67.

_____ (1990) *Selected Poems 1940–1989* (London: Penguin).

Dansey, Harry (1974) *Te Raukura* (Auckland: Longman Paul).

D'Aponte, Mimi Gisolfi (ed.) (1999) *An Anthology of Native American Plays* (New York: Theatre Communications Group).

Davenport, Kiana (1993) 'Dragon Seed', in Jessica Hagedorn (ed.), *Charlie Chan is Dead: An Anthology of Contemporary Asian American Fiction* (New York: Penguin), pp. 94–101.

Davis, Tom, and Davis, Lydia (1960) *Makutu* (London: Michael Joseph).

Deleuze, Gilles, and Guattari, Félix (1986) *Kafka: Toward a Minor Literature*, trans. D. Polan (Minneapolis: University of Minnesota Press).

Delrez, Marc (2002) *Manifold Utopia: The Novels of Janet Frame* (Amsterdam: Rodopi).

DeLoughrey, Elizabeth, and Hall, S. (1999) 'Beginning from a Centre: An Interview with Patricia Grace', *New Zealand Books* 9.1: 13–14.

Denoon, Donald, Mein-Smith, Philippa, and Wyndham, Marivic (eds.) (2000) *A History of Australia, New Zealand and the Pacific* (Oxford: Blackwell).

Dibblin, Jane (1988) *Day of Two Suns: US Nuclear Testing and the Pacific Islanders* (London: Virago).

Dirlik, Arif (1998) 'Globalism and the Politics of Place', *Development* 41.2: 7–13.

Domett, Alfred (1872) *Ranolf and Amohia: A South-Sea Day-Dream* (London: Smith Elder).

Douglas, Bronwen (1999) 'Art as Ethno-Historical Text: Science, Representation and Indigenous Presence in Eighteenth and Nineteenth Century Oceanic Voyage Literature', in N. Thomas and D. Losche (eds.), *Double Vision: Art Histories and Colonial Histories in the Pacific* (Cambridge: Cambridge University Press), pp. 65–99.

Douglas, Mary (1966) *Purity and Danger: An Analysis of Concepts of Pollution and Taboo* (London: Routledge).

Duff, Alan (1993) *Maori: The Crisis and the Challenge* (Auckland: Harper-Collins).

—— (1994 [1990]) *Once Were Warriors* (Auckland: Tandem).

—— (1996) *What Becomes of the Broken Hearted?* (Auckland: Vintage).

—— (1999) *Out of the Mist and Steam: A Memoir* (Auckland: Tandem).

Dumont d'Urville, Jules-Sébastian-César (1832) 'Sur les îles du Grand Océan', *Bulletin de la Société de Géographie* 17: 1–21.

Edmond, Rod (1990) ' "Kiss My Arse!": Epeli Hau'ofa and the Politics of Laughter', *Journal of Commonwealth Literature* 25.2: 143–55.

—— (1997) *Representing the South Pacific: Colonial Discourse from Cook to Gauguin* (Cambridge: Cambridge University Press).

—— (2002) 'The Pacific/Tahiti: Queen of the South Sea Isles', in P. Hulme and T. Youngs (eds.), *The Cambridge Companion to Travel Writing* (Cambridge: Cambridge University Press), pp. 139–55.

Edmond, Rod, and Smith, Vanessa (2003) 'Introduction', in R. Edmond and V. Smith (eds.), *Islands in History and Representation* (London: Routledge), pp. 1–18.

Ellis, Juniper (1994) 'A Postmodernism of Resistance: Albert Wendt's "Black Rainbow" ', *Ariel* 25.4: 101–14.

—— (1997) ' "The Techniques of Storytelling": An Interview with Albert Wendt', *Ariel* 28.3: 79–94.

—— (2003) ' "Niugini i bekem tok": Creolizing Global English in Papua New Guinean Literature', *Mosaic* 36.2: 33–52.

Ellis, William (1969 [1829]) *Polynesian Researches* (Rutland: Charles E. Tuttle).

Enos, Apisai (1972) 'Niugini Literature: A View from the Editor', *Kovave* 4.1: 46–9.

Eri, Vincent (1973 [1970]) *The Crocodile* (Harmondsworth: Penguin).

Fairburn, A. R. D. (June 1934) 'Some Aspects of New Zealand Art and Letters', *Art in New Zealand*: 216–17.

Fanon, Frantz (1967 [1961]) *The Wretched of the Earth* (London: Penguin).

Fifi'i, Jonathan (1989) *From Pig-theft to Parliament: My Life between Two Worlds* (Suva: Institute of Pacific Studies).

Figiel, Sia (1995) 'The Poet (as a Girl)', *Printout* 9: 15–17.

_____ (1996a) *Where We Once Belonged* (Auckland: Pasifika).

_____ (1996b) *The Girl in the Moon Circle* (Suva: Mana).

_____ (1998) *To a Young Artist in Contemplation* (Suva: Pacific Writing Forum).

_____ (1999) *They Who Do Not Grieve* (Auckland: Vintage).

Firth, Stewart (1997a) 'Colonial Administration and the Invention of the Native', in Denoon *et al.* (eds.), *The Cambridge History of the Pacific Islanders* (Cambridge: Cambridge University Press), pp. 253–88.

_____ (1997b) 'The War in the Pacific', in Denoon *et al.* (eds.), *The Cambridge History of the Pacific Islanders* (Cambridge: Cambridge University Press), pp. 291–323.

Firth, Stewart, and Von Strokirch, Karin (1997) 'A Nuclear Pacific', in Denoon *et al.* (eds.), *The Cambridge History of the Pacific Islanders* (Cambridge: Cambridge University Press), pp. 324–58.

Fischer, Steven R. (2005a) *A History of the Pacific Islands* (Basingstoke and New York: Palgrave).

_____ (2005b) *Island at the End of the World: The Turbulent History of Easter Island* (London: Reaktion Books).

Forsdick, Charles, and Murphy, David (2003) *Francophone Postcolonial Studies: A Critical Introduction* (London: Arnold).

Frame, Janet (1985 [1957]) *Owls Do Cry* (London: The Women's Press).

_____ (1966) *A State of Siege* (New York: George Braziller).

_____ (1990 [1989]) *An Angel at My Table: The Complete Autobiography* (London: The Women's Press).

_____ (1992 [1988]) *The Carpathians* (Auckland: Vintage).

Freeman, Derek (1984 [1983]) *Margaret Mead and Samoa: The Making and Unmaking of an Anthropological Myth* (Harmondsworth: Pelican).

_____ (1999 [1998]) *The Fateful Hoaxing of Margaret Mead: A Historical Analysis of Her Samoan Research* (Boulder and Oxford: Westview).

Fuchs, Miriam (1993) 'Reading Towards the Indigenous Pacific: Patricia Grace's *Potiki*, a Case Study', *SPAN* 36.2: 566–83.

Fuemana, Dianna (2004) *Mapaki* (Wellington: The Play Press).

Gardiner, Wira (1992) *Te Mura o te Ahi: The Story of the Maori Battalion* (Auckland: Reed).

Garrett, Simon (ed.) (1991) *He Reo Hou: 5 Plays by Maori Playwrights* (Wellington: Playmarket).

Gaskell, Ian (2001) 'Introduction', in Ian Gaskell (ed.), *Beyond Ceremony: An Anthology of Drama from Fiji* (Suva: Institute of Pacific Studies and Pacific Writing Forum), 5–8.

—— (2002) 'Introduction', in Larry Thomas, *To Let You Know and Other Plays* (Suva: Pacific Writing Forum), pp. i–xiv.

Gauguin, Paul (1985 [1919]) *Noa Noa*, ed. Nicholas Waldey (Oxford: Phaidon).

Gibbons, Peter (1998) 'Non-Fiction', in T. Sturm (ed.), *The Oxford History of New Zealand Literature*, 2nd edn. (Auckland: Oxford University Press), pp. 31–118.

Gilbert, Helen (ed.) (2001) *Postcolonial Plays: An Anthology* (London: Routledge).

Gilroy, Paul (1993) *The Black Atlantic* (Cambridge, MA: Harvard University Press).

Gope, Pierre (2001) *The Last Nightfall* (Noumea: Grain de Sable; Suva: Institute of Pacific Studies).

Gorodé, Déwé (2004a) *Sharing as Custom Provides: Selected Poems of Déwé Gorodé*, ed. and trans. Raylene Ramsay and Deborah Walker (Canberra: Pandanus).

—— (2004b) *The Kanak Apple Season: Selected Short Fiction of Déwé Gorodé*, ed. and transl. Peter Brown (Canberra: Pandanus).

Goss, J., and Lindquist, B. (2000) 'Placing Movers: An Overview of the Asian-Pacific Migration System', *The Contemporary Pacific* 12.2: 385–414.

Grace, Patricia (1975) *Waiariki and Other Stories* (Auckland: Longman Paul).

—— (1978a) 'The Maori in Literature', in M. King (ed.), *Tihe Mauri Ora: Aspects of Maoritanga* (Hong Kong: Methuen), pp. 80–3.

—— (1978b) *Mutuwhenua: The Moon Sleeps* (Auckland: Penguin).

—— (1980) *The Dream Sleepers and Other Stories* (Auckland: Longman Paul).

—— (1986) *Potiki* (Auckland: Penguin).

—— (1987) *Electric City and Other Stories* (Auckland: Penguin).

—— (1992) *Cousins* (Auckland: Penguin).

—— (1994) *Collected Stories* (Auckland: Penguin).

—— (1998) *Baby No-Eyes* (Auckland: Penguin).

—— (1999) 'Influences on Writing', in V. Hereniko and R. Wilson (eds.), *Inside Out: Literature, Cultural Politics, and Identity in the New Pacific* (Lanham and Boulder: Rowman and Littlefield), pp. 65–73.

—— (2001) *Dogside Story* (Auckland: Penguin).

—— (2004) *Tu: A Novel* (Honolulu: University of Hawai'i Press).

Grace-Smith, Briar (1999) *Purapurawhetū* (Wellington: Huia).

Griffen, Arlene (ed.) (1997a) *With Heart and Nerve and Sinew: Post-coup Writing from Fiji* (Suva: Christmas Club).

Griffen, Arlene (1997*b*) 'A Pacific Novel: The Example of Epeli Hauʻofa', *Dreadlocks* 1: 149–74.

Grimshaw, Beatrice (1907) *From Fiji to the Cannibal Islands* (London: Thomas Nelson).

Hagedorn, Jessica (ed.) (1993) *Charlie Chan is Dead: an Anthology of Contemporary Asian American Fiction* (New York: Penguin).

Hall, Dana Naone (ed.) (1985) *Mālama: Hawaiian Land and Water* (Honolulu: Bamboo Ridge Press).

Hall, Stuart (1997) 'The Local and the Global: Globalization and Ethnicity', in Anthony D. King (ed.), *Culture, Globalization and the World-System: Contemporary Conditions for the Representation of Identity* (University of Minnesota Press), pp. 19–40.

Hamasaki, Richard (1993) 'Mountains in the Sea: The Emergence of Contemporary Hawaiian Poetry in English', in P. Sharrad (ed.), *Readings in Pacific Literature* (Wollongong: New Literatures Research Centre), pp. 190–207.

—— (2000) *From the Spider Bone Diaries: Poems and Songs* (Honolulu: Kalamakū).

Hanson, A. (1989) 'The Making of the Maori: Culture Invention and its Logic', *American Anthropologist* 91: 890–902.

Hardt, Michael, and Negri, Antonio (2001) *Empire* (Harvard: Harvard University Press).

—— (2004) *Multitude: War and Democracy in the Age of Empire* (New York: Penguin).

Harlow, Ray (1989) 'Ka: The Maori Injunctive', in R. B. Harlow, and R. Hooper (eds.), *VICAL 1: Oceanic Languages* (Auckland: Linguistic Society of New Zealand), pp. 197–210.

—— (2005) 'Māori: Introduction', in A. Bell, R. Harlow, and D. Starks (eds.), *Languages of New Zealand* (Wellington: Victoria University Press), pp. 59–66.

Hauʻofa, Epeli (1975) 'Anthropology and Pacific Islanders', *Oceania* 45.4: 283–89.

—— (1983) *Tales of the Tikongs* (Auckland: Longman Paul).

—— (1987) *Kisses in the Nederends* (Auckland: Penguin).

—— (1993) 'Our Sea of Islands', in E. Waddell, V. Naidu, and E. Hauʻofa (eds.), *A New Oceania: Rediscovering Our Sea of Islands* (Suva: University of the South Pacific), pp. 2–18.

—— (1998) 'The Ocean In Us', *The Contemporary Pacific* 10.2: 391–410.

—— (27 September 2000) Opening address for the Red Wave Collective exhibition at the James Harvey Gallery, Sydney. A promotional pamphlet for the Oceania Centre for Arts and Culture includes sections of this address; see www.usp.ac.fj//fileadmin/files/others/vakavuku/oceania-centre.pdf

Hayes, G. (1991) 'Migration, Metascience, and Development in Policy in Island Polynesia', *The Contemporary Pacific* 3.1: 1–58.

Heim, Otto (1998) *Writing Along Broken Lines: Violence and Ethnicity in Contemporary Maori Fiction* (Auckland: Auckland University Press).

Hempenstall, Peter, and Rutherford, Noel (1984) *Protest and Dissent in the Colonial Pacific* (Suva: Institute of Pacific Studies).

Hereniko, Vilsoni (1989) *The Monster and Other Plays* (Suva: Mana).

—— (1993) 'Comic Theatre of Samoa: An Interview with John Kneubuhl', *Mānoa* 5.1: 99–105.

—— (1995) *Woven Gods: Female Clowns and Power in Rotuma* (Honolulu: University of Hawai'i Press).

—— (1998) *Two Plays: A Child For Iva/Sera's Choice* (Suva: Mana).

—— (2001) 'Interview with Vilsoni Hereniko', in Ian Gaskell (ed.), *Beyond Ceremony* (Suva: Institute of Pacific Studies and Pacific Writing Forum), pp. 86–92.

Hereniko, Vilsoni, and Teaiwa, Teresia (1993) *Last Virgin in Paradise* (Suva: Mana).

Holt, Jill (16 August 1997) 'Celestial Mixture', *Listener*: 48.

Holt, John Dominis (1964) *On Being Hawaiian* (Honolulu: Topgallant).

—— (1976) *Waimea Summer* (Honolulu: Topgallant).

Hulme, Keri (1986 [1983]) *The Bone People* (London: Picador).

Hyde, Robin (1993 [1938]) *The Godwits Fly*, ed. Gloria Rawlinson (Auckland: Auckland University Press).

Ihimaera, Witi (1972) *Pounamu, Pounamu* (Auckland: Heinemann).

—— (1973) *Tangi* (London: Heinemann).

—— (1974) *Whanau* (Auckland: Heinemann).

—— (1977) *The New Net Goes Fishing* (London: Heinemann).

—— (1982) 'Maori Life and Literature: A Sensory Perception', *Turnbull Library Record* 15.1: 45–55.

—— (1987) *The Whale Rider* (Auckland: Heinemann).

—— (1988 [1986]) *The Matriarch* (Auckland: Picador).

—— (1989) *Dear Miss Mansfield: A Tribute to Kathleen Mansfield Beauchamp* (Auckland: Viking).

—— (1991) 'A Maori Perspective', *Journal of New Zealand Literature* 9: 53–4.

—— (1997) *The Dream Swimmer* (Auckland: Penguin).

—— (2000*a*) *The Uncle's Story* (Auckland: Penguin).

—— (2000*b*) *Woman Far Walking* (Auckland: Huia).

Innes, C. L. (1995) 'Conspicuous Consumption: Corruption and the Body Politic in the Writing of Ayi Kwei Armah and Ama Ata Aidoo', in A. Gurnah (ed.), *Essays on African Writing 2: Contemporary Literature* (London: Heinemann), pp. 1–18.

Jackson, MacD. P. (1998) 'Poetry', in T. Sturm (ed.), *The Oxford History of New Zealand Literature in English*, 2nd edn (Auckland: Oxford University Press), pp. 394–524.

James, Adeola (1996) *PNG Women Writers: An Anthology* (Melbourne: Longman Australia).

JanMohamed, A. R. (1992) 'Worldliness-Without-World, Homelessness-As-Home: Toward a Definition of the Specular Border Intellectual', in M. Sprinker (ed.), *Edward Said: A Critical Reader* (London: Blackwell), pp. 96–120.

Jolly, Margaret (1996) 'Introduction', in R. L. Stevenson, *South Sea Tales*, ed. Margaret Jolly (Oxford: Oxford University Press), pp. ix–xxxiii.

Jones, Alison, Herda, P., and Suaalii, T. M. (eds.) (2000) *Bitter Sweet: Indigenous Women in the Pacific* (Dunedin: University of Otago Press).

Jones, Lawrence (1998) 'The Novel', in Terry Sturm (ed.), *The Oxford History of New Zealand Literature in English*, 2nd edn (Auckland: Oxford University Press), pp. 119–244.

Kahoʻolawe Island Reserve Commission (1995) 'Kahoʻolawe Island Reserve: A Hawaiian Cultural Sanctuary', *Mānoa* 7.1: 18–24.

Kalahele, Imaikalani (2002) *Kalahele: Poetry and Art by Imaikalani Kalahele* (Honolulu: Kalamakū Press).

Kasaipwalova, John (1972) 'Betel Nut is Bad Magic for Airplanes', in Ulli Beier (ed.), *The Night Warrior and Other Stories from Papua New Guinea* (Melbourne: Jacaranda Press), pp. 83–90. Reprinted in Roberta Rubenstein and Charles R. Larson (eds.) (1993) *Worlds of Fiction* (New York: Macmillan), pp. 613–19.

Keown, Michelle (1998) 'The Whare Whakairo as Symbol of Maori Identity', *SPAN* 47: 39–56.

—— (1999) ' "Gauguin is Dead": Sia Figiel and the Representation of the Polynesian Female Body', *SPAN* 48–49: 91–107.

—— (2000a) 'Interview with Patricia Grace', *Kunapipi* 22.2: 54–63.

—— (2000b) 'Ihimaera's Maori Map: The Topography of Maori Cultural Identity in Contemporary Maori Writing in English', in I. Conrich and D. Wood (eds.), *New Zealand: A Pastoral Paradise?* (Nottingham: Kakapo), pp. 69–90.

—— (2001) 'Freeing the Ancestors: An Interview with Epeli Hauʻofa', *Ariel* 32.1: 71–80.

—— (2002) 'The Samoan Sisyphus: Camus and Colonialism in Albert Wendt's *Leaves of the Banyan Tree*', *Journal of Commonwealth Literature* 37.1: 49–64.

—— (2003) 'Māori or English? The Politics of Language in Patricia Grace's *Baby No-Eyes*', in Christian Mair (ed.), *The Politics of English as a World Language* (Amsterdam: Rodopi), pp. 419–29.

—— (2005) *Postcolonial Pacific Writing: Representations of the Body* (London: Routledge).

Kightley, Oscar, and Small, Simon (2005) *Fresh Off the Boat* (Wellington: The Play Press).

King, Michael (2001 [2000]) *Wrestling with the Angel: A Life of Janet Frame* (London: Picador).

—— (2003) *The Penguin History of New Zealand* (Auckland: Penguin).

Kjellgren, Eric (1993) 'Rousseau and Hobbes in the Pacific: Western Literary Visions of Polynesia and Melanesia', *Mana* 10.1: 95–111.

Kneubuhl, John (1997) Think of a Garden *and Other Plays* (Honolulu: University of Hawai'i Press).

Kneubuhl, Victoria Nalani (2002) *Hawai'i Nei: Island Plays* (Honolulu: University of Hawai'i Press).

Kouka, Hone (1994) *Ngā Tāngata Toa* (Wellington: Victoria University Press).

—— (1997 [1996]) *Waiora* (Wellington: Huia).

—— (1999) 'Introduction', in Hone Kouka (ed.), *Ta Matou Mangai: Three Plays of the 1990s* (Wellington: Victoria University Press), pp. 9–28.

Krauth, Nigel (1993) 'Unfolding like Petals: the Developing Definition of the Writer's Role in Modern Papua New Guinean Literature', in Paul Sharrad (ed.), *Readings in Pacific Literature* (Wollongong: New Literatures Research Centre), pp. 52–62.

Krishnaswamy, R. (1995) 'Mythologies of Migrancy: Postcolonialism, Postmodernism and the Politics of (Dis)location', *Ariel* 26.1: 125–46.

Krupa, V. (1982) *The Polynesian Languages* (London: Routledge).

Lal, Brij V. (2004) '*Girmit*, History, Memory', in Brij V. Lal (ed.), *Bittersweet: the Indo-Fijian Experience* (Canberra: Pandanus), pp. 1–29.

Lamb, Jonathan (1999) 'The Idea of Utopia in New Zealand', in K. Neumann, N. Thomas, and H. Ericksen (eds.), *Quicksands: Foundational Histories in Australia and Aotearoa New Zealand* (Sydney: University of New South Wales Press), pp. 79–97.

Lee, Deborah, and Salas, Antonia (eds.) (1999) *Unfaithing U.S. Colonialism* (Berkeley: PACTS).

Lindstrom, Lamont, and White, Geoffrey M. (1993) 'Singing History: Island Songs from the Pacific War', in P. J. C. Dark and R. G. Rose (eds.) *Artistic Heritage in a Changing Pacific* (Honolulu: University of Hawai'i Press), pp. 185–96.

Lomas, Rongotai (1987) 'A First For the Maori: *Ngati*', *Illusions* 5: 2–5.

London, Jack (2003 [1911]) *The Cruise of the Snark* (Washington, DC: National Geographic Society).

—— (1939 [1911]) *South Seas Tales* (London: Methuen).

—— (1912) *The House of Pride and Other Tales of Hawaii* (London: Mills and Boon).

—— (2003 [1918]) *The Red One and Other Stories* (Charleston, SC: Booksurge).

Loti, Pierre (1929 [1880]) *Le Mariage de Loti* (Edinburgh: Dunedin).

Lynch, John (1998) *Pacific Languages: An Introduction* (Honolulu: University of Hawai'i Press).

McKenzie, D. F. (1999 [1986]) *Bibliography and the Sociology of Texts* (Cambridge: Cambridge University Press).

McKenzie, Stuart (February 1995) 'Warrior Cast: Stuart McKenzie talks to Lee Tamahori', *Artforum*: 64–7; 104–5.

McLeod, Aorewa, and Nola, Nina (1998) 'The Absent Presence: the Silenced Voice of the "Other" Woman in New Zealand Fiction', in Rosemary Du Plessis and Lynne Alice (eds.), *Feminist Thought in Aotearoa/New Zealand* (Auckland: Oxford University Press), pp. 12–20.

McLeod, John (2000) *Beginning Postcolonialism* (Manchester: Manchester University Press).

McMullin, Dan Taulapapa (1999) 'My Mother, My Grandmother and I', in Deborah Lee and Antonia Salas (eds.), *Unfaithing U.S. Colonialism* (Berkeley: PACTS), pp. 112–22.

—— (2000) 'The Bat', 'The Doll', and 'O Kaulaiku' in Quang Boa and Hanya Yanagihara (eds.), *Take Out: Queer Writing from Asian Pacific America* (New York: Asian American Writers' Workshop), pp. 257–61.

—— (2001*a*) 'Sunday', in Susie Bright (ed.), *Best American Erotica 2001* (New York: Simon and Schuster), pp. 107–114.

—— (2001*b*) 'Untitled, to J. K. Kauanui', http://downwindproductions.com /poem.html

—— (2004) *A Drag Queen Named Pipi* (Honolulu: Tinfish).

—— (2005) ' "The fire that devours me": Tahitian spirituality and activism in the poetry of Henri Hiro', *International Journal of Francophone Studies* 8.3: 341–57.

McNaughton, Howard (1998) 'Drama', in Terry Sturm (ed.) *The Oxford History of New Zealand Literature in English*, 2nd edn (Auckland: Oxford University Press), pp. 321–93.

Macpherson, Cluny (1992) 'Economic and Political Restructuring and the Sustainability of Migrant Remittances: The Case of Western Samoa', *The Contemporary Pacific* 4.1: 109–35.

—— (1999) 'Will the "Real" Samoans Please Stand Up? Issues in Diasporic Samoan Identity', *New Zealand Geographer* 55.2: 50–9.

McRae, Jane (1991) 'Maori Literature: A Survey', in T. Sturm (ed.), *The Oxford History of New Zealand Literature in English* (Oxford: Oxford University Press), pp. 1–24.

Maka'a, Julian (1985) *The Confession and Other Stories* (Suva: Institute of Pacific Studies).

Maning, F. E. (1906 [1863]) *Old New Zealand* (Christchurch: Whitcombe and Tombs). Available online at www.nzetc.org/tm/scholarly/tei-ManPake.html

Mansfield, Katherine (2002) *Selected Stories*, ed. Angela Smith (Oxford: Oxford University Press).

Marsh, Selina Tusitala (1997) 'A distinct voice, uncovering others', rev. of *Where We Once Belonged*, by Sia Figiel, *New Zealand Books* 7.2: 4–5.

—— (1999) 'Theory "versus" Pacific Islands Writing: Toward a *Tama'ita'i* Criticism in the Works of Three Pacific Islands Woman Poets', in V. Hereniko and R. Wilson (eds.), *Inside Out: Literature, Cultural Politics, and Identity in the New Pacific* (Lanham: Rowman and Littlefield), pp. 337–56.

Martin, Helen (1995) 'Lee Tamahori: Once Were Warriors', *The Big Picture* 5: 3–5.

Maugham, Somerset (1968 [1921]) *The Trembling of a Leaf* (London: Heron Books).

Mead, Margaret (1943 [1928]) *Coming of Age in Samoa* (Harmondsworth: Penguin).

Melbourne, Hirini (1991) 'Whare Whakairo: Maori "Literary" Traditions', in G. McGregor and M. Williams (eds.), *Dirty Silence: Aspects of Language and Literature in New Zealand* (Oxford: Oxford University Press), pp. 129–41.

Meleisea, Malama (1987) *Lāgaga: A Short History of Western Samoa* (Suva: Institute of Pacific Studies).

Melville, Herman (2001 [1846]) *Typee: A Peep at Polynesian Life* (New York: Random House).

Michener, James (1973 [1946]) *Tales of the South Pacific* (New York: Fawcett).

Mishra, Sudesh (1994) 'Lila', *Meanjin* 53.4: 649–55.

—— (2002) *Diaspora and the Difficult Art of Dying* (Dunedin: Otago University Press).

Mishra, Vijay (1977) 'Indo-Fijian Fiction: Towards an Interpretation', *World Literature Written in English* 16.2: 395–408.

—— (1992) 'The Girmit Ideology Revisited: Fiji Indian Literature', in Emmanuel Nelson (ed.), *Reworlding: The Literature of the Indian Diaspora* (New York, Westport (CT) and London: Greenwood), pp. 1–12.

Mita, Merata (1992) 'The Soul and the Image', in Jonathan Dennis and Jan Bieringa (eds.), *Film in Aotearoa New Zealand* (Wellington: Victoria University Press), pp. 36–54.

Molisa, Grace Mera (1983) *Black Stone* (Suva: Mana).

—— (1989) *Black Stone II* (Port Vila: Black Stone).

Moon, Paul (1996) review of *Ka Whawhai Tonu Matou: Struggle Without End*, by Ranginui Walker, *Deep South* 2.1: www.otago.ac.nz/DeepSouth/vol2no1/review.html

Moore-Gilbert, Bart (1997) *Postcolonial Theory: Contexts, Practices, Politics* (London: Verso).

Mosel, Ulrike, and Hovdhaugen, Even (1992) *Samoan Reference Grammar* (Oslo: Scandinavian University Press).

Mugler, France, and Lynch, John (1996) 'Language and Education in the Pacific', in Mugler and Lynch (eds.), *Pacific Languages in Education* (Suva: Institute of Pacific Studies), pp. 1–9.

Mulgan, John (1939) *Man Alone* (London: Selwyn and Blount).

Murdoch, Adlai, and Donadey, Anne (2005) (eds.) *Postcolonial Theory and Francophone Literary Studies* (Gainesville: University Press of Florida).

Murdoch, Claire (Spring 2003) 'Holy Sea-Cow', *Landfall* 206: 97–105.

Murray, Stuart (1997) 'Introduction', in Stuart Murray (ed.), *Not on Any Map: Essays on Postcoloniality and Cultural Nationalism* (Exeter: University of Exeter Press), pp. 1–18.

_____ (1998) *Never a Soul at Home: New Zealand Literary Nationalism and the 1930s* (Wellington: Victoria University Press).

Naipaul, V. S. (1969) *The Mimic Men* (Harmondsworth: Penguin).

_____ (2001) 'Two Worlds', Nobel Prize in Literature acceptance speech, http://nobelprize.org/literature/laureates/2001/naipaul-lecture-e.html

Nandan, Satendra (1985) *Voices in the River: Poems 1974–1984* (Suva: Vision International).

_____ (1991) *The Wounded Sea* (Sydney: Simon and Schuster).

_____ (2000) *Fiji: Paradise in Pieces*, ed. Anthony Mason (Adelaide: CRNLE).

_____ (2001) *Requiem for a Rainbow: A Fijian Indian Story* (Canberra: Pacific Indian Publications).

Nicole, Robert (1999) 'Resisting Orientalism: Pacific Literature in French', in Hereniko and Wilson (eds.), *Inside Out: Literature, Cultural Politics, and Identity in the New Pacific* (Lanham and Boulder: Rowman and Littlefield), pp. 265–90.

_____ (2001) *The Word, the Pen, and the Pistol: Literature and Power in Tahiti* (New York: State University of New York Press).

O'Donnell, David (2004) 'Introduction' to Makerita Urale, *Frangipani Perfume* and Dianna Fuemana, *Mapaki* (Wellington: The Play Press), pp. i–x.

O'Donnell, David, and Tweddle, Bronwyn (2003) 'Naked Samoans: Pacific Island Voices in the Theatre of Aotearoa/New Zealand', *Performance Research* 8.1: 51–60.

Orange, Claudia (1987) *The Treaty of Waitangi* (Wellington: Allen and Unwin).

Pearson, David (2001) *The Politics of Ethnicity in Settler Societies: States of Unease* (London: Palgrave).

Pearson, W. H. (1982) 'Witi Ihimaera and Patricia Grace', in Cherry Hankin (ed.), *Critical Essays on the New Zealand Short Story* (Auckland: Heinemann), pp. 166–84.

_____ (1984) *Rifled Sanctuaries: Some Views of the Pacific Islands in Western Literature* (Auckland: Auckland University Press).

Petersen, K. H., and Rutherford, A. (eds.) (1986) *A Double Colonisation: Colonial and Post-Colonial Women's Writing* (Sydney: Dangaroo).

Phelps, Conrad (1985) 'First writers' workshop on Easter Island', *Notes on Literacy* 45: 19–25.

Pi'ilani (2001 [1906]) *The True Story of Kaluaikoolau as Told by His Wife, Piilani*, trans. Frances N. Frazier (Lihue, HI: Kauai Historical Society).

Prasad, Mohit (2001) *Eating Mangoes* (Suva: Pacific Writing Forum).

Prasad, Rameshwar (2003) rev. of *Dauka Puraan*, by Subramani, *Fijian Studies* 1.1: www.fijianstudies.org/dload/vol1no1/review_Dauka_Puraan_by_rameshwar_Prasad.pdf

Pratt, Mary Louise (1992) *Imperial Eyes: Travel Writing and Transculturation* (London and New York: Routledge).

Pratt, Rev. George (1984 [1893]) *A Grammar and Dictionary of the Samoan Language* (Papakura: R. McMillan).

Pule, John (1992) *The Shark that Ate the Sun* (Auckland: Penguin).

——— (1998) *Burn My Head in Heaven* (Auckland: Penguin).

Rousseau, Jean-Jacques (1958 [1754]) *A Discourse on Inequality*, trans. Maurice Cranston (Harmondsworth: Penguin).

Royal, Te Ahukaramū Charles (1997) 'Te Whare Tapere: Towards a Model for Māori and/or Tribal Theatre', unpublished paper, www.orotokare.org.nz/Pdf/Stoutlecture.pdf#search=%22whare%20tapere%22

——— (2004) 'Ōrotokare: Art, Story, Motion; Towards Indigenous Theatre and Performing Arts', unpublished paper, www.orotokare.org.nz/Pdf/OrotokareConfPaper.pdf#search=%22whare%20tapere%22

Rushdie, Salman (1988) *The Satanic Verses* (London: Viking).

——— (1991) *Imaginary Homelands: Essays and Criticism 1981–1991* (London: Granta).

Said, Edward (1995 [1978]) *Orientalism* (London: Penguin).

Sakoda, Kent, and Siegel, Jeff (2003) *Pidgin Grammar: An Introduction to the Creole Language of Hawai'i* (Honolulu: Bess Press).

Salmond, Anne (1991) *Two Worlds: First Meetings between Maori and Europeans, 1642–1772* (Honolulu: University of Hawai'i Press).

Satchell, William (1914) *The Greenstone Door* (New York: MacMillan).

Sharrad, Paul (1990) 'Imagining the Pacific', *Meanjin* 49.4: 597–606.

——— (2003) *Albert Wendt and Pacific Literature: Cirling the Void* (Auckland: Auckland University Press).

Sinavaiana-Gabbard, Caroline (1999) 'Where the Spirits Laugh Last: Comic Theatre in Samoa', in V. Hereniko and R. Wilson (eds.) *Inside Out: Literature, Cultural Politics, and Identity in the New Pacific* (Lanham: Rowman and Littlefield), pp. 183–205.

——— (2001) *Alchemies of Distance* (Suva: Institute of Pacific Studies and Honolulu: Tinfish).

Sinclair, Keith (1986) *A Destiny Apart: New Zealand's Search for National Identity* (Wellington: Allen and Unwin).

Smith, Angela (2002) 'Introduction', in Katherine Manfield, *Selected Stories*, ed. A. Smith (Oxford: Oxford University Press), pp. ix–xxxii.

Smith, Bernard (1985 [1960]) *European Vision and the South Pacific* (New Haven and London: Yale University Press).

Smith, Vanessa (1998) *Literary Culture and the Pacific: Nineteenth-Century Textual Encounters* (Cambridge: Cambridge University Press).

Soaba, Russell (1977) *Wanpis* (Madang: Kristen Pres).

Spickard, Paul (2002) 'Introduction: Pacific Diaspora?', in P. Spickard, J. L. Rondilla, and D. H. Wright (eds.), *Pacific Diaspora: Island Peoples in the United States and Across the Pacific* (Honolulu: University of Hawai'i Press), pp. 1–27.

Spitz, Chantal (1991) *L'île des Rêves Écrasés* (Papeete: Au Vent Des Iles).

Spivak, Gayatri (1988) 'Can the Subaltern Speak?', in Cary Nelson and Larry Grossberg (eds.), *Marxism and the Interpretation of Culture* (Urbana: University of Illinois Press), pp. 271–313.

——— (1999) *A Critique of Postcolonial Reason* (Cambridge, MA.: Harvard University Press).

Spurr, David (1993) *The Rhetoric of Empire: Colonial Discourse in Journalism, Travel Writing, and Imperial Administration* (Durham and London: Duke University Press).

Staff, Bryan (1993) 'Initiation Rites', *On Film* 10.8: 9.

Stead, C. K. (1994) *The Singing Whakapapa* (Auckland: Penguin).

——— (2002) *Kin of Place: Essays on 20 New Zealand Writers* (Auckland: Auckland University Press).

Stella, Regis (1999) 'Reluctant Voyages into Otherness: Practice and Appraisal in Papua New Guinean Literature', in V. Hereniko and R. Wilson (eds.), *Inside Out: Literature, Cultural Politics, and Identity in the New Pacific* (Lanham: Rowman and Littlefield), pp. 221–30.

Stevenson, R. L. (1987) *Tales of the South Seas*, ed. Jenni Calder (Edinburgh: Canongate).

——— (1996) *South Sea Tales*, ed. R. Jolly (Oxford and New York: Oxford University Press).

Stow, Randolph (1991 [1979]) *Visitants* (London: Minerva).

Subramani (1988) *The Fantasy Eaters* (Washington, DC: Three Continents Press).

——— (1992) *South Pacific Literature: From Myth to Fabulation*, 2nd edn (Suva: Institute of Pacific Studies, University of the South Pacific).

——— (1995) *Altering Imagination* (Suva: Fiji Writers' Association).

——— (1996) Interview with Sia Figiel, appended to *The Girl in the Moon Circle*, by Sia Figiel (Suva: Mana), pp. 121–32.

——— (2001) *Dauka Puraan* (New Delhi: Star Publications).

——— (2003) *Pacific Epistemologies, Monograph Series 1* (Suva: Pacific Writing Forum), pp. 1–14. First published in *The Contemporary Pacific* 13.1 (2001): 149–62.

Sullivan, Robert (1999) *Star Waka* (Auckland: Auckland University Press).

Sumner, Barbara (23 August 1999) 'From Their Reactions, I See Who People Are', *Independent* (London): Monday Review, 7.

Talib, Ismail S. (2002) *The Language of Postcolonial Literatures: an Introduction* (London and New York: Routledge).

Taouma, Lisa (2002) 'Gettin' Jiggy With It: The Evolving of Pasifika Dance in New Zealand', in Sean Mallon and Pandora Fulimalo Pereira (eds.), *Pacific Art Niu Sila: The Pacific Dimension of Contemporary New Zealand Arts* (Wellington: Te Papa Press), pp. 133–45.

Tauroa, Hiwi, and Tauroa, Pat (1986) *Te Marae: A Guide to Customs and Protocol* (Auckland: Reed).

Tausky, Thomas (1991) 'Stories that Show Them Who They Are: An Interview with Patricia Grace', *Australian and New Zealand Studies in Canada* 6: 90–102.

Teaiwa, Teresia (1999) 'Reading Gauguin's *Noa Noa* with Hau'ofa's *Kisses in the Nederends*: Militourism, Feminism and the "Polynesian" Body', in V. Hereniko and R. Wilson (eds.), *Inside Out: Literature, Cultural Politics, and Identity in the New Pacific* (Lanham and Boulder: Rowman and Littlefield), pp. 249–63.

Te Awekotuku, Ngahuia (1989) *Tahuri* (Auckland: New Women's Press). (Four stories from the collection have been reprinted: 'Auntie Marleen' appears in *Te Ao Marama 3* (Ihimaera (ed.) 1993), while 'Paretipua', 'Old Man Tuna', and 'Watching the Big Girls' appear in the *Vintage Book of International Lesbian Fiction* (Holoch and Nestle (eds.) 1999).)

—— (1992) 'Kia Mau, Kia Manawanui—We Will Never Go Away: Experiences of a Māori Lesbian Feminist', in Rosemary Du Plessis (ed.), *Feminist Voices: Women's Studies Texts for Aotearoa/New Zealand* (Auckland: Oxford University Press), pp. 278–89.

—— (2003) *Ruahine: Mythic Women* (Wellington: Huia).

Thaman, Konai Helu (1999) *Songs of Love: New and Selected Poems, 1974–1999* (Suva: Mana).

Thieme, John (ed.) (1996) *The Arnold Anthology of Post-Colonial Literatures in English* (London: Arnold).

Theroux, Paul (1992) *The Happy Isles of Oceania* (London: Hamish Hamilton).

Thomas, Larry (2001) 'Looking Back and Moving On', in I. Gaskell (ed.), *Beyond Ceremony: An Anthology of Drama from Fiji* (Suva: Institute of Pacific Studies; Pacific Writing Forum), pp. 117–19.

—— (2002) To Let You Know *and Other Plays* (Suva: Pacific Writing Forum).

Tiffin, Helen (1997) 'The Body in the Library: Identity, Opposition and the Settler-Invader Woman', in M. Delrez and B. Ledent (eds.), *The Contact and the Culmination* (Liège: University of Liège), pp. 271–80.

Trask, Haunani-Kay (1999a) *From a Native Daughter: Colonialism and Sovereignty in Hawai'i*, rev. edn. (Honolulu: University of Hawai'i Press).

Trask, Haunani-Kay (1999b) *Light in the Crevice Never Seen,* rev. edn. (Corvallis, OR: Calyx).

_____ (1999c) 'Decolonizing Hawaiian Literature', in Vilsoni Hereniko and Rob Wilson (eds.), *Inside Out: Literature, Cultural Politics, and Identity in the New Pacific* (Lanham: Rowman and Littlefield), pp. 167–82.

_____ (2002) *Night is a Sharkskin Drum* (Honolulu: University of Hawai'i Press).

Treadaway, Julian (2002) *Fifi'i* (Suva: Institute of Pacific Studies).

Tupuola, AnneMarie (2000) 'Learning Sexuality: Young Samoan Women', in A. Jones, P. Herda, and T. M. Suaalii (eds.), *Bitter Sweet: Indigenous Women in the Pacific* (Dunedin: University of Otago Press), pp. 61–72.

Turner, Stephen (2000) 'Colonialism Continued: Producing the Self for Export', in J. Docker and G. Fischer (eds.), *Race, Colour and Identity in Australia and New Zealand* (Sydney: University of New South Wales Press), pp. 218–28.

Tuwhare, Hone (1972) *Sap-Wood and Milk: Poems by Hone Tuwhare* (Dunedin: Caveman).

_____ (1994 [1993]) *Deep River Talk: Collected Poems* (Honolulu: University of Hawai'i Press).

Urale, Makerita (2004) *Frangipani Perfume* (Wellington: The Play Press).

Va'ai, S. M. T. (1999) *Literary Representations in Western Polynesia: Colonialism and Indigeneity* (Apia: National University of Samoa).

Vercoe, Caroline (2002) 'Art Niu Sila: Contemporary Pacific Art in New Zealand', in Sean Mallon and Pandora Fulimalo Pereira (eds.), *Pacific Art Niu Sila: The Pacific Dimension of Contemporary New Zealand Arts* (Wellington: Te Papa Press), pp. 191–207.

Waddell, Eric, Naidu, Vijay, and Hau'ofa, Epeli (eds.) (1993) *A New Oceania: Rediscovering Our Sea of Islands* (Suva: 'School of Social and Economic Development).

Waite, Geoffrey (1992) *Aoteareo: Speaking for Ourselves* (Wellington: Learning Media).

Walker, Ranginui (August 1994) 'Te Karanga: Getting Real', a review of Lee Tamahori's *Once Were Warriors, Metro*: 134–5.

_____ (2004) *Ka Whawhai Tonu Matou: Struggle Without End,* 2nd edn (Auckland: Penguin).

Wallis, Mary (1983 [1851]) *Life in Feejee: Five Years Among the Cannibals* (Suva: Fiji Museum).

Wat, John H. Y., and Desha, Meredith M. (eds.) (2003) *Heo Leo Hou/A New Voice: Hawaiian Playwrights* (Honolulu: Bamboo Ridge Press).

Watters. R. (1987) 'Mirab Societies and Bureaucratic Elites', in A. Hooper, S. Britton, R. Crocombe, J. Huntsman, and C. Macpherson (eds.), *Class and Culture in the South Pacific* (Suva: Institute of Pacific Studies), pp. 32–54.

Webster, Stephen (1998) *Patrons of Maori Culture: Power, Theory and Ideology in the Maori Renaissance* (Dunedin: University of Otago Press).

Wendt, Albert (1965) ' "Guardians and Wards" : A Study of the Origins, Causes, and the First Two Years of the Mau in Western Samoa', MA thesis (Victoria University of Wellington), available online at www.nzetc.org/tm/scholarly/tei-WenGua.html

—— (1973) *Sons for the Return Home* (Auckland: Longman Paul).

—— (1974) *Flying Fox in a Freedom Tree* (Auckland: Longman Paul).

—— (1976a) 'Towards a New Oceania', *Mana Review* 1.1: 49–60.

—— (1976b) *Inside Us the Dead: Poems 1961 to 1974* (Auckland: Longman Paul).

—— (1979) *Leaves of the Banyan Tree* (Auckland: Longman Paul).

—— (ed.) (1980) *Lali: A Pacific Anthology* (Auckland: Longman Paul).

—— (1981) 'Don't Generalise about the South Pacific', *Aid Research Newsletter*: 4–6.

—— (1983) 'Three Faces of Samoa: Mead's, Freeman's and Wendt's', *Pacific Islands Monthly* 54.4: 10–14; 69.

—— (1987 [1977]) *Pouliuli* (Auckland: Penguin).

—— (1991) *Ola* (Auckland: Penguin).

—— (1992) *Black Rainbow* (Auckland: Penguin).

—— (ed.) (1995a) *Nuanua: Pacific Writing in English since 1980* (Auckland: Auckland University Press).

—— (1995b) 'Pacific Maps and Fiction(s): A Personal Journey', in S. Perera (ed.), *Asian and Pacific Inscriptions: Identities, Ethnicities, Nationalities* (Bundoora: spec. book issue of *Meridian* 14.2): 13–44.

—— (1996) 'Tatauing the Post-Colonial Body', *SPAN* 42–43: 15–29.

—— (2002) 'Robocop in Long Bay', *Landfall* 203: 76–90.

—— (2003a) *The Mango's Kiss* (Auckland: Vintage).

—— (2003b) 'Tusitala: The Legend, the Writer and the Literature of the Pacific', in R. Robinson (ed.), *Robert Louis Stevenson: His Best Pacific Writings* (Auckland: Streamline), pp. 9–11.

—— (2004) *The Songmaker's Chair* (Auckland: Huia).

—— Sullivan, R., and Whaitiri, R. (eds.) (2003) *Whetu Moana: An Anthology of Polynesian Poetry* (Auckland: Auckland University Press).

Williams, John (1998 [1837]) *A Narrative of Missionary Enterprises in the South Seas* (Rarotonga: Cook Islands Library and Museum Society).

Williams, Mark (1990) *Leaving the Highway: Six Contemporary Novelists* (Auckland: Auckland University Press).

—— (1997) 'Crippled by Geography? New Zealand Nationalisms', in S. Murray (ed.), *Not on Any Map: Essays on Postcoloniality and Cultural Nationalism* (Exeter: University of Exeter Press), pp. 19–42.

252 · References

Wilson, Rob (1999a) 'Introduction: Toward Imagining a New Pacific', in V. Hereniko and R. Wilson (eds.), *Inside Out: Literature, Cultural Politics, and Identity in the New Pacific* (Boulder and New York: Rowman and Littlefield), pp. 1–14.

—— (1999b) 'Bloody Mary Meets Lois-Ann Yamanaka: Imagining Hawaiian Locality, from *South Pacific* to Bamboo Ridge and Beyond', in V. Hereniko and R. Wilson (eds.), *Inside Out: Literature, Cultural Politics, and Identity in the New Pacific* (Lanham: Rowman and Littlefield), pp. 357–80.

—— (2000) *Reimagining the American Pacific: From* South Pacific *to* Bamboo Ridge *and Beyond* (Durham and London: Duke University Press).

—— (2002) Review of *Hembemba: Rivers of the Forest*, by Steven Winduo, *The Contemporary Pacific* 14.2: 509.

Winduo, Steven (1990) 'Papua New Guinea Writing Today: The Growth of a Literary Culture', *Mānoa* 2.1: 37–41.

Wood, Briar (2006) 'In Spirits' Voices: An Interview with Steven Winduo', *Journal of Postcolonial Writing* 42.1: 84–93.

Yamanaka, Lois-Ann (1993) *Saturday Night at the Pahala Theatre* (Honolulu: Bamboo Ridge).

Young, Robert (2001) *Postcolonialism: An Historical Introduction* (Oxford: Blackwell).

INDEX